Harnessing the Power of Firebase and Google Cloud Platform: A Comprehensive Guide for Developers

Kameron Hussain and Frahaan Hussain

Published by Sonar Publishing, 2024.

While every precaution has been taken in the preparation of this book, the publisher assumes no responsibility for errors or omissions, or for damages resulting from the use of the information contained herein.

HARNESSING THE POWER OF FIREBASE AND GOOGLE CLOUD PLATFORM: A COMPREHENSIVE GUIDE FOR DEVELOPERS

First edition. October 13, 2024.

Copyright © 2024 Kameron Hussain and Frahaan Hussain.

ISBN: 979-8224172627

Written by Kameron Hussain and Frahaan Hussain.

Harnessing the Power of Firebase and Google Cloud Platform

FIRST EDITION

A COMPREHENSIVE GUIDE FOR DEVELOPERS

Table of Contents

1. Organizing Projects and Resources

2. Managing Budgets and Billing

3. Monitoring and Logging

4. Implementing Access Controls and Security

5. Automating Deployment and CI/CD Pipelines

Security Best Practices for Firebase and GCP Applications

1. Securing User Authentication and Identity Management

2. Managing Access Control with IAM and Firebase Security Rules

3. Data Protection and Encryption

4. Securing Backend Services and APIs

5. Regularly Testing and Updating Security Measures

Scaling Applications Seamlessly

1. Understanding Horizontal vs. Vertical Scaling

2. Planning for Scalability in Firebase and GCP

3. Optimizing Databases for Scalability

4. Handling Traffic Spikes with Auto-Scaling

5. Leveraging Serverless Computing for Scalability

6. Automating Scaling with Infrastructure as Code (IaC)

Glossary of Firebase & GCP Terms

Resources for Further Learning

1. Official Documentation

2. Online Courses

3. Tutorial Websites

4. Community Forums

5. GitHub Repositories

6. Books and E-Books

7. Blogs and Newsletters

8. Conferences and Events

Sample Projects and Code Snippets

1. Real-Time Chat Application with Firebase Firestore

2. E-Commerce Platform with Firebase Authentication and Firestore

3. Image Recognition App with Firebase ML Kit and Cloud Storage

4. Fitness Tracking App with Firebase Realtime Database

Firebase & GCP API Reference Guide

1. Firebase Authentication API

2. Firestore Database API

3. Firebase Cloud Functions API

4. Firebase Cloud Storage API

5. Google Cloud Compute Engine API

6. Google Cloud Storage API

7. Google Cloud Pub/Sub API

8. Google Cloud BigQuery API

Frequently Asked Questions

1. Getting Started with Firebase and GCP

2. Billing and Pricing

3. Authentication and User Management

4. Data Management and Storage

5. Hosting and Deployment

6. Integrating Firebase with Google Cloud

7. Advanced Topics: Machine Learning and AI

8. Security and Compliance

9. Scaling and Performance

Preface

In an era where mobile and web application development is constantly evolving, the need for robust, scalable, and easy-to-integrate solutions has become paramount. Firebase and Google Cloud Platform (GCP) offer an unmatched synergy for developers aiming to build high-quality applications with minimal backend concerns. Together, these platforms provide a comprehensive suite of tools that allow for seamless integration, quick deployment, and reliable scaling. This book delves deep into how Firebase and GCP can be leveraged to create powerful, data-driven applications that meet the demands of modern users.

The journey begins with an introduction to Firebase and GCP, setting the stage for understanding how these two platforms complement each other. From there, you will be guided through the process of setting up both environments, exploring Firebase Authentication, Firestore databases, and Cloud Functions. Each chapter builds on the previous, gradually leading you into more advanced territories such as machine learning integrations and best practices for maintaining and scaling your applications.

Whether you are a beginner looking to understand the fundamentals or an experienced developer aiming to refine your skills, this book provides a structured approach to mastering Firebase and GCP. Through real-world examples, case studies, and step-by-step tutorials, you will gain the confidence to take your application development skills to the next level.

Chapter 1: Introduction to Firebase and GCP

Overview of Firebase

FIREBASE IS A COMPREHENSIVE development platform that provides a wide range of tools and services to help developers build and deploy applications. Initially launched as a Backend-as-a-Service (BaaS) for mobile apps, Firebase has since evolved into a powerful suite that supports web apps and offers extensive features such as authentication, real-time databases, cloud functions, analytics, and more.

Firebase's core strength lies in its ability to handle backend tasks, allowing developers to focus on front-end development and user experience. It provides real-time data synchronization, which is crucial for applications requiring live data updates, such as chat applications, collaborative tools, and live dashboards. Additionally, Firebase offers robust solutions for handling user authentication, cloud storage, and serverless computing, making it an ideal choice for developers seeking a complete backend solution without the overhead of managing servers.

Firebase Real-time Database

ONE OF FIREBASE'S FLAGSHIP features is its real-time database, which stores and syncs data across all clients in real time. The real-time database is a NoSQL cloud database that provides real-time data syncing, enabling applications to update immediately across all devices. This makes it particularly useful for applications that require live updates, such as multiplayer games, collaborative document editing tools, and live comment feeds.

```javascript
// Example of Firebase Real-time Database

import { initializeApp } from "firebase/app";

import { getDatabase, ref, set } from "firebase/database";

const firebaseConfig = {

apiKey: "YOUR_API_KEY",

authDomain: "YOUR_PROJECT_ID.firebaseapp.com",

databaseURL: "https://YOUR_PROJECT_ID.firebaseio.com",

projectId: "YOUR_PROJECT_ID",

storageBucket: "YOUR_PROJECT_ID.appspot.com",

messagingSenderId: "YOUR_MESSAGING_SENDER_ID",

appId: "YOUR_APP_ID",

};

const app = initializeApp(firebaseConfig);

const database = getDatabase(app);

// Write data to Firebase

function writeUserData(userId, name, email) {

set(ref(database, 'users/' + userId), {

username: name,

email: email,

});
```

```
}
```

Firebase Firestore

IN ADDITION TO THE real-time database, Firebase also offers Firestore, a flexible, scalable database for app development. Firestore is a NoSQL document-oriented database that provides real-time data synchronization and offline support, making it a more advanced option for complex applications. Firestore allows for richer querying and offers better scalability compared to the real-time database, making it suitable for larger applications that require sophisticated data handling.

```
// Example of Firebase Firestore

import { getFirestore, collection, addDoc } from "firebase/firestore";

const db = getFirestore();

async function addUser(name, email) {

try {

const docRef = await addDoc(collection(db, "users"), {

username: name,

email: email,

});

console.log("Document written with ID: ", docRef.id);

} catch (e) {

console.error("Error adding document: ", e);
```

}

}

Introduction to Google Cloud Platform (GCP)

GCP IS A SUITE OF CLOUD computing services that runs on the same infrastructure Google uses internally for its end-user products, such as Google Search and YouTube. GCP provides a range of services including compute power, storage, databases, machine learning, and networking. By integrating with Firebase, GCP enables developers to build, deploy, and scale applications with greater flexibility and control over their infrastructure.

GCP offers advanced tools and services for big data, artificial intelligence, and machine learning, allowing developers to incorporate AI-powered features into their applications. With GCP's global network, developers can scale their applications across regions, ensuring high availability and low latency for users worldwide.

Key GCP Services

Google Compute Engine

GOOGLE COMPUTE ENGINE (GCE) is a scalable, high-performance virtual machine service that allows you to run custom virtual machines on Google's infrastructure. GCE provides flexible configurations, allowing you to choose the optimal amount of memory, CPUs, and storage for your workloads.

Google Kubernetes Engine

GOOGLE KUBERNETES ENGINE (GKE) is a managed Kubernetes service that allows you to deploy, manage, and scale containerized applications using Kubernetes, the leading open-source system for automating deployment, scaling, and management of containerized applications.

Google Cloud Storage

GOOGLE CLOUD STORAGE is a unified object storage solution that offers high durability, availability, and scalability. It supports a wide range of storage classes, enabling developers to choose the right balance between cost and performance for their storage needs.

By combining Firebase and GCP, developers can leverage Firebase's ease of use with GCP's powerful infrastructure and machine learning capabilities, creating robust applications that are prepared for scalability, reliability, and global reach.

The subsequent sections of this chapter will explore the synergy and integration between Firebase and GCP, the benefits of using them together, and how they can be applied to real-world scenarios.

Firebase and GCP: Synergy and Integration

THE INTEGRATION BETWEEN Firebase and Google Cloud Platform (GCP) creates a powerful ecosystem that supports a wide range of application needs, from mobile and web development to complex machine learning and big data processing. Firebase provides the core functionalities required to build, manage, and deploy applications quickly, while GCP offers advanced infrastructure and services that help scale applications and optimize performance. This section explores how Firebase and GCP work together, their complementary strengths, and the practical steps for integrating the two platforms effectively.

Understanding the Core Synergy

FIREBASE IS OFTEN SEEN as the frontend for rapid application development, offering real-time databases, authentication, and hosting, which are essential for creating engaging user experiences. On the other hand, GCP provides robust backend infrastructure, including Compute Engine, BigQuery, and AI services, which handle complex computations, data analysis, and storage at scale.

By linking Firebase and GCP, you can leverage Firebase's user-friendly frontend services and complement them with GCP's advanced backend solutions. This synergy not only enhances the capabilities of your applications but also streamlines your development process by centralizing your application's needs within a single ecosystem.

Linking Firebase with GCP

TO INTEGRATE FIREBASE with GCP, you need to link your Firebase project with a corresponding GCP project. This process enables you to access GCP services directly from your Firebase console and vice versa. Linking projects also facilitates shared access to resources such as Cloud Storage, BigQuery, and IAM roles across both platforms.

Step-by-Step Guide to Linking Firebase with GCP

1. **Create a Firebase Project:**

o Navigate to the Firebase Console.

o Click on **Add Project**, enter a project name, and follow the prompts to create your Firebase project.

2. **Link to a GCP Project:**

o In the Firebase Console, go to **Project Settings**.

o Under the **Integrations** tab, find the **Google Cloud Platform (GCP)** section.

o Click on **Link Project** and choose an existing GCP project or create a new one.

3. **Enable Required APIs:**

o Once linked, you may need to enable additional GCP APIs depending on the services you intend to use. For example, if you plan to use BigQuery, navigate to the Google Cloud Console, select your project, and enable the BigQuery API.

4. **Set Up Billing and Permissions:**

o Linking Firebase with GCP requires setting up billing to access certain services. In the Google Cloud Console, navigate to **Billing** and link a billing account to your project.

○ Configure IAM roles to manage permissions. You can assign roles such as **Firebase Admin** or **Storage Admin** to control access levels for team members.

Integrating Firebase Authentication with GCP Identity Platform

FIREBASE AUTHENTICATION can be extended using GCP's Identity Platform, which offers a more advanced identity and access management solution. The Identity Platform provides multi-factor authentication, identity federation, and additional security features that enhance Firebase Authentication's capabilities.

Adding Identity Platform to Firebase Authentication

TO ENABLE IDENTITY Platform features, follow these steps:

1. **Enable Identity Platform**:

○ In the Google Cloud Console, go to **APIs & Services > Library**.

○ Search for **Identity Platform** and click **Enable**.

2. **Configure Authentication Providers**:

○ In the Identity Platform settings, you can configure a range of authentication providers, including SAML, OpenID Connect, and more. This allows you to support enterprise-level authentication needs.

3. **Integrate with Firebase Authentication**:

○ Once configured, you can access Identity Platform features through Firebase Authentication, enabling options such as phone authentication, social logins, and more advanced multi-factor authentication (MFA).

4. Use Custom Authentication Providers:

○ With Identity Platform, you can set up custom authentication providers that allow you to create unique login experiences based on your application's needs.

```
// Example of enabling multi-factor authentication

import { initializeApp } from "firebase/app";

import { getAuth, signInWithPhoneNumber, RecaptchaVerifier }
from "firebase/auth";

const firebaseConfig = {

apiKey: "YOUR_API_KEY",

authDomain: "YOUR_PROJECT_ID.firebaseapp.com",

projectId: "YOUR_PROJECT_ID",

};

const app = initializeApp(firebaseConfig);

const auth = getAuth(app);

auth.useDeviceLanguage();

// Initialize reCAPTCHA

window.recaptchaVerifier                    =                    new
RecaptchaVerifier('recaptcha-container', {
```

```
'size': 'invisible',

'callback': function(response) {

// Handle reCAPTCHA success

}

}, auth);

const phoneNumber = "+1234567890";

const appVerifier = window.recaptchaVerifier;

signInWithPhoneNumber(auth, phoneNumber, appVerifier)

.then((confirmationResult) => {

const verificationCode = window.prompt("Please enter the
verification code sent to your phone");

return confirmationResult.confirm(verificationCode);

})

.catch((error) => {

console.error("Error during sign-in:", error);

});
```

Data Management with Firestore and BigQuery

FIRESTORE IS AN EXCELLENT solution for storing real-time data, but for extensive data analysis, GCP's BigQuery offers more powerful querying capabilities. You can export data from Firestore to BigQuery for in-depth analytics and reporting.

Setting Up Firestore Data Export to BigQuery

1. **Enable BigQuery:**

   ○ In the Google Cloud Console, navigate to **BigQuery** and enable the API if it's not already enabled.

2. **Link Firestore to BigQuery:**

   ○ In the Firebase Console, go to **Firestore**, and under **Usage**, select **Export Data**.

   ○ Choose BigQuery as the export destination and select your GCP project and BigQuery dataset.

3. **Run Queries in BigQuery:**

   ○ Once data is exported, you can query it using SQL syntax in BigQuery. This enables you to perform complex analyses, generate reports, and visualize data trends.

—EXAMPLE QUERY TO COUNT documents by status in BigQuery

SELECT status, COUNT(*) as document_count

FROM `your_project.your_dataset.your_collection`

GROUP BY status;

Combining Cloud Functions with GCP Services

FIREBASE CLOUD FUNCTIONS can call GCP services, enabling you to extend your application with functionalities like sending emails through SendGrid, analyzing data with Cloud Vision, or processing data with Cloud Dataflow.

Example: Using Cloud Functions to Trigger GCP Services

1. **Create a Cloud Function**:

o In the Firebase Console, go to **Functions** and create a new function. Write the function to trigger on specific events such as database changes, authentication events, or HTTP requests.

2. **Call GCP Service**:

o Within the function, use the GCP client library to interact with the desired service. For instance, you could trigger a Google Cloud Storage bucket to process images or invoke a machine learning model on AI Platform.

3. **Deploy and Monitor**:

o Deploy your function and monitor it from the Firebase Console. Use GCP's Stackdriver for detailed logging and error tracking.

```
// EXAMPLE CLOUD FUNCTION to process images in Cloud Storage

const functions = require("firebase-functions");

const { Storage } = require("@google-cloud/storage");

const storage = new Storage();
```

```
exports.processImage                                    =
functions.storage.object().onFinalize(async (object) => {

const bucketName = object.bucket;

const filePath = object.name;

const bucket = storage.bucket(bucketName);

// Processing logic here

});
```

Conclusion

THE INTEGRATION BETWEEN Firebase and GCP offers developers a unique blend of simplicity and power. Firebase simplifies frontend and mobile application development, while GCP's backend services provide the infrastructure necessary to handle demanding workloads, from big data to AI-driven solutions. By combining these platforms, you can build scalable, reliable, and feature-rich applications with a streamlined development process. In the next sections, we will explore the practical applications of these integrations and how they can be applied to real-world scenarios.

Benefits of Using Firebase and GCP Together

THE COMBINATION OF Firebase and Google Cloud Platform (GCP) offers a plethora of advantages that make it an ideal solution for developers aiming to build scalable, secure, and efficient applications. By leveraging the strengths of both platforms, developers can streamline their workflows, enhance user experiences, and reduce operational complexity. This section outlines the key benefits of integrating Firebase with GCP, covering aspects such as scalability, cost efficiency, security, and development speed.

1. Scalability and Performance

ONE OF THE MOST SIGNIFICANT advantages of combining Firebase and GCP is the ability to scale applications seamlessly. Firebase services like Firestore and Firebase Hosting are designed to handle real-time updates and high traffic, while GCP provides additional scalability options through services like Google Compute Engine (GCE), Google Kubernetes Engine (GKE), and Cloud Spanner.

Autoscaling with Google Kubernetes Engine (GKE)

FOR APPLICATIONS THAT require container orchestration, GKE offers a managed Kubernetes environment that supports autoscaling. This ensures that your application can automatically adjust to traffic spikes and optimize resource usage.

```
# Example Kubernetes deployment with autoscaling in GKE

apiVersion: apps/v1

kind: Deployment

metadata:

name: my-app

spec:

replicas: 1

selector:
```

```yaml
    matchLabels:

      app: my-app

  template:

    metadata:

      labels:

        app: my-app

    spec:

      containers:

      - name: my-app-container

        image: gcr.io/my-project/my-app-image
```

```yaml
APIVERSION: AUTOSCALING/v1

kind: HorizontalPodAutoscaler

metadata:

  name: my-app-autoscaler

spec:

  scaleTargetRef:

    apiVersion: apps/v1

    kind: Deployment

    name: my-app
```

minReplicas: 1

maxReplicas: 10

targetCPUUtilizationPercentage: 80

This example configures an autoscaler for a Kubernetes deployment, ensuring that the application scales between 1 and 10 replicas based on CPU utilization. By deploying applications on GKE, developers can handle varying levels of user demand without compromising performance.

2. Cost Efficiency

FIREBASE AND GCP OFFER flexible pricing models that help manage costs effectively. Firebase provides generous free tiers for many of its services, which is particularly beneficial for startups and small projects. As your application scales, GCP allows you to optimize costs through various mechanisms such as preemptible instances, committed use contracts, and sustained-use discounts.

Utilizing Firebase's Free Tier

FIREBASE'S FREE TIER includes many essential services such as Firebase Authentication, Firestore, and Firebase Hosting. For instance, the free tier of Firebase Hosting allows up to 10 GB of data transfer per month, making it suitable for low to moderate traffic applications. Firestore also provides a free monthly quota, which can handle initial usage and prototyping.

Managing Costs with GCP's Preemptible VMs

GCP OFFERS PREEMPTIBLE virtual machines, which are short-lived VMs available at a fraction of the cost of standard VMs.

These are ideal for workloads that are fault-tolerant and can be interrupted, such as batch processing, testing, or non-urgent tasks.

```python
# Example of creating a preemptible VM using Google Cloud Python client

from google.cloud import compute_v1

def create_preemptible_instance(project_id, zone, instance_name):

    instance_client = compute_v1.InstancesClient()

    machine_type = f"zones/{zone}/machineTypes/e2-standard-2"

    instance = compute_v1.Instance()

    instance.name = instance_name

    instance.machine_type = machine_type

    instance.scheduling = compute_v1.Scheduling(preemptible=True)

    instance.network_interfaces = [compute_v1.NetworkInterface(name="global/networks/default")]

    operation = instance_client.insert(project=project_id, zone=zone, instance_resource=instance)

    return operation
```

By using preemptible instances, developers can significantly reduce their cloud computing costs without compromising on computational power.

3. Enhanced Security

FIREBASE AND GCP OFFER robust security features, allowing developers to protect their applications and user data comprehensively. Firebase provides built-in security measures such as Firebase Authentication and Firestore security rules, which simplify the process of securing access to resources. GCP further enhances security with advanced tools like Identity and Access Management (IAM), Cloud Armor, and the Identity Platform.

Implementing Fine-Grained Access Control with IAM

GCP'S IAM ALLOWS DEVELOPERS to implement fine-grained access control for various services, ensuring that users and applications have the minimum required permissions. This can be especially useful when managing multiple team members and services within a project.

Example of an IAM policy for a GCP project

bindings:

- role: roles/storage.admin

members:

- user:admin@example.com

- role: roles/storage.objectViewer

members:

-

serviceAccount:my-service-account@my-project.iam.gserviceaccount.c

In this example, the storage.admin role is granted to an admin user, while the storage.objectViewer role is assigned to a service account. By applying IAM roles at the project or service level, developers can enforce strict access policies and protect sensitive data.

4. Rapid Development and Deployment

FIREBASE IS DESIGNED with rapid development in mind, offering features such as Firebase Hosting, Firebase Functions, and Firebase Authentication, which streamline common tasks in application development. With Firebase, developers can quickly deploy static and dynamic web applications, set up user authentication, and build serverless functions that respond to HTTP requests or database changes.

Streamlined Deployment with Firebase Hosting

FIREBASE HOSTING ALLOWS developers to deploy web applications with a single command. Firebase Hosting supports both single-page applications and static sites, providing SSL, custom domains, and built-in CDN integration to optimize performance.

Command to deploy an application to Firebase Hosting

firebase deploy—only hosting

After running this command, Firebase automatically handles SSL configuration and content delivery, allowing the application to go live in minutes. For more complex applications, Firebase Functions can be combined with Firebase Hosting to serve dynamic content, while still maintaining a streamlined deployment process.

5. Advanced Analytics and Monitoring

FIREBASE AND GCP TOGETHER provide comprehensive analytics and monitoring tools that help developers gain insights into user behavior, application performance, and resource usage. Firebase offers Firebase Analytics for tracking user interactions, while GCP's Cloud Monitoring and Cloud Logging provide detailed metrics and logs for backend services.

Tracking User Engagement with Firebase Analytics

FIREBASE ANALYTICS automatically captures key user events and allows developers to define custom events to gain deeper insights into user interactions. These insights can be used to improve user experience, optimize features, and enhance marketing strategies.

```
// Example of logging a custom event with Firebase Analytics

import { getAnalytics, logEvent } from "firebase/analytics";

const analytics = getAnalytics();

logEvent(analytics, 'select_content', {

content_type: 'image',

item_id: 'P12453'

});
```

Real-Time Monitoring with Cloud Monitoring

GCP'S CLOUD MONITORING service provides real-time visibility into the health and performance of your GCP services.

It supports alerting and integrates with Stackdriver Logging for a comprehensive monitoring solution.

```python
# Example of creating a monitoring alert in Python

from google.cloud import monitoring_v3

def create_alert_policy(project_id, display_name):

client = monitoring_v3.AlertPolicyServiceClient()

alert_policy = monitoring_v3.AlertPolicy(

display_name=display_name,

conditions=[monitoring_v3.AlertPolicy.Condition(

display_name="CPU Usage",

condition_threshold=monitoring_v3.AlertPolicy.Condition.MetricThres

filter='metric.type="compute.googleapis.com/instance/cpu/
utilization"',

comparison=monitoring_v3.ComparisonType.COMPARISON_GT,

threshold_value=0.8,

duration={"seconds": 900},

)

)],

combiner=monitoring_v3.AlertPolicy.ConditionCombinerType.AND

)

project_name = f"projects/{project_id}"
```

```
client.create_alert_policy(name=project_name,
alert_policy=alert_policy)
```

Conclusion

THE INTEGRATION OF Firebase and GCP unlocks an array of benefits that can transform the way applications are built and managed. By combining Firebase's simplicity and GCP's power, developers can achieve remarkable efficiency, cost savings, and security, all while ensuring that applications are highly scalable and user-centric. As development needs evolve, Firebase and GCP continue to provide flexible solutions that support growth and innovation, making them a formidable duo in the cloud ecosystem.

Real-World Applications of Firebase and GCP

THE COMBINATION OF Firebase and Google Cloud Platform (GCP) provides an ideal environment for building diverse types of applications, from mobile apps to complex backend services. Firebase's focus on frontend services pairs well with GCP's extensive backend infrastructure, offering a well-rounded ecosystem for building, deploying, and managing applications. This section explores real-world scenarios and use cases that highlight the strengths of Firebase and GCP when used together, demonstrating how these platforms can support various industries and application types.

1. Mobile and Web Applications with Real-Time Data

FIREBASE IS PARTICULARLY well-suited for applications that require real-time data synchronization, such as social media platforms, messaging apps, and collaborative tools. Its Realtime

Database and Firestore services allow developers to build apps where data changes reflect immediately across all clients, creating a seamless experience for users.

Example: Building a Real-Time Chat Application

IN A REAL-TIME CHAT application, Firebase Authentication can be used for user sign-in, while Firestore serves as the database for storing messages and user information. Firebase Functions can be used to handle message notifications and updates. GCP can complement this setup by providing additional services such as Cloud Storage for storing media files, BigQuery for analytics, and Pub/Sub for messaging at scale.

```
// Firestore structure for a chat app

// Collections: users, messages, chats

import { getFirestore, collection, addDoc, serverTimestamp } from "firebase/firestore";

const db = getFirestore();

// Add a new message to the "messages" collection

async function sendMessage(chatId, userId, messageContent) {

try {

await addDoc(collection(db, 'chats', chatId, 'messages'), {

userId: userId,

content: messageContent,

timestamp: serverTimestamp(),
```

```
});

} catch (e) {

console.error("Error sending message: ", e);

}

}
```

In this example, messages are added to a Firestore subcollection under a specific chat, making it easy to query and display them in real time. Firebase's built-in support for Firestore listeners ensures that the chat interface updates automatically whenever a new message is added.

2. E-commerce Applications with Scalable Backend

FOR E-COMMERCE APPLICATIONS, Firebase and GCP provide a robust, scalable platform that can handle high traffic, real-time inventory updates, and secure transactions. Firebase Authentication simplifies user sign-up and login, while Firestore or Cloud SQL can be used for storing product and order data. GCP can further enhance the application with services like Cloud Functions for server-side logic, Cloud Spanner for highly scalable database needs, and BigQuery for customer and sales analytics.

Implementing Server-Side Order Processing with Cloud Functions

IN AN E-COMMERCE SCENARIO, Cloud Functions can be used to handle order processing, inventory updates, and payment confirmations. For example, when a user places an order, a Firebase Cloud Function can be triggered to process the order, update inventory, and send notifications.

```javascript
const functions = require("firebase-functions");

const admin = require("firebase-admin");

admin.initializeApp();

const db = admin.firestore();

exports.processOrder =
functions.firestore.document("orders/{orderId}")

.onCreate(async (snap, context) => {

const orderData = snap.data();

// Update inventory based on the order

const batch = db.batch();

orderData.items.forEach(item => {

const productRef =
db.collection('products').doc(item.productId);

batch.update(productRef, {

stock: admin.firestore.FieldValue.increment(-item.quantity)

});

});

await batch.commit();

console.log("Order processed and inventory updated");

});
```

In this example, the processOrder function is triggered whenever a new document is added to the orders collection. The function updates the stock count for each product in the order, ensuring that inventory levels are always up-to-date.

3. IoT and Smart Home Applications

FOR IOT AND SMART HOME applications, Firebase and GCP offer scalable, real-time data handling and device management solutions. Firebase can manage user authentication, real-time updates, and front-end services, while GCP provides the infrastructure for processing large volumes of data from IoT devices, performing analytics, and managing device connectivity through services like Cloud IoT Core.

Using Firebase for Real-Time Data and GCP for IoT Device Management

IN A SMART HOME APPLICATION, Firebase Realtime Database or Firestore can be used to handle real-time device state updates, while GCP's Cloud IoT Core can manage device connectivity and messaging. Data from devices can be sent to BigQuery for analysis, and Firebase can deliver real-time updates to user interfaces, enabling users to control and monitor their devices through a web or mobile app.

```
// Example of updating device state in Firebase

import { getDatabase, ref, set } from "firebase/database";

const db = getDatabase();

function updateDeviceState(deviceId, state) {

set(ref(db, 'devices/' + deviceId), {
```

```
state: state,

lastUpdated: Date.now()

});

}
```

Here, device states are stored in the Firebase Realtime Database, allowing the application to reflect changes immediately across all user devices. This setup is well-suited for scenarios where real-time control and monitoring are crucial, such as home automation or industrial IoT applications.

4. Machine Learning-Powered Applications

FIREBASE AND GCP CAN be used together to develop machine learning (ML) applications that personalize user experiences, provide recommendations, and perform real-time data analysis. Firebase ML provides easy-to-integrate ML capabilities for mobile apps, while GCP offers powerful services such as AI Platform, AutoML, and Cloud Vision for more complex ML workloads.

Example: Image Recognition with Firebase ML and GCP's Cloud Vision

FOR AN APPLICATION that requires image recognition, Firebase ML Kit can be used to integrate basic ML capabilities on the client side, while GCP's Cloud Vision API can handle more advanced image analysis. This hybrid approach ensures that the application can perform on-device ML tasks quickly while leveraging GCP for more intensive processing.

```
# Example of using Cloud Vision API with Python
```

```python
from google.cloud import vision

def analyze_image(image_path):

client = vision.ImageAnnotatorClient()

with open(image_path, 'rb') as image_file:

content = image_file.read()

image = vision.Image(content=content)

response = client.label_detection(image=image)

for label in response.label_annotations:

print(label.description, label.score)
```

This example shows how to use the Cloud Vision API to analyze images. By integrating this functionality with Firebase, the application can upload images to Cloud Storage and trigger Cloud Functions to analyze the images using Cloud Vision, delivering the results back to the user in real time.

5. Analytics and Data-Driven Decision Making

ANALYTICS IS A VITAL part of any modern application, providing insights into user behavior, application performance, and business metrics. Firebase Analytics provides out-of-the-box tracking for mobile and web applications, while GCP's BigQuery and Data Studio offer advanced data processing and visualization capabilities.

Using Firebase Analytics with BigQuery for Advanced Insights

FIREBASE ANALYTICS can be integrated with BigQuery, allowing you to run custom SQL queries on your analytics data for more detailed insights. This enables developers to track user engagement, retention, and other key metrics, helping to make data-driven decisions to improve the application.

—Example BigQuery query to analyze user retention

```
SELECT

user_pseudo_id,

COUNT(DISTINCT event_date) AS active_days

FROM

`project-id.analytics.dataset.events_YYYYMMDD`

GROUP BY

user_pseudo_id

HAVING

active_days > 1

ORDER BY

active_days DESC;
```

This query calculates the number of active days for each user, helping to identify the most engaged users. By leveraging BigQuery's powerful query capabilities, developers can gain actionable insights into how users interact with their applications.

Conclusion

THE REAL-WORLD APPLICATIONS of Firebase and GCP are vast, spanning industries and use cases that range from real-time data applications and e-commerce platforms to IoT and machine learning solutions. By harnessing the power of Firebase and GCP together, developers can build robust, scalable, and feature-rich applications that are ready to meet the demands of today's users. These examples demonstrate the flexibility and strength of the Firebase-GCP ecosystem, making it a go-to choice for developing modern applications across diverse sectors.

Chapter 2: Setting Up Firebase and GCP Environments

Creating a Firebase Project

SETTING UP A FIREBASE project is the initial step to leveraging Firebase services for building web and mobile applications. Firebase provides a user-friendly interface and integration with Google Cloud Platform (GCP), making it an ideal choice for developers looking to build scalable, real-time apps with minimal setup. In this section, we'll walk through the detailed steps of creating a Firebase project, configuring essential settings, and understanding Firebase's structure.

1. Prerequisites

BEFORE STARTING WITH Firebase, ensure you have:

- A Google account.

- Access to the Firebase Console (https://console.firebase.google.com).

- Basic understanding of the Firebase services and GCP architecture.

2. Navigating to the Firebase Console

TO BEGIN, OPEN YOUR web browser and go to https://console.firebase.google.com. The Firebase Console is the central hub for managing all Firebase services and projects. Here, you can create, configure, and monitor your Firebase project.

3. Creating a New Firebase Project

1. **Sign In**: Log in to your Google account if you haven't already. Once signed in, you'll be directed to the Firebase Console.

2. **Start a New Project**: Click on **"Add Project"**. This initiates the Firebase project creation process. You'll be prompted to provide a project name. Choose a descriptive name that reflects your application's purpose. For example, if you're building a chat application, you might name it **"ChatApp"**.

3. **Enable Google Analytics (Optional)**: You'll be asked whether to enable Google Analytics for your project. Google Analytics offers valuable insights into user behavior and engagement. If you plan to use it, select **"Enable Google Analytics for this project"**. Otherwise, you can skip this step.

4. **Configure Google Analytics Settings**: If you enable Analytics, select or create a Google Analytics account and configure region-specific settings. Analytics data is crucial for understanding your users and optimizing your app.

5. **Create Project**: Click **"Create Project"** to finalize. Firebase will take a few moments to set up the necessary infrastructure.

4. Exploring Firebase Project Structure

ONCE YOUR PROJECT IS created, you'll be taken to the **Firebase Project Overview** page. Let's explore the key sections:

- **Project Overview**: This section gives a snapshot of your project. Here, you can find your project's name, project ID, and a summary of services enabled.

- **Develop Section**: The Develop section includes Firebase's core tools like Authentication, Firestore, and Storage. These are the essential building blocks for app development.

- **Build Section**: This is where you'll find tools related to app performance and quality, such as Firebase Crashlytics and Performance Monitoring.

- **Release & Monitor Section**: Tools for managing app releases and monitoring analytics, including App Distribution and Firebase Analytics.

5. Configuring Project Settings

NAVIGATE TO THE **Project Settings** by clicking the gear icon in the top left corner of the Firebase Console. Here, you can customize settings related to your project:

- **General Settings**: In this section, you can view your project's details, including project name, project ID, and public settings. You can also manage linked accounts, such as Google Cloud accounts associated with the project.

- **Billing Settings**: Firebase offers a free tier, but for advanced services, you'll need to upgrade your plan. Configure your billing settings here to ensure your project has access to necessary services without interruptions.

- **Service Accounts**: Firebase automatically creates service accounts to interact with other Google Cloud services. These accounts are essential for app security and permissions management.

6. Adding Firebase SDK to Your App

TO USE FIREBASE SERVICES in your application, integrate the Firebase SDK. Firebase supports various platforms, including iOS, Android, and Web. Below is a step-by-step guide for integrating Firebase SDK into a web application.

Adding Firebase SDK to a Web Application

1. **Go to Project Settings**: Navigate to the **Project Settings** page and scroll down to **Your Apps**.
2. **Add App**: Select **Add App** and choose **Web** as your platform. Follow the instructions to register your app, including providing an app nickname and optional App ID.
3. **Get Firebase Config Object**: After registering the app, Firebase will generate a **Config Object** that includes your API Key, Project ID, and other essential information. Copy this config object.

INITIALIZE FIREBASE in Your App:

Add the Firebase SDK to your web app by pasting the following script tags into your HTML file:

html

Copy code

```
<!—Firebase App (the core Firebase SDK) is always required and must be listed first—>
```

```html
<script          src="https://www.gstatic.com/firebasejs/9.0.0/
firebase-app.js"></script>

<!—Add Firebase products that you want to use—>

<script          src="https://www.gstatic.com/firebasejs/9.0.0/
firebase-auth.js"></script>

<script          src="https://www.gstatic.com/firebasejs/9.0.0/
firebase-firestore.js"></script>
```

Then, initialize Firebase using the Config Object:

```javascript
// Your web app's Firebase configuration

const firebaseConfig = {

apiKey: "YOUR_API_KEY",

authDomain: "YOUR_PROJECT_ID.firebaseapp.com",

projectId: "YOUR_PROJECT_ID",

storageBucket: "YOUR_PROJECT_ID.appspot.com",

messagingSenderId: "YOUR_MESSAGING_SENDER_ID",

appId: "YOUR_APP_ID"

};

// Initialize Firebase

const app = firebase.initializeApp(firebaseConfig);
```

1.

7. Next Steps

AT THIS POINT, YOUR Firebase project is set up, and you're ready to explore Firebase's features and integrate services like Authentication, Firestore, and Storage. Firebase's integration with Google Cloud makes it easy to scale as your app grows, providing you with powerful tools to manage and deploy your application.

With your Firebase project created and configured, you can now proceed to connect it to a Google Cloud project and further customize settings for specific services in Firebase and GCP. The following sections in this chapter will cover setting up your Google Cloud project and linking it with Firebase for a seamless development experience.

Introduction to Firebase Console and Key Features

THE FIREBASE CONSOLE is the central hub for managing all aspects of your Firebase project. It provides a user-friendly interface to configure, deploy, and monitor various Firebase services. Whether you're building a mobile app, a web app, or both, the Firebase Console simplifies the management of backend infrastructure and offers integrated tools to enhance app performance, monitor user engagement, and scale seamlessly.

In this section, we'll dive deep into the Firebase Console, exploring its key features and functionalities. By the end of this section, you'll have a comprehensive understanding of how to navigate the console, access essential tools, and configure various Firebase services to meet your app development needs.

1. Navigating the Firebase Console

UPON ACCESSING HTTPS://console.firebase.google.com, you'll be directed to the Firebase Console homepage. Here, you can view all your existing projects or create a new one. Once you've selected a project, you'll be taken to the **Project Overview** page, which acts as the entry point to all Firebase services. Key sections of the Firebase Console include:

- **Develop Section**: This section houses core Firebase services like **Authentication**, **Firestore Database**, **Realtime Database**, **Storage**, and **Hosting**. These services provide essential backend support for your applications.

- **Build Section**: Here, you'll find tools related to app quality, including **Crashlytics**, **Performance Monitoring**, **Test Lab**, and more. These tools are designed to help you monitor and improve app stability and performance.

- **Release & Monitor Section**: This section focuses on the deployment and monitoring of your applications. It includes tools like **Analytics**, **App Distribution**, **Cloud Messaging**, and **Remote Config**, allowing you to manage app versions, analyze user behavior, and deploy targeted content.

- **Engage Section**: Firebase offers a range of tools to engage users, including **A/B Testing**, **In-App Messaging**, and **Predictions**. These features allow you to optimize user experience through targeted experiments and personalized messaging.

Each section contains specific tools and services that are integral to Firebase's functionality. Let's delve into some of these key areas and understand their capabilities.

2. Key Features of Firebase Console

a. Authentication

FIREBASE AUTHENTICATION supports multiple sign-in methods, including email/password, Google Sign-In, Facebook Login, Twitter Login, and more. To access the **Authentication** service:

1. Navigate to the **Develop** section and select **Authentication**.
2. Click on **Get Started**. You'll be prompted to enable a sign-in method.
3. Choose a sign-in provider. For instance, to enable **Email/Password** authentication, click **Edit** beside the provider, toggle **Enable**, and click **Save**.

Firebase Authentication simplifies user sign-up and sign-in processes, providing secure authentication methods with minimal code.

b. Firestore Database

FIRESTORE IS FIREBASE'S scalable NoSQL cloud database for storing and syncing data in real-time. Firestore supports offline data persistence, allowing users to access data even without a network connection. To start using Firestore:

1. Go to **Develop > Firestore Database**.

2. Click **Create Database** and choose a mode (either **Production** or **Test** mode). For development, **Test mode** allows read and write access for 30 days.

3. Configure your database location to optimize performance based on where your users are located.

Firestore uses collections and documents to store data, offering flexibility in data structure and robust querying capabilities.

c. Storage

FIREBASE STORAGE PROVIDES a secure way to upload and download files such as photos, videos, and other user-generated content. It's built for scalability and integrates seamlessly with Firebase Authentication for access control. To configure Firebase Storage:

1. Under **Develop**, select **Storage** and click **Get Started**.
2. Choose your storage location and click **Done**.
3. Upload a file by clicking **Upload File**. You can also create folders to organize files within your storage bucket.

Firebase Storage includes client libraries for easy integration across platforms, supporting large file uploads and resumable uploads for network resilience.

d. Hosting

FIREBASE HOSTING IS a static web hosting service that's quick to set up and supports custom domains and SSL certificates. It's optimized for serving static content and single-page applications. To deploy your app to Firebase Hosting:

1. Navigate to **Develop > Hosting**.
2. Click **Get Started** and follow the steps to install Firebase CLI if you haven't already.

Initialize your project using Firebase CLI by running:

bash

firebase init hosting

Select your Firebase project, specify the public directory (usually public), and configure settings as prompted. Once configured, deploy your app with:

bash

firebase deploy

1.

Firebase Hosting supports custom domain configuration and provides free SSL certificates, making it a robust solution for hosting web applications.

3. Monitoring and Analytics in Firebase Console

a. Analytics

FIREBASE ANALYTICS provides detailed insights into user behavior, allowing you to track metrics such as active users, session duration, and user demographics. To access analytics:

1. Go to **Release & Monitor > Analytics**.
2. Firebase automatically tracks events like app opens, user engagement, and in-app purchases. You can also define custom events to track specific user actions.

Analytics data is invaluable for understanding user behavior, optimizing user experience, and making data-driven decisions for app improvements.

b. Crashlytics

FIREBASE CRASHLYTICS is a powerful tool for monitoring app crashes and performance issues. It provides real-time crash reports with insights into why the crash occurred, allowing you to quickly address issues. To set up Crashlytics:

1. Navigate to **Build > Crashlytics** and click **Set up Crashlytics**.

Integrate the Crashlytics SDK into your app. For Android apps, add the following dependencies to your build.gradle file:

gradle

Copy code

implementation 'com.google.firebase:firebase-crashlytics'
   1.

2. Initialize Crashlytics in your app's entry point. Crashlytics will automatically log crashes and report them to the Firebase Console.

Crashlytics enables you to prioritize issues based on impact and provides detailed stack traces to expedite debugging.

c. Performance Monitoring

FIREBASE PERFORMANCE Monitoring offers insights into app performance, including app startup time, network latency, and screen rendering times. It allows you to identify bottlenecks and optimize performance for a smoother user experience. To enable Performance Monitoring:

1. Go to **Build** > **Performance Monitoring** and click **Start Monitoring**.

Integrate the Performance Monitoring SDK by adding the following dependency to your app:

implementation 'com.google.firebase:firebase-perf'

Firebase Performance Monitoring includes out-of-the-box metrics and lets you define custom metrics for granular performance insights.

4. Integrating Firebase Console with Google Cloud Platform

FIREBASE INTEGRATES seamlessly with Google Cloud Platform (GCP), allowing you to extend Firebase's capabilities with GCP services like BigQuery, Cloud Functions, and AI/ML services. You can link your Firebase project to a GCP project for access to advanced GCP tools:

1. Go to **Project Settings** in the Firebase Console.
2. Click on **Integrations** and select **Link to Google Cloud Platform**.
3. Follow the prompts to link your Firebase project with an existing GCP project or create a new one.

By integrating with GCP, you can leverage advanced cloud services for machine learning, data analytics, and scalable backend infrastructure.

5. Next Steps in Firebase Console

THE FIREBASE CONSOLE is a comprehensive platform that covers all aspects of app development, deployment, and monitoring. Familiarize yourself with the console to take full advantage of Firebase's capabilities. In the next section, we'll explore how to set up a Google Cloud project, link it to your Firebase project, and manage billing and cloud resources for seamless integration with Google Cloud Platform.

Setting Up a Google Cloud Project

GOOGLE CLOUD PLATFORM (GCP) provides a wide array of services and tools that enable developers to build, deploy, and manage applications in the cloud. Setting up a Google Cloud project is a foundational step for leveraging GCP services and integrating them with Firebase. In this section, we'll explore the process of creating a Google Cloud project, configuring essential settings, and understanding the GCP Console's core functionalities.

1. Overview of Google Cloud Platform

GOOGLE CLOUD PLATFORM offers a comprehensive suite of cloud computing services, including infrastructure as a service (IaaS), platform as a service (PaaS), and software as a service (SaaS) solutions. These services support a wide range of application development needs, from data storage and machine learning to networking and security.

To manage these resources, GCP utilizes **Projects** as the central organizational unit. Each project contains settings, permissions, and billing information for all associated resources and services. Understanding how to create and configure a GCP project is essential for any developer working within the Google ecosystem.

2. Creating a Google Cloud Project

TO GET STARTED, FOLLOW these steps to create a new project on Google Cloud:

1. **Sign In to Google Cloud Console**: Open https://console.cloud.google.com and sign in with your Google account. If you're new to GCP, you may need to agree to the terms of service before proceeding.

2. **Navigate to the Project Selector**: In the GCP Console, click on the project selector at the top of the page. This dropdown lists all your existing projects. To create a new project, select **New Project** from the dropdown menu.

3. **Configure Project Details**:

○ **Project Name**: Enter a name for your project. This name should reflect the purpose or scope of the project, such as **"E-commerceApp"** or **"MachineLearningProject"**.

○ **Project ID**: GCP automatically generates a unique project ID based on the project name. This ID is immutable and globally unique across Google Cloud. You can use the default ID or customize it, but once set, it cannot be changed.

○ **Billing Account**: Select a billing account or create a new one if you don't have an existing account. A billing account is necessary to access GCP's paid services beyond the free tier.

○ **Location**: If your organization has organizational units, select the appropriate one. Otherwise, leave it as **No organization**.

4. **Create the Project**: Click **Create** to finalize. GCP will take a few moments to set up the new project and redirect you to the project's dashboard.

3. Exploring the GCP Console

AFTER CREATING YOUR project, you'll be taken to the **GCP Console Dashboard**, where you can manage and monitor all aspects of your project. Let's explore some key areas within the GCP Console:

• **Dashboard**: This provides an overview of your project, including recent activities, resources, and billing information. You can customize the dashboard to display widgets for specific services, such as **Compute Engine**, **Cloud Storage**, or **BigQuery**.

• **Navigation Menu**: On the left-hand side, the navigation menu lists all GCP services. Services are grouped into categories like **Compute**, **Storage**, **Database**, **Networking**, and **AI & Machine Learning**. Select any service to access its settings, documentation, and configuration options.

● **API & Services**: Accessed via the **Navigation Menu** under **APIs & Services**, this section allows you to enable or disable APIs, view usage reports, and manage credentials. Most GCP services require enabling the corresponding API before use.

● **IAM & Admin**: Google Cloud uses **Identity and Access Management (IAM)** to control permissions for project resources. In this section, you can add users, assign roles, and set permissions at both the project and resource levels.

● **Billing**: The **Billing** section lets you manage billing accounts, view usage reports, and set up budgets and alerts. GCP offers a free tier and credits for new users, making it accessible for initial experimentation and development.

4. Configuring IAM Permissions

PROPERLY CONFIGURING IAM permissions is crucial for maintaining security and controlling access to GCP resources. Google Cloud IAM allows you to assign roles to users, groups, or service accounts with specific permissions. Here's how to configure IAM roles in your project:

1. **Navigate to IAM**: In the GCP Console, go to **IAM & Admin > IAM**. You'll see a list of all users and service accounts with access to your project.

2. **Add Members**: To add a new member, click **Add**. Enter the user's email address and assign one or more roles. Common roles include:

○ **Viewer**: Provides read-only access to all project resources.

○ **Editor**: Allows read-write access to all resources.

○ **Owner**: Grants full control over all resources, including billing.

3. **Assign Custom Roles** (Optional): If predefined roles don't meet your needs, you can create custom roles with specific permissions. Under **IAM & Admin > Roles**, click **Create Role**. Define permissions based on the actions required by the user or application.

4. **Service Accounts**: For applications and automated scripts, use service accounts instead of personal user accounts. Service accounts are linked to specific resources and provide a secure way to access GCP services. Create service accounts under **IAM & Admin > Service Accounts**.

5. Enabling GCP APIs and Services

MOST GCP SERVICES REQUIRE enabling specific APIs to access them. For example, to use **Cloud Storage**, you must enable the **Cloud Storage API**. Here's how to enable APIs:

1. **Go to APIs & Services**: In the navigation menu, select **APIs & Services > Library**.
2. **Search for the API**: Enter the API name, such as **Cloud Storage API**, in the search bar. Click on the API in the search results.
3. **Enable the API**: Click **Enable** to activate the API for your project. Repeat this process for any other APIs you

need.

GCP provides detailed documentation and pricing information for each API, allowing you to understand usage limits and potential costs before enabling services.

6. Setting Up Billing and Budgets

BILLING MANAGEMENT is a critical aspect of GCP project configuration. By setting budgets and alerts, you can avoid unexpected charges and monitor your spending:

1. **Navigate to Billing**: Go to **Billing** in the navigation menu. If you haven't linked a billing account, you'll need to do so before proceeding.
2. **Set Up a Budget**: Under **Billing**, select **Budgets & Alerts**. Click **Create Budget**, choose a name, and set a spending limit based on your expected usage.
3. **Configure Alerts**: Define thresholds for email alerts. For example, you can set alerts at 50%, 90%, and 100% of your budget to receive notifications when approaching your spending limit.
4. **Billing Reports**: Access detailed billing reports under **Billing > Reports**. You can filter by service, project, or time frame to gain insights into your usage patterns and costs.

7. Linking Google Cloud Project to Firebase

LINKING YOUR GCP PROJECT to Firebase allows you to use Firebase's powerful app development tools while taking advantage of GCP's advanced services. To link projects:

1. **Go to Firebase Console:** Open

https://console.firebase.google.com and select your Firebase project.

2. **Project Settings**: Click on the gear icon to access **Project Settings**. Under the **General** tab, scroll down to **Google Cloud Platform (GCP) Resource Location**.

3. **Link Project**: Click **Link to Google Cloud Platform Project** and select your GCP project from the list. Confirm the link to establish the connection.

4. **Confirm Integration**: Once linked, you can access GCP services directly from the Firebase Console. For example, use **BigQuery** for advanced analytics or **Cloud Functions** for serverless backend logic.

8. Using Google Cloud Shell for Advanced Management

GOOGLE CLOUD SHELL provides a command-line environment directly in the GCP Console, allowing you to manage resources, deploy applications, and automate tasks. To use Cloud Shell:

1. **Activate Cloud Shell**: Click the **Cloud Shell** icon in the top right corner of the GCP Console. A terminal will open at the bottom of the screen.

Access GCP Resources: Use gcloud commands to manage your project. For example, to list all enabled APIs, enter:

gcloud services list

1.

2. **Deploy Applications**: With Cloud Shell, you can deploy applications, configure resources, and execute scripts without leaving the GCP Console.

9. Next Steps in Google Cloud Platform

SETTING UP A GOOGLE Cloud project is an essential step in integrating Firebase with GCP services. By configuring IAM permissions, enabling APIs, and linking your project to Firebase, you can leverage both platforms for a seamless development experience. In the next section, we'll explore linking Firebase to GCP in more detail, including advanced cloud resource management and monitoring for optimal performance and scalability.

Linking Firebase to GCP

LINKING FIREBASE TO Google Cloud Platform (GCP) is a powerful way to extend the capabilities of your Firebase project by leveraging the advanced services provided by GCP. This connection enables Firebase to utilize a broader range of Google Cloud services, such as BigQuery for advanced analytics, Cloud Storage for extensive file management, and Cloud Functions for serverless architecture. In this section, we'll walk through the process of linking Firebase with GCP, configuring essential settings, and understanding how to manage and optimize linked services effectively.

1. Why Link Firebase with GCP?

FIREBASE AND GCP INTEGRATION is advantageous for developers who require additional cloud resources that aren't natively available within Firebase alone. Some key benefits include:

- **Advanced Analytics**: With BigQuery, you can conduct complex data analyses and visualize app data for deeper insights beyond Firebase Analytics.

- **Scalability**: Leverage GCP's infrastructure, such as Cloud SQL and Compute Engine, to handle large-scale data storage and processing needs.

- **Security and Compliance**: Utilize GCP's security tools and compliance certifications to protect user data and meet regulatory requirements.

By linking Firebase to GCP, you can unlock these benefits and seamlessly scale your applications as your user base grows.

2. Prerequisites for Linking Firebase to GCP

BEFORE STARTING, MAKE sure you have:

- A Firebase project set up.

- A GCP project with billing enabled.

- Owner or Editor permissions on both Firebase and GCP projects.

With these prerequisites, you can proceed to link Firebase and GCP projects through the Firebase Console.

3. Linking a Firebase Project to a GCP Project

1. **Open Firebase Console**: Navigate to https://console.firebase.google.com and select the Firebase project you wish to link.

2. **Access Project Settings**: In the Firebase Console, click on the gear icon next to **Project Overview** and select **Project Settings** from the dropdown menu.

3. **Link to GCP Project**: Scroll down to the **Google Cloud Platform (GCP) Resource Location** section. Click **Link to Google Cloud Platform Project**.

4. **Select or Create a GCP Project**:

○ If you already have a GCP project, select it from the list. The list will display only those projects where you have the required permissions.

○ If you need to create a new GCP project, follow the on-screen instructions to set one up. This will involve providing a project name, ID, and billing information.

5. **Confirm the Link**: After selecting the GCP project, review the details and confirm the link. This process may take a few moments as Firebase configures necessary settings.

ONCE LINKED, FIREBASE and GCP will automatically synchronize resources, allowing you to access GCP services from within Firebase and vice versa.

4. Configuring Firebase to Use GCP Services

WITH FIREBASE AND GCP now linked, you can begin configuring Firebase to utilize various GCP services. Here's a look at some of the commonly used integrations:

a. BigQuery for Advanced Analytics

BIGQUERY PROVIDES ROBUST tools for querying large datasets, making it ideal for in-depth analysis of app usage and performance data.

1. **Enable BigQuery Integration**: In the Firebase Console, navigate to **Analytics** and select **BigQuery**. Click **Link** to enable BigQuery export.
2. **Select Data to Export**: Choose which datasets to export to BigQuery. Firebase Analytics data, including events and user properties, are available for export. You can also export Crashlytics data for detailed error analysis.
3. **Access Data in BigQuery**: Once enabled, Firebase will automatically sync data to BigQuery, where you can create custom queries and visualize data. Use SQL queries to filter, aggregate, and analyze app data.

b. Cloud Storage for Extensive File Management

WHILE FIREBASE STORAGE is sufficient for most use cases, linking with Google Cloud Storage provides additional flexibility and storage options.

1. **Access Google Cloud Storage**: In the Firebase Console, go to **Storage** and select **Buckets**. You'll see a list of linked Google Cloud Storage buckets.
2. **Create and Manage Buckets**: If needed, create new storage buckets directly within GCP. To do this, navigate to the **Google Cloud Console** and select **Storage > Create Bucket**. Define bucket settings like location, storage class, and access permissions.

Integrate Cloud Storage with Firebase App: Use the Firebase SDK to upload and download files. Here's an example of how to upload a file using JavaScript:

```
const storageRef = firebase.storage().ref();
```

```
const fileRef = storageRef.child('images/myImage.jpg');

fileRef.put(file).then((snapshot) => {

console.log('Uploaded a file!');

});
```

1. **Manage Access and Permissions**: Use IAM settings in GCP to control access to Cloud Storage buckets, ensuring secure file storage and retrieval.

c. Cloud Functions for Serverless Computing

FIREBASE CLOUD FUNCTIONS can be enhanced with GCP Cloud Functions for greater scalability and functionality.

Enable Cloud Functions in Firebase: In the Firebase Console, go to **Functions** and click **Get Started**. Install the Firebase CLI and initialize Cloud Functions by running:

bash

Copy code

```
firebase init functions
```

1.

Write and Deploy Functions: Firebase Cloud Functions use Node.js. You can write functions to handle events like user sign-ups, Firestore updates, and more. Deploy functions with:

```
firebase deploy—only functions
```

1.

2. **Integrate with Other GCP Services**: You can extend

functions to access GCP services like **Cloud Pub/Sub** for messaging or **Cloud Vision** for image recognition. Use service accounts to authenticate your functions with these services securely.

d. Cloud SQL for Relational Data

FOR APPLICATIONS REQUIRING relational databases, Cloud SQL offers fully managed MySQL, PostgreSQL, and SQL Server instances.

1. **Create a Cloud SQL Instance**: In the Google Cloud Console, navigate to **SQL > Create Instance**. Choose a database engine and configure instance settings such as region, machine type, and storage.
2. **Connect Firebase App to Cloud SQL**: Use the Firebase Admin SDK or standard database clients to connect your app to Cloud SQL. Define environment variables for credentials and connection strings in your app's backend code.
3. **Manage Databases and Users**: Use the Cloud SQL interface to manage databases, configure backups, and add users. Set permissions for secure database access.

5. Monitoring and Managing Linked Firebase and GCP Projects

MONITORING LINKED PROJECTS is essential for maintaining security, optimizing performance, and controlling costs. Firebase and GCP provide various tools for monitoring and managing resources:

a. Cloud Monitoring for Performance Insights

CLOUD MONITORING OFFERS dashboards, metrics, and alerts for Firebase and GCP resources.

1. **Set Up Monitoring Dashboards**: In the GCP Console, navigate to **Monitoring** and create custom dashboards for services like Firestore, Cloud Functions, and BigQuery.
2. **Define Alerts**: Configure alerts for key metrics, such as CPU usage or database latency. Set thresholds and choose notification channels like email or Slack for real-time updates.
3. **Use Logs Explorer**: Access Logs Explorer in the Google Cloud Console for detailed logs on Firebase functions, Cloud SQL queries, and more. Use filters to pinpoint specific events or errors.

b. IAM for Secure Access Management

IDENTITY AND ACCESS Management (IAM) controls user permissions for both Firebase and GCP services.

1. **Review IAM Permissions**: Regularly review and update IAM roles for Firebase and GCP projects. Use predefined roles like **Owner**, **Editor**, and **Viewer**, or create custom roles for specific use cases.
2. **Use Service Accounts for Applications**: For secure application access, create service accounts with the least privileges necessary. Download JSON keys for authentication and securely store them.
3. **Monitor Access Logs**: Use Cloud Audit Logs to track IAM activity, such as role changes or service account

access. Audit logs provide transparency and help detect unauthorized access.

c. Billing Management for Cost Control

TO MANAGE COSTS EFFECTIVELY, Firebase and GCP provide tools for setting budgets, monitoring expenses, and optimizing resource usage.

1. **Set Budgets and Alerts**: In the GCP Console, go to **Billing** and create budgets for your linked project. Set alerts for 50%, 75%, and 100% of the budget to prevent overspending.
2. **Analyze Billing Reports**: Use the **Reports** section under Billing to track expenses by service. Identify high-cost services and optimize or scale down where possible.
3. **Use the Cost Management API**: For advanced cost management, use the Cost Management API to automate budget tracking and generate custom expense reports.

6. Best Practices for Firebase and GCP Integration

TO MAXIMIZE THE BENEFITS of Firebase and GCP integration, consider the following best practices:

- **Optimize Resource Allocation**: Regularly review and adjust resource allocations, such as database instances and storage buckets, based on usage patterns to avoid unnecessary costs.

- **Implement Security Best Practices**: Use IAM roles, service accounts, and encryption to secure resources.

Regularly update permissions and audit access logs for compliance.

- **Automate Deployments with CI/CD**: Set up continuous integration and continuous delivery pipelines for Firebase and GCP projects. Use tools like Cloud Build to automate testing and deployment.

By following these best practices, you can ensure a secure, scalable, and cost-effective environment for your application. In the next section, we'll explore billing and resource management in more detail, providing tips on how to optimize your Firebase and GCP projects for sustainability and growth.

Managing Billing and Cloud Resources

EFFECTIVE BILLING AND resource management are essential components of any project on Google Cloud Platform (GCP) and Firebase. Properly managing billing helps you avoid unexpected costs and ensures that your application remains sustainable as it scales. This section covers the fundamentals of billing, budgeting, and resource optimization in both Firebase and GCP, with step-by-step instructions for setting up billing alerts, analyzing costs, and optimizing resource usage.

1. Setting Up Billing in Google Cloud Platform

BILLING IN GCP IS MANAGED at the project level, which allows for detailed tracking and reporting. You can set up a billing account during the initial project creation or add one later.

a. Creating and Linking a Billing Account

1. **Access the GCP Console**: Go to https://console.cloud.google.com and navigate to **Billing**.

2. **Create a New Billing Account**: If you do not have an existing billing account, you will need to create one. Click **Manage Billing Accounts** and select **Create Account**. Follow the prompts to provide necessary details, including payment information.

3. **Link Billing Account to Project**: Once created, link your billing account to your project. In the **Billing** section, choose **Account Management** and select your project from the dropdown menu. Click **Link Billing Account** and choose the appropriate account.

4. **Enable Cost Management Features**: After linking, you can enable additional cost management tools like **Budgets & Alerts** and **Cost Reporting** to keep track of your spending.

b. Understanding Billing Account Settings

A BILLING ACCOUNT IN GCP includes several important settings:

- **Billing Contacts**: Ensure that you add billing contacts who will receive notifications about expenses and invoices.

- **Payment Settings**: Configure your payment methods and schedule. You can choose between automatic payments (default) and manual payments if supported in your region.

- **Billing Export**: Enable billing export to BigQuery for detailed analysis. This feature allows you to export billing data and analyze costs over time, which is essential for projects with complex usage patterns.

2. Setting Up Budgets and Alerts

BUDGETS AND ALERTS are critical for controlling costs and avoiding billing surprises. GCP provides robust tools for setting up budgets and configuring email alerts based on budget thresholds.

a. Creating a Budget

1. **Go to Budgets & Alerts**: In the **Billing** section of the GCP Console, select **Budgets & Alerts**.
2. **Create a New Budget**: Click **Create Budget**. Choose a name for your budget and specify the scope. You can set the budget at the project level or choose specific services.
3. **Define Budget Amount and Period**: Set a budget amount that aligns with your expected spending. You can define budgets based on a fixed amount or previous spend trends. Specify whether the budget should reset monthly, quarterly, or annually.
4. **Set Alert Thresholds**: Configure alert thresholds, such as 50%, 75%, and 90% of the budget. Alerts can be sent via email or integrated with tools like Slack for real-time notifications.

b. Managing Alerts

- **Configure Multiple Recipients**: To ensure key stakeholders are informed, add multiple recipients to alert notifications. This can include technical and financial contacts.

● **Integration with Google Chat**: For real-time alerts, integrate notifications with Google Chat or other communication tools through webhooks.

● **Review Alert History**: Regularly review alert history to understand spending patterns and adjust thresholds accordingly.

3. Monitoring and Analyzing Billing Reports

BILLING REPORTS IN GCP provide detailed insights into spending across services and projects. You can filter reports by service, time period, and project to gain a granular view of expenses.

a. Accessing Billing Reports

1. **Navigate to Billing Reports**: In the **Billing** section, click **Reports**. Here, you'll see an overview of your spending over time.
2. **Filtering Data by Services and Projects**: Use the filters at the top of the page to narrow down data by service (e.g., **Compute Engine, BigQuery**) or by specific projects. This allows you to identify high-cost services and optimize accordingly.
3. **View Trends and Usage Patterns**: The **Trends** tab displays spending patterns over time. You can adjust the date range to view daily, monthly, or yearly trends. Identifying spikes in usage can help you adjust resource allocation and mitigate unnecessary expenses.

4. **Download Billing Data**: For in-depth analysis, download billing data as a CSV file or export it to BigQuery. This provides the flexibility to create custom reports and visualize spending with tools like Data Studio.

b. Analyzing Billing Data with BigQuery

1. **Enable Billing Export to BigQuery**: In the **Billing** section, go to **Billing Export** and choose **BigQuery Export**. Select your project and specify the dataset to store billing data.

WRITE SQL QUERIES FOR Cost Analysis: Once billing data is available in BigQuery, you can write SQL queries to analyze costs. For example, the following query retrieves total spending per service:

```sql
SELECT

service.description AS Service,

SUM(cost) AS Total_Cost

FROM

`project.billing_dataset.gcp_billing_export`

WHERE

usage_start_time >= '2024-01-01' AND usage_end_time <= '2024-12-31'

GROUP BY

Service
```

ORDER BY

Total_Cost DESC;

    1.

2. **Visualize Data in Data Studio**: Connect BigQuery to Google Data Studio for advanced visualization. Create dashboards to track spending in real-time and set up automated email reports for regular updates.

4. Optimizing Resource Usage

OPTIMIZING RESOURCE usage involves scaling services based on demand, leveraging cost-effective options, and utilizing monitoring tools to identify inefficient resource allocation.

a. Scaling Services with Autoscaler

AUTOSCALER IS A GCP feature that automatically adjusts the number of VM instances based on usage patterns. This ensures that you're only paying for resources when needed.

1. **Enable Autoscaler for Compute Engine**: Go to **Compute Engine > Instance Groups**. Select an instance group and enable **Autoscaling**.
2. **Configure Autoscaling Policies**: Define policies based on CPU usage, load balancing, or custom metrics. You can set minimum and maximum instance counts to control costs.
3. **Monitor Autoscaling Activity**: Use **Cloud Monitoring** to track autoscaling activity and adjust policies as needed. This ensures efficient scaling and cost savings.

b. Using Preemptible VM Instances

PREEMPTIBLE VM INSTANCES are cost-effective alternatives for non-critical workloads. These instances are significantly cheaper than regular VMs but may be terminated by Google Cloud with a short notice.

1. **Create a Preemptible VM Instance**: In **Compute Engine**, select **Create Instance** and choose **Preemptible** under the pricing options.
2. **Configure VM for Fault-Tolerant Workloads**: Use preemptible instances for batch processing, data analysis, or other tasks that can tolerate interruptions.
3. **Leverage Instance Templates**: For ease of deployment, create instance templates that specify preemptible instances. This allows for quick scaling of fault-tolerant tasks.

5. Managing Firebase Billing

FIREBASE OFFERS A FREE tier, but as your app scales, you may need to upgrade to a paid plan. Firebase billing is integrated with GCP, allowing you to manage Firebase costs through the GCP Console.

a. Understanding Firebase Pricing Tiers

FIREBASE PRICING IS divided into three tiers:

- **Spark Plan**: Free tier with limited usage of Firebase services, such as limited storage and authentication.

- **Blaze Plan**: Pay-as-you-go pricing based on actual usage. Ideal for scaling apps with unpredictable usage patterns.

- **Flame Plan** (Deprecated): Flat-rate pricing model, though it has been phased out in favor of Blaze.

b. Estimating Firebase Costs

1. **Use the Firebase Pricing Calculator**: The Firebase website provides a calculator for estimating costs based on usage. Input values for services like Firestore, Authentication, and Hosting to get an estimate.

2. **Review Usage in Firebase Console**: In the Firebase Console, navigate to **Usage and Billing** to see detailed usage metrics. This section shows data for services like Firestore, Cloud Functions, and Realtime Database.

3. **Set Quotas for Resources**: To control costs, configure quotas for services in the GCP Console under **IAM & Admin > Quotas**. Setting quotas prevents overuse of services that could lead to unexpected expenses.

c. Tracking Firebase Usage with Cloud Monitoring

1. **Set Up Monitoring Alerts**: In the Firebase Console, link to **Cloud Monitoring** for detailed insights into Firebase resource usage. Configure alerts for critical metrics, such as Firestore reads/writes or Cloud Functions invocations.

2. **Create Dashboards for Firebase Services**: Use Cloud Monitoring to create dashboards that display key Firebase metrics. This allows for real-time monitoring and quick adjustments if usage spikes unexpectedly.

3. **Use Cloud Logging for Debugging**: Enable **Cloud Logging** to track logs for Firebase services. Logs provide detailed information about resource usage and can help troubleshoot issues affecting costs.

6. Best Practices for Cost Management

TO MAINTAIN A COST-effective Firebase and GCP project, follow these best practices:

- **Regularly Review Billing Reports**: Schedule monthly reviews of billing reports to identify trends and adjust budgets.

- **Use Resource Labels**: Apply labels to resources for easy cost allocation and categorization. Labels can help track costs associated with specific projects, departments, or clients.

- **Automate Cost Management**: Use the **Billing API** to automate cost tracking and reporting. Automate budget creation and alerting to maintain proactive control over expenses.

- **Consider Committed Use Contracts**: For predictable workloads, consider GCP's committed use contracts for discounts on resources like Compute Engine and Cloud SQL.

- **Review Free Tier Limits**: Ensure you're maximizing the use of free tier limits for both Firebase and GCP services, and only scale when usage consistently exceeds free tier allowances.

By applying these strategies, you can optimize your Firebase and GCP projects for cost efficiency, ensuring that your app remains sustainable and scalable over time. In the next chapter, we will explore Firebase Authentication and Cloud Identity, focusing on best practices for secure and scalable user authentication.

Chapter 3: Firebase Authentication and Cloud Identity

Introduction to Firebase Authentication

FIREBASE AUTHENTICATION provides a robust, secure, and flexible way to handle user authentication for your applications. By leveraging Firebase Authentication, developers can easily integrate multiple authentication methods, including email/password, phone, Google, Facebook, Twitter, and more, without having to implement custom authentication systems. Firebase Authentication also allows for anonymous sign-in and custom authentication solutions, which makes it a versatile choice for applications with diverse authentication requirements.

Firebase Authentication is built on top of Google Cloud Platform (GCP) infrastructure, meaning it is designed to handle large-scale applications with high availability, security, and performance. In this section, we will explore Firebase Authentication's key features, the various ways it can be implemented, and how it integrates with Google Cloud Identity services to provide a unified and secure authentication experience for your users.

Key Features of Firebase Authentication

FIREBASE AUTHENTICATION offers the following essential features:

- **Multiple Authentication Providers**: Firebase supports various popular authentication methods such as email/password, phone authentication, and social logins (Google, Facebook, Twitter, GitHub, etc.). This provides flexibility and convenience for users by allowing them to sign in using their preferred method.

● **Anonymous Authentication**: Firebase allows users to authenticate without requiring any credentials. This is useful for applications where users may want to explore features without signing up, and it also enables easy conversion to permanent accounts later on.

● **Custom Authentication System**: With Firebase Authentication, developers can implement a custom authentication system using a secure token generated on their server, enabling more complex authentication scenarios.

● **Integration with Google Cloud Identity**: Firebase Authentication integrates seamlessly with Google Cloud Identity, enabling centralized user management, secure access control, and unified authentication across multiple Google Cloud services.

● **Built-In User Management**: Firebase provides a user management system that allows developers to manage users, reset passwords, verify email addresses, and more. This helps streamline the management of user accounts and improves the user experience.

Setting Up Firebase Authentication

BEFORE IMPLEMENTING Firebase Authentication, you need to ensure that your Firebase project is set up correctly. Follow these steps:

1. **Create a Firebase Project**: In the Firebase console, click

on **"Add Project"** and follow the on-screen instructions to create a new Firebase project.

2. **Enable Firebase Authentication**: Navigate to the **"Authentication"** section in the Firebase console and click **"Get Started"**. This enables the Firebase Authentication service for your project.

3. **Configure Authentication Providers**: In the **"Sign-in Method"** tab, select the authentication providers you want to enable (e.g., Email/Password, Google, Facebook, etc.) and configure them according to your needs.

Implementing Email/Password Authentication

EMAIL/PASSWORD AUTHENTICATION is one of the most common methods, as it provides a straightforward way for users to create an account and sign in. Below is an example of how to implement email/password authentication using Firebase in a JavaScript-based web application.

// Import Firebase

import firebase from "firebase/app";

import "firebase/auth";

// Initialize Firebase

const firebaseConfig = {

apiKey: "your-api-key",

authDomain: "your-auth-domain",

projectId: "your-project-id",

storageBucket: "your-storage-bucket",

```javascript
  messagingSenderId: "your-messaging-sender-id",

  appId: "your-app-id"

};

firebase.initializeApp(firebaseConfig);

// Function to Sign Up a New User

const signUp = (email, password) => {

  firebase.auth().createUserWithEmailAndPassword(email,
  password)

  .then((userCredential) => {

    // User signed up successfully

    console.log("User signed up:", userCredential.user);

  })

  .catch((error) => {

    // Handle sign up errors

    console.error("Error during sign up:", error);

  });

};

// Function to Sign In a User

const signIn = (email, password) => {

  firebase.auth().signInWithEmailAndPassword(email, password)

  .then((userCredential) => {
```

```
// User signed in successfully
console.log("User signed in:", userCredential.user);
})
.catch((error) => {
// Handle sign in errors
console.error("Error during sign in:", error);
});
};

// Function to Sign Out the User
const signOut = () => {
firebase.auth().signOut()
.then(() => {
// User signed out successfully
console.log("User signed out");
})
.catch((error) => {
// Handle sign out errors
console.error("Error during sign out:", error);
});
};
```

In this code:

- **signUp**: Creates a new user account with the specified email and password.

- **signIn**: Signs in an existing user with the specified email and password.

- **signOut**: Signs out the currently signed-in user.

Social Authentication Providers

FIREBASE MAKES IT EASY to integrate social login providers such as Google, Facebook, and Twitter. For example, to implement Google sign-in, you would configure Google as a provider in the Firebase console and then use the following code:

```
// Configure Google Provider

const googleProvider = new firebase.auth.GoogleAuthProvider();

// Function to Sign In with Google

const signInWithGoogle = () => {

firebase.auth().signInWithPopup(googleProvider)

.then((result) => {

// Google user signed in successfully

console.log("Google user signed in:", result.user);

})

.catch((error) => {

// Handle sign in errors
```

```
console.error("Error during Google sign in:", error);

});

};
```

This allows users to sign in with their Google account seamlessly. The process for Facebook, Twitter, and other providers is similar—just replace GoogleAuthProvider with the relevant provider.

Custom Authentication with Tokens

FIREBASE SUPPORTS CUSTOM authentication tokens, enabling applications to integrate their own authentication mechanisms. This can be done by creating a secure token on your server and then using it to authenticate with Firebase:

```
// Function to Sign In with Custom Token

const signInWithCustomToken = (token) => {

firebase.auth().signInWithCustomToken(token)

.then((userCredential) => {

// User signed in with custom token

console.log("User signed in with custom token:", userCredential.user);

})

.catch((error) => {

// Handle custom token sign-in errors

console.error("Error during custom token sign in:", error);
```

```
});
```

```
};
```

Best Practices for User Authentication and Security

IMPLEMENTING AUTHENTICATION securely is crucial. Here are some best practices to consider:

- **Use HTTPS**: Always ensure your app is served over HTTPS to secure data in transit, especially sensitive user information like passwords.

- **Enforce Strong Passwords**: Use Firebase Authentication's built-in password strength policies or implement custom validation logic to enforce strong password creation.

- **Implement Multi-Factor Authentication (MFA)**: Firebase Authentication offers support for MFA, which provides an additional layer of security for user accounts.

- **Monitor Sign-In Attempts**: Use Firebase Authentication logging and monitoring features to detect suspicious sign-in activity and block unauthorized access.

- **Regularly Update Dependencies**: Keep your Firebase SDK and other dependencies up to date to benefit from the latest security patches and improvements.

By following these steps and best practices, you can ensure that your application's authentication system is secure, reliable, and provides a seamless user experience. Firebase Authentication, when combined with the power of GCP, offers a comprehensive and scalable solution for user identity management.

Implementing Email, Google, and Social Logins

IMPLEMENTING VARIOUS sign-in options is one of the core strengths of Firebase Authentication. This section will cover the process of setting up and integrating email/password, Google, and social logins like Facebook and Twitter. By allowing multiple ways for users to authenticate, you can provide a more flexible and user-friendly experience.

Firebase provides built-in support for these providers, streamlining the process of integrating them into your app and allowing users to sign in with their existing accounts on these platforms.

Configuring Email and Password Authentication

EMAIL AND PASSWORD authentication is a popular choice for many applications, as it allows users to create an account with minimal information. Firebase Authentication makes it easy to enable and implement this method. Here's how to configure it:

1. **Enable Email/Password Authentication**: In the Firebase Console, navigate to the **Authentication** section, click on **Sign-in method**, and enable **Email/Password**.
2. **Create and Sign In Users with Email/Password**: With Firebase's JavaScript SDK, you can easily create and sign in users using the following code.

// Import Firebase

```javascript
import firebase from "firebase/app";

import "firebase/auth";

// Function to Sign Up a New User

const signUpWithEmail = (email, password) => {

firebase.auth().createUserWithEmailAndPassword(email,
password)

.then((userCredential) => {

console.log("User signed up:", userCredential.user);

})

.catch((error) => {

console.error("Error during sign up:", error);

});

};

// Function to Sign In an Existing User

const signInWithEmail = (email, password) => {

firebase.auth().signInWithEmailAndPassword(email, password)

.then((userCredential) => {

console.log("User signed in:", userCredential.user);

})

.catch((error) => {

console.error("Error during sign in:", error);
```

```
});
```

```
};
```

These functions allow users to create an account and log in with their email and password. The createUserWithEmailAndPassword and signInWithEmailAndPassword methods return a userCredential object containing user information upon success.

Integrating Google Sign-In

ENABLING GOOGLE SIGN-In provides a quick and convenient way for users to authenticate using their Google accounts. This is especially useful for applications targeting a wide audience, as many users already have Google accounts.

1. **Enable Google Sign-In in Firebase Console**: In the Firebase Console, go to **Authentication** > **Sign-in method** and enable **Google**. Configure the Google sign-in options if needed.
2. **Implement Google Sign-In**: Here's an example of how to integrate Google Sign-In in your app:

```
// Configure Google Provider

const googleProvider = new firebase.auth.GoogleAuthProvider();

// Function to Sign In with Google

const signInWithGoogle = () => {

firebase.auth().signInWithPopup(googleProvider)

.then((result) => {

console.log("Google user signed in:", result.user);
```

```
})
```

```
.catch((error) => {
```

```
console.error("Error during Google sign in:", error);
```

```
});
```

```
};
```

When a user signs in with Google, Firebase opens a pop-up window where the user can select their Google account. Upon successful authentication, Firebase returns a user object containing the user's details, which can be accessed for further customization in your application.

Integrating Facebook Login

FACEBOOK LOGIN IS ANOTHER popular choice for many applications. Firebase's built-in support for Facebook login makes it straightforward to integrate.

1. **Enable Facebook Login in Firebase Console**: In the Firebase Console, go to **Authentication > Sign-in method** and enable **Facebook**. You will need to provide your Facebook App ID and App Secret.

2. **Set Up Facebook App:**

○ Go to theFacebook Developer Console[1] and create a new app.

○ Add **Facebook Login** to the app and configure the necessary settings.

---

1. https://developers.facebook.com/

○ Copy the **App ID** and **App Secret** to the Firebase Console.

3. **Implement Facebook Login**: Here's an example code to sign in with Facebook:

```
// Configure Facebook Provider

const facebookProvider = new firebase.auth.FacebookAuthProvider();

// Function to Sign In with Facebook

const signInWithFacebook = () => {

firebase.auth().signInWithPopup(facebookProvider)

.then((result) => {

console.log("Facebook user signed in:", result.user);

})

.catch((error) => {

console.error("Error during Facebook sign in:", error);

});

};
```

Implementing Twitter Login

TWITTER LOGIN CAN ALSO be easily implemented using Firebase. Twitter authentication works similarly to other social providers but requires setting up a Twitter Developer Account.

1. **Enable Twitter Login in Firebase Console**: In the Firebase Console, go to **Authentication** > **Sign-in method** and enable **Twitter**. You will need to provide your Twitter API Key and API Secret Key.

2. **Set Up Twitter App**:

○ Go to theTwitter Developer Console[2] and create a new app.

○ Obtain your **API Key** and **API Secret Key** and enter them into the Firebase Console.

3. **Implement Twitter Login**: Here's how you can sign in users with Twitter:

```javascript
// Configure Twitter Provider

const twitterProvider = new firebase.auth.TwitterAuthProvider();

// Function to Sign In with Twitter

const signInWithTwitter = () => {

firebase.auth().signInWithPopup(twitterProvider)

.then((result) => {

console.log("Twitter user signed in:", result.user);

})

.catch((error) => {

console.error("Error during Twitter sign in:", error);
```

---

2. https://developer.twitter.com/

```
});
```

```
};
```

Managing Authentication State

AFTER IMPLEMENTING these authentication methods, managing the user's authentication state becomes essential. Firebase provides an onAuthStateChanged listener, which is triggered whenever the user's sign-in state changes.

```
// Function to Monitor Auth State Changes

firebase.auth().onAuthStateChanged((user) => {

if (user) {

console.log("User is signed in:", user);

} else {

console.log("No user is signed in.");

}

});
```

The onAuthStateChanged function helps in maintaining the user's authentication state across the application and allows for personalized experiences based on whether the user is signed in or out.

Handling Errors and Security

HANDLING ERRORS CORRECTLY is essential for providing a smooth user experience. Firebase provides detailed error codes for different sign-in scenarios, such as incorrect passwords or disabled accounts. For example:

```
firebase.auth().signInWithEmailAndPassword(email, password)

.catch((error) => {

if (error.code === 'auth/wrong-password') {

console.error("Wrong password.");

} else if (error.code === 'auth/user-not-found') {

console.error("User not found.");

} else {

console.error("Error during sign in:", error);

}

});
```

Security Considerations:

- **HTTPS**: Ensure that your app uses HTTPS to encrypt data in transit.

- **App Restriction**: Configure OAuth providers with restricted access to specific domains or IP addresses.

- **Error Monitoring**: Enable error monitoring with Firebase's integrated monitoring tools to detect issues early.

- **Rate Limiting**: Implement rate limiting on your authentication endpoints to prevent abuse.

Conclusion

WITH FIREBASE AUTHENTICATION, integrating multiple sign-in methods into your application is straightforward and highly customizable. By offering email/password, Google, Facebook, and Twitter sign-in options, you can provide a seamless and flexible authentication experience for your users. Following best practices for security and error handling ensures that your application remains secure and user-friendly. Firebase's integration with Google Cloud Identity further enhances its capabilities, making it a robust solution for managing user identities at scale.

Advanced Authentication with Custom Tokens

IN SOME CASES, YOU may need to implement a custom authentication system that integrates with Firebase Authentication. This can include scenarios where you have an existing user database or when using Firebase as part of a larger, multi-platform infrastructure. Custom tokens provide a way to authenticate users on Firebase using an external authentication system, allowing for greater flexibility and control over user management.

Firebase custom tokens enable you to generate a secure token on your server, which your application can then use to authenticate with Firebase. This section will guide you through the process of creating and managing custom tokens, exploring how they can be integrated with Firebase Authentication for advanced authentication needs.

Understanding Custom Tokens in Firebase

CUSTOM TOKENS ALLOW Firebase to authenticate users from a trusted backend server. These tokens:

- Are **JWTs (JSON Web Tokens)** signed with a service account's private key, which securely identifies users to Firebase.

- Allow you to integrate with any authentication provider, as long as you can generate the token on your server.

- Are ideal for existing user systems where you want to maintain control over the authentication flow.

Using custom tokens, you can assign specific roles and permissions to users, control user sessions, and integrate Firebase Authentication seamlessly with your existing infrastructure.

Setting Up Your Server to Generate Custom Tokens

TO CREATE CUSTOM TOKENS, you need to set up your server with the Firebase Admin SDK. Here's how to generate a custom token on a Node.js server:

Install the Firebase Admin SDK:

npm install firebase-admin

Initialize the Firebase Admin SDK: Import the SDK and initialize it with your service account credentials, which can be downloaded from the Firebase Console under **Project Settings > Service Accounts.**

javascript

Copy code

```
const admin = require('firebase-admin');

const serviceAccount = require('path/to/serviceAccountKey.json');

admin.initializeApp({

credential: admin.credential.cert(serviceAccount)

});
```

Generate a Custom Token: Use the createCustomToken method to create a token. The method accepts the user's unique identifier and an optional payload containing custom claims for role-based access control.

javascript

Copy code

```
// Function to Generate Custom Token

const generateCustomToken = async (uid, additionalClaims) => {

try {

const token = await admin.auth().createCustomToken(uid, additionalClaims);

console.log('Custom token created:', token);

return token;

} catch (error) {

console.error('Error creating custom token:', error);
```

```
}

};

// Example Usage

const uid = 'some-unique-user-id';

const additionalClaims = { role: 'admin' };

generateCustomToken(uid, additionalClaims);
```

In this example, uid is a unique identifier for the user, and additionalClaims is an optional object containing additional information, such as user roles, which can be used for authorization purposes.

Authenticating with Firebase Using Custom Tokens

ONCE THE CUSTOM TOKEN is generated on your server, you can send it to the client, where it can be used to authenticate with Firebase Authentication. The client uses signInWithCustomToken to authenticate with Firebase.

```
// Firebase Client-Side Code

firebase.auth().signInWithCustomToken(customToken)

.then((userCredential) => {

console.log('User signed in with custom token:', userCredential.user);

})

.catch((error) => {

console.error('Error signing in with custom token:', error);
```

```
});
```

When the client signs in with the custom token, Firebase will create a new user session or update an existing session, depending on the token and the user's details.

Using Custom Claims for Role-Based Access Control

CUSTOM CLAIMS IN FIREBASE allow you to add user-specific data directly into the authentication token. This is particularly useful for implementing role-based access control (RBAC). For example, you might have roles such as admin, editor, or viewer, which dictate different levels of access within your application.

Setting Custom Claims

YOU CAN SET CUSTOM claims on a user's authentication token from your server using the Firebase Admin SDK:

```
// Assigning Custom Claims

const setCustomUserClaims = async (uid) => {

try {

await admin.auth().setCustomUserClaims(uid, { role: 'admin' });

console.log('Custom claims set for user:', uid);

} catch (error) {

console.error('Error setting custom claims:', error);

}
```

```javascript
};

// Example Usage

setCustomUserClaims('user-id-123');
```

Accessing Custom Claims on the Client

ON THE CLIENT SIDE, you can access the custom claims after the user signs in. Custom claims are part of the user's ID token and can be accessed as follows:

```javascript
firebase.auth().currentUser.getIdTokenResult()

.then((idTokenResult) => {

// Read custom claims

const role = idTokenResult.claims.role;

if (role === 'admin') {

console.log('User has admin privileges');

} else {

console.log('User role:', role);

}

})

.catch((error) => {

console.error('Error getting ID token result:', error);

});
```

This example shows how to check if the user has admin privileges by examining the custom claims in the ID token.

Refreshing Custom Claims

FIREBASE AUTOMATICALLY refreshes the ID token every hour, so changes to custom claims might take up to an hour to propagate. To force a refresh, you can use the getIdToken method with the true parameter:

firebase.auth().currentUser.getIdToken(true)

.then((token) => {

console.log('ID token refreshed:', token);

});

Advanced Custom Authentication Flows

CUSTOM TOKENS PROVIDE the flexibility to integrate with various authentication systems. Here are a few advanced use cases for custom tokens:

1. **Single Sign-On (SSO) Integration**: If your application uses an SSO provider, you can generate custom tokens based on the user's SSO session, allowing for a unified login experience across multiple applications.
2. **Third-Party Authentication**: Custom tokens can be used to authenticate users with third-party services that do not have direct Firebase support. For example, integrating Firebase Authentication with enterprise identity providers or legacy authentication systems.
3. **Multi-Tenant Applications**: With custom claims, you can differentiate users across multiple tenants by assigning

each user a tenant attribute. This is useful for SaaS applications that serve different organizations.

4. **Temporary Access Tokens**: Custom tokens can be used to provide temporary access to a resource. For instance, you might issue a custom token that grants access to a specific resource for a limited time.

Security Considerations for Custom Authentication

USING CUSTOM TOKENS introduces additional security considerations. Here are some best practices to keep in mind:

- **Secure Your Service Account**: The private key of your Firebase service account should be kept secure and should never be hard-coded in your application. Use environment variables or secure storage solutions.

- **Use HTTPS**: Always use HTTPS when transmitting tokens between your server and client to prevent token interception.

- **Set Token Expiry**: Implement logic on your server to expire tokens after a certain period, especially for tokens with elevated privileges or sensitive claims.

- **Monitor Usage**: Track the usage of custom tokens and monitor for unusual patterns that might indicate abuse. Firebase's built-in logging can be useful for this.

- **Rotate Keys Regularly**: Regularly rotate your private keys and update your Firebase service account credentials to reduce the risk of compromise.

Conclusion

CUSTOM TOKENS PROVIDE a powerful way to integrate Firebase Authentication with a variety of external systems and scenarios. By using custom tokens, you can authenticate users from any provider, assign roles with custom claims, and integrate with third-party authentication systems seamlessly. While implementing custom tokens requires additional server-side setup, the flexibility and control they offer make them invaluable for advanced authentication scenarios. As you continue to explore custom authentication, be mindful of security best practices to ensure that your application remains secure and reliable.

Integrating Firebase Authentication with GCP Identity

INTEGRATING FIREBASE Authentication with Google Cloud Platform (GCP) Identity services allows you to leverage the power of Google's comprehensive identity management solutions. This integration provides enhanced security, scalability, and control over user access across multiple Google Cloud services. By combining Firebase Authentication with Google Identity and Access Management (IAM), Cloud Identity, and GCP Identity-Aware Proxy (IAP), you can build a unified authentication system that supports both user and service identity management.

Overview of GCP Identity Services

GCP OFFERS A SUITE of identity services that can complement Firebase Authentication:

- **Google Identity and Access Management (IAM):** Manages permissions and access control for Google

Cloud resources. With IAM, you can define roles and policies to control user and service access.

- **Cloud Identity**: Extends Google IAM by providing user directory and group management features, allowing for centralized identity and access management across your organization.

- **Identity-Aware Proxy (IAP)**: Secures web applications and resources by enforcing identity-based access control, providing seamless access for authenticated users.

Setting Up Google Identity and Access Management (IAM)

IAM IS AN ESSENTIAL component for managing access to your Google Cloud resources. By using IAM with Firebase Authentication, you can create detailed access control policies and assign permissions to users and services. Here's how to get started:

1. **Enable IAM for Your Project**: In the Google Cloud Console, navigate to **IAM & Admin** and enable IAM if it's not already enabled for your project.

Create IAM Roles and Assign Permissions: IAM allows you to define roles with specific permissions for each service. You can create custom roles or use predefined roles provided by Google.

bash

Copy code

Create a custom role using gcloud CLI

```
gcloud iam roles create customRoleName \

—project your-project-id \

—title "Custom Role Title" \

—permissions="list,of,permissions"
```

1.

Assign IAM Roles to Users or Service Accounts: Assign roles to individual users, groups, or service accounts as needed. This can be done via the Google Cloud Console or by using the gcloud command-line tool.

```
# Assign a role to a user

gcloud projects add-iam-policy-binding your-project-id \

—member="user:user@example.com" \

—role="roles/customRoleName"
```

1.

2. **Integrate Firebase Users with IAM Policies**: Use Firebase Authentication's user tokens to create IAM policies that allow or deny access based on user attributes, such as roles or groups stored in custom claims.

Using Cloud Identity for Enhanced User Management

CLOUD IDENTITY PROVIDES a comprehensive solution for managing users, groups, and devices across your organization. By connecting Cloud Identity with Firebase Authentication, you can unify user management, enforce security policies, and simplify identity governance.

1. **Set Up Cloud Identity**: Sign up for Cloud Identity in the Google Admin Console. If you have an existing Google Workspace account, Cloud Identity may already be available.
2. **Manage User Directories and Groups**: Cloud Identity allows you to manage user profiles, group memberships, and security policies. You can synchronize user data from other directory services, such as Active Directory or LDAP.

Integrate Firebase Authentication with Cloud Identity: Using Firebase Authentication's custom claims feature, you can map user attributes to specific roles or groups within Cloud Identity, enabling granular access control.

```
// Assign Cloud Identity group claims to a user

admin.auth().setCustomUserClaims(uid, { cloudIdentityGroup: 'group-id' });
```

1.

2. **Implement Group-Based Access Control**: With group-based access control, you can enforce different access levels for users based on their group memberships within Cloud Identity. This allows for centralized management of permissions across your Firebase and GCP resources.

Securing Resources with Identity-Aware Proxy (IAP)

IDENTITY-AWARE PROXY (IAP) is a GCP service that enables you to secure applications and resources by enforcing identity-based access controls. IAP works with Firebase

Authentication to provide single sign-on (SSO) capabilities and restrict access based on user identities.

1. **Enable IAP for Your Application**: In the Google Cloud Console, navigate to **Security > Identity-Aware Proxy** and enable IAP for your project. You'll need to set up an OAuth consent screen and configure your OAuth credentials.

Configure IAP Policies for Firebase Users: IAP policies allow you to specify which users or groups have access to specific resources. You can create IAP policies based on Firebase Authentication attributes, such as user email or custom claims.

```
# Create an IAP policy binding for a user

gcloud iap web add-iam-policy-binding \

—resource-type=backend-services \

—resource-id=your-backend-service-id \

—member="user:user@example.com" \

—role="roles/iap.httpsResourceAccessor"
```
1.

Integrate IAP with Firebase Authentication: When a user attempts to access a protected resource, IAP checks the user's identity and authorization. If authenticated, IAP forwards the user's token to the application, which can then be validated using Firebase Authentication's SDK.

```
// Verify IAP token on your backend

const token = request.headers['x-goog-iap-jwt-assertion'];
```

```
admin.auth().verifyIdToken(token)

.then((decodedToken) => {

console.log("IAP user verified:", decodedToken);

})

.catch((error) => {

console.error("Error verifying IAP token:", error);

});
```
1.

Automating Access Control with GCP IAM Policies and Firebase Rules

FIREBASE OFFERS SECURITY rules that allow you to enforce fine-grained access control directly in Firebase. When combined with IAM policies, you can automate access control based on user attributes and Firebase Authentication's custom claims.

Create Firebase Security Rules Based on IAM Roles: Firebase Security Rules can reference custom claims, allowing you to control access based on IAM roles and policies.

```
// Example Firebase security rules using custom claims

{

"rules": {

"documents": {

"$docId": {

".read": "auth.token.role === 'admin'",
```

```
".write": "auth.token.role === 'editor'"
```

```
}
```

```
}
```

```
}
```

```
}
```
1.

Automate Access Control with Conditional IAM Policies: By using conditional IAM policies, you can automate access control decisions based on user attributes, such as location, device type, or time of day.

bash

Copy code

```
# Example conditional IAM policy

gcloud iam policies create \

—condition="request.time
timestamp('2024-12-31T23:59:59Z')" \

—role="roles/viewer" \

—member="user:user@example.com"
```
1.

2. **Integrate Firebase Rules with GCP IAM for Unified Policies**: Use Firebase Security Rules and IAM policies together to enforce both application-level and resource-level security, ensuring that access control is consistently applied across your Firebase and GCP resources.

Best Practices for Integrating Firebase Authentication with GCP Identity

TO ENSURE A SECURE and scalable integration between Firebase Authentication and GCP Identity services, consider the following best practices:

- **Use Custom Claims Sparingly**: While custom claims provide flexibility, they can increase the size of the user's ID token. Use only essential claims and consider using Cloud Identity or IAM for more complex access control.

- **Regularly Review IAM Policies**: Continuously review and audit IAM policies to ensure that users have only the permissions they need, following the principle of least privilege.

- **Leverage Group-Based Access Control**: Using groups in Cloud Identity simplifies permission management and ensures consistency across multiple users.

- **Monitor Access and Audit Logs**: Enable access logging and audit trails to monitor user activity and detect any unauthorized access attempts. Google Cloud's Audit Logs and Firebase Analytics can be useful tools for this purpose.

- **Implement Multi-Factor Authentication (MFA)**: Enforce MFA for sensitive resources and users with elevated privileges. Firebase Authentication supports MFA for email and phone verification, which can be combined with GCP Identity features.

Conclusion

INTEGRATING FIREBASE Authentication with Google Cloud Platform Identity services provides a powerful and flexible approach to managing user identities and access control. By leveraging IAM, Cloud Identity, and IAP, you can build a secure and scalable authentication system that extends across Firebase and GCP resources. This integration allows for centralized user management, improved security, and a seamless user experience, making it ideal for complex applications with diverse identity requirements. As you implement this integration, follow best practices to ensure the security and reliability of your authentication system, and take full advantage of the capabilities offered by GCP Identity services.

Best Practices for User Authentication and Security

USER AUTHENTICATION and security are fundamental aspects of application development. Ensuring a secure and user-friendly authentication process can help build trust and protect sensitive user data. Firebase Authentication provides a robust platform for implementing various authentication methods, but adhering to best practices is essential for maximizing security and optimizing the user experience. This section covers the best practices for user authentication and security when using Firebase Authentication, along with tips on how to effectively manage users, secure data, and comply with privacy regulations.

1. Enforcing Strong Password Policies

ONE OF THE PRIMARY methods of authentication is email/ password login. To enhance security, you should enforce strong password policies:

- **Minimum Length**: Require passwords to have a minimum length, typically at least 8 characters.

- **Complexity Requirements**: Enforce complexity by requiring a mix of uppercase and lowercase letters, numbers, and special characters.

- **Password Blacklisting**: Consider implementing a password blacklist to prevent users from choosing commonly used or easily guessable passwords.

Firebase Authentication doesn't provide a built-in mechanism for password complexity, but you can enforce these rules in your application before passing the password to Firebase:

```
// Example password validation function

const isValidPassword = (password) => {

const                          regex                          =
/^(?=.*[a-z])(?=.*[A-Z])(?=.*\d)(?=.*[\W_]).{8,}$/;

return regex.test(password);

};

const signUp = (email, password) => {

if (isValidPassword(password)) {
```

```
firebase.auth().createUserWithEmailAndPassword(email,
password)

.then((userCredential) => {

console.log("User signed up:", userCredential.user);

})

.catch((error) => {

console.error("Error during sign up:", error);

});

} else {

console.error("Password        does        not        meet        complexity
requirements.");

}

};
```

2. Implementing Multi-Factor Authentication (MFA)

MULTI-FACTOR AUTHENTICATION (MFA) adds an extra layer of security by requiring users to provide additional verification, such as a code sent to their phone or email. Firebase Authentication supports MFA for email and phone number verification, which can be enabled in high-security applications.

To enable phone-based MFA, follow these steps:

1. **Set Up Phone Authentication in the Firebase Console:** Go to the Firebase Console, navigate to **Authentication >**

Sign-in method, and enable **Phone** as a provider.

Request Phone Number Verification: Use Firebase's signInWithPhoneNumber method to send a verification code to the user's phone:

```
// Initialize Recaptcha

const recaptchaVerifier = new firebase.auth.RecaptchaVerifier('recaptcha-container', {

size: 'invisible',

});

// Request Verification Code

const requestPhoneVerification = (phoneNumber) => {

firebase.auth().signInWithPhoneNumber(phoneNumber, recaptchaVerifier)

.then((confirmationResult) => {

// Store confirmationResult to complete verification later

window.confirmationResult = confirmationResult;

console.log("Verification code sent to:", phoneNumber);

})

.catch((error) => {

console.error("Error sending verification code:", error);

});

};
```

1.

Verify the Code: After the user receives the code, verify it to complete authentication:

```
// Confirm Verification Code

const verifyCode = (code) => {

confirmationResult.confirm(code)

.then((result) => {

console.log("Phone number verified, user signed in:", result.user);

})

.catch((error) => {

console.error("Error verifying code:", error);

});

};
```

3. Securing User Data with Encryption

ENCRYPTION IS ESSENTIAL for protecting sensitive user data, such as passwords and personal information. Firebase Authentication automatically encrypts data in transit, but you should also:

- **Encrypt Sensitive Data at Rest**: For sensitive data stored in databases (e.g., Firestore or Realtime Database), consider encrypting it before saving it to ensure security even if data is accessed improperly.

- **Use HTTPS for All Communications**: Ensure that all communications between your application and

Firebase use HTTPS to prevent interception of data in transit.

For custom data encryption, you can use the crypto library in Node.js, for example:

```javascript
// Example of encrypting data with AES-256

const crypto = require('crypto');

const algorithm = 'aes-256-cbc';

const key = crypto.randomBytes(32);

const iv = crypto.randomBytes(16);

const encrypt = (text) => {

let cipher = crypto.createCipheriv(algorithm, Buffer.from(key), iv);

let encrypted = cipher.update(text);

encrypted = Buffer.concat([encrypted, cipher.final()]);

return iv.toString('hex') + ':' + encrypted.toString('hex');

};

const decrypt = (text) => {

let textParts = text.split(':');

let iv = Buffer.from(textParts.shift(), 'hex');

let encryptedText = Buffer.from(textParts.join(':'), 'hex');

let decipher = crypto.createDecipheriv(algorithm, Buffer.from(key), iv);
```

```
let decrypted = decipher.update(encryptedText);

decrypted = Buffer.concat([decrypted, decipher.final()]);

return decrypted.toString();

};
```

4. Implementing Secure Token Management

FIREBASE AUTHENTICATION uses JSON Web Tokens (JWT) to manage sessions and authentication. For secure token management:

Verify Tokens on the Server: When users make authenticated requests to your backend, always verify their ID tokens to ensure they are legitimate. Firebase provides server-side SDKs to help with this:

```
// Verify ID Token with Firebase Admin SDK

const verifyToken = async (idToken) => {

try {

const decodedToken = await admin.auth().verifyIdToken(idToken);

console.log("Token verified:", decodedToken);

} catch (error) {

console.error("Error verifying token:", error);

}

};
```

-

  - **Set Short Expiration for Tokens**: Configure tokens with a short expiration time to minimize risks if a token is compromised.

  - **Rotate Keys Regularly**: If using custom tokens, rotate the private keys used to sign tokens regularly.

5. Enforcing User Access Control with Custom Claims

USE FIREBASE AUTHENTICATION'S custom claims to enforce access control and implement role-based authorization. Custom claims are set on the server and define the user's access level, such as admin, editor, or viewer.

Setting Custom Claims

```
// SET CUSTOM CLAIMS with Firebase Admin SDK

const setUserClaims = async (uid) => {

try {

await admin.auth().setCustomUserClaims(uid, { role: 'editor' });

console.log("Custom claims set for user:", uid);

} catch (error) {

console.error("Error setting custom claims:", error);

}

};
```

Accessing Custom Claims on the Client

AFTER THE USER SIGNS in, retrieve their custom claims to implement role-based access in your application:

firebase.auth().currentUser.getIdTokenResult()

.then((idTokenResult) => {

console.log("User role:", idTokenResult.claims.role);

})

.catch((error) => {

console.error("Error retrieving custom claims:", error);

});

6. Monitoring and Auditing User Activity

MONITORING USER ACTIVITY is essential for detecting suspicious behavior and maintaining security. Firebase Authentication integrates with Google Cloud's audit logging and monitoring tools:

- **Enable Audit Logging**: Configure Google Cloud Logging to track user sign-in attempts and other authentication events.

- **Monitor Anomalies**: Use Firebase Analytics and Cloud Monitoring to detect unusual patterns, such as multiple failed login attempts, which may indicate an attack.

7. Complying with Privacy Regulations

WHEN HANDLING USER authentication, it's essential to comply with privacy regulations such as GDPR and CCPA:

- **Implement User Data Controls**: Provide users with the ability to delete their accounts or request data deletion, as required by privacy laws.

- **Minimize Data Collection**: Only collect the data necessary for authentication and avoid storing unnecessary personal information.

- **Secure Data Storage**: Use Firebase's built-in data storage options, which comply with various privacy standards, and ensure all data is encrypted and securely managed.

Conclusion

ADHERING TO THESE BEST practices for user authentication and security ensures that your application is well-protected against common threats and provides a safe experience for users. By enforcing strong password policies, implementing MFA, encrypting data, and following secure token management practices, you can create a secure authentication system that enhances user trust. Additionally, by integrating Firebase Authentication with GCP Identity services and following privacy regulations, you can ensure compliance and build a scalable, reliable system for managing user identities.

Chapter 4: Firebase Firestore and Google Cloud Databases

Overview of Firebase Firestore

FIREBASE FIRESTORE is a NoSQL, document-oriented database that provides real-time synchronization and offline support for mobile and web applications. As a cloud-hosted database, Firestore allows developers to store, query, and sync data seamlessly across multiple clients. Firestore is part of Google's Firebase platform and is fully integrated with Google Cloud Platform (GCP), making it a flexible and scalable solution for building modern applications.

Firestore organizes data into collections and documents. A collection is a container of documents, and each document contains fields mapping to values. Unlike traditional relational databases, Firestore does not have tables or rows, and its structure is much more dynamic and flexible. It's designed to support both simple data, such as user profiles, and complex, hierarchical data structures, such as chat messages or product catalogs.

One of Firestore's standout features is its ability to synchronize data across clients in real time. This means that when data is updated in the database, all connected clients receive the updated data almost instantaneously. This is particularly useful for collaborative apps, such as messaging, gaming, or document editing, where multiple users need to see updates immediately.

Firestore also offers offline support, allowing clients to continue accessing and modifying data even when they are not connected to the internet. When connectivity is restored, Firestore automatically synchronizes the local data with the server, ensuring that changes are properly merged and consistent across all devices.

In this section, we will delve into Firestore's architecture, explore its core features, and examine some of the key considerations for data modeling. We will also look at how Firestore integrates with other Google Cloud databases and tools to offer a comprehensive data management solution.

Key Concepts in Firebase Firestore

TO EFFECTIVELY USE Firestore, it's important to understand its key concepts:

- **Documents**: The basic unit of data in Firestore, akin to a record in a relational database. Documents contain fields, which are key-value pairs, and they can store different types of data, such as strings, numbers, arrays, maps, and nested documents.

- **Collections**: Groups of documents. A collection can contain any number of documents, but it cannot directly contain other collections.

- **Subcollections**: Collections that are nested within a document. Firestore allows for an unlimited level of nesting, enabling complex data structures.

- **Realtime Updates**: Firestore's ability to sync data across clients in real time. When a document is updated, all clients listening to changes on that document receive the update immediately.

- **Offline Support**: Firestore caches data locally, allowing users to read and write data even when they are offline. The data is synchronized with the server once connectivity is restored.

- **Security Rules**: Firestore provides fine-grained access control through security rules, allowing you to restrict access based on user roles, document fields, and other conditions.

- **Queries**: Firestore supports powerful querying capabilities, including filtering, sorting, and combining multiple queries.

Creating a Firestore Database

TO GET STARTED WITH Firestore, you'll need to create a Firebase project and enable Firestore:

1. Go to the Firebase Console and sign in with your Google account.
2. Create a new Firebase project or select an existing one.
3. In the Firebase Console, navigate to the "Firestore Database" section and click on "Create Database."
4. Choose a location for your Firestore database. Firestore offers two database options: **Firestore in Native mode** and **Firestore in Datastore mode**. Native mode is optimized for real-time updates and mobile/web use cases, while Datastore mode is optimized for server-side use and integrates well with Google Cloud's legacy Datastore service.
5. Select the appropriate mode and click "Next." Follow the on-screen instructions to complete the setup.

Once your Firestore database is set up, you can begin creating collections and documents, and use Firestore's SDKs to interact with your data from your mobile or web applications.

Adding Data to Firestore

FIRESTORE ALLOWS YOU to add data by creating documents within collections. You can add data using the Firebase SDK in various programming languages. Here is an example in JavaScript:

```javascript
// Initialize Firestore

const db = firebase.firestore();

// Reference a collection

const usersCollection = db.collection('users');

// Add a new document with a generated ID

usersCollection.add({

firstName: 'John',

lastName: 'Doe',

email: 'john.doe@example.com',

age: 25

})

.then((docRef) => {

console.log('Document written with ID: ', docRef.id);

})

.catch((error) => {
```

```
console.error('Error adding document: ', error);

});
```

In this example, we create a new document in the users collection with fields for firstName, lastName, email, and age. The add() method automatically generates a unique document ID. Alternatively, you can specify a custom ID using the doc() method.

Querying Data in Firestore

FIRESTORE SUPPORTS various querying operations, such as filtering, sorting, and combining multiple queries. Queries in Firestore are shallow, meaning they only retrieve documents from the collection being queried, not from any nested subcollections. Here are some examples of common query operations:

Simple Query

TO RETRIEVE ALL DOCUMENTS in a collection:

```
db.collection('users').get()

.then((querySnapshot) => {

querySnapshot.forEach((doc) => {

console.log(`${doc.id} => ${doc.data()}`);

});

})

.catch((error) => {

console.log('Error getting documents: ', error);
```

```
});
```

Filtered Query

TO FILTER DOCUMENTS based on specific field values, use the where() method:

```
db.collection('users')

.where('age', '>=', 18)

.get()

.then((querySnapshot) => {

querySnapshot.forEach((doc) => {

console.log(`${doc.id} => ${doc.data()}`);

});

})

.catch((error) => {

console.log('Error getting documents: ', error);

});
```

In this example, we retrieve all users aged 18 or older.

Sorting Results

TO SORT QUERY RESULTS, use the orderBy() method:

```
db.collection('users')

.orderBy('lastName', 'asc')
```

```
.get()

.then((querySnapshot) => {

querySnapshot.forEach((doc) => {

console.log(`${doc.id} => ${doc.data()}`);

});

})

.catch((error) => {

console.log('Error getting documents: ', error);

});
```

This query sorts the users by their last name in ascending order.

Real-Time Data with Firestore

FIRESTORE'S REAL-TIME capabilities allow you to listen for changes in your data. Here's an example of how to set up a real-time listener in JavaScript:

```
db.collection('users')

.onSnapshot((querySnapshot) => {

querySnapshot.forEach((doc) => {

console.log(`${doc.id} => ${doc.data()}`);

});

});
```

The onSnapshot() method sets up a listener that triggers whenever there are changes in the users collection. This is useful for applications that require real-time data synchronization, such as chat apps or collaborative tools.

Conclusion

FIRESTORE IS A POWERFUL and flexible NoSQL database that is well-suited for real-time applications. Its integration with Firebase and Google Cloud Platform allows for seamless scaling, robust security, and a range of tools for optimizing performance. Understanding Firestore's core concepts and capabilities will enable you to build data-driven applications that are efficient, scalable, and responsive to user interactions.

Data Modeling in Firestore

DATA MODELING IS A crucial aspect of developing efficient and scalable applications with Firestore. Unlike relational databases, which use a structured schema with tables and columns, Firestore is a NoSQL document database. It organizes data into collections and documents, allowing for a flexible, schema-less approach to data storage. However, this flexibility comes with the responsibility of designing a data model that suits the needs of your application while maintaining optimal performance.

In this section, we will explore the principles and best practices of data modeling in Firestore. We will discuss how to structure data to support your app's features, how to handle relationships between data entities, and how to optimize your data model for performance. Additionally, we will examine techniques for managing large datasets, dealing with hierarchical data, and maintaining consistency across your application.

Key Concepts in Firestore Data Modeling

TO DESIGN AN EFFECTIVE data model in Firestore, it's essential to understand a few core concepts:

- **Collections and Documents**: Firestore organizes data into collections and documents. A collection is a container for documents, and each document contains key-value pairs. Collections can only contain documents, not other collections. However, each document can contain subcollections, allowing for deep nesting and complex structures.

- **Denormalization**: Unlike relational databases, where data is typically normalized to minimize redundancy, Firestore often requires denormalized data models. This means duplicating data across multiple documents to avoid complex joins and to facilitate faster queries.

- **Nested Data**: Firestore allows for nested data structures, where documents contain subcollections or maps. This enables you to represent hierarchical data within a single document, making it easier to retrieve related data in one query.

- **Atomic Transactions and Batching**: Firestore supports atomic transactions and batch writes, which allow you to perform multiple operations as a single unit. This is essential for maintaining data consistency, especially when dealing with complex data structures or relationships.

Structuring Data for Common Use Cases

IN FIRESTORE, THE WAY you structure your data depends heavily on your application's requirements. Here are some common patterns for organizing data in Firestore:

1. Flat Data Structure for Simple Use Cases

FOR SIMPLE DATA THAT doesn't require complex relationships, a flat structure is usually sufficient. Each document contains all the necessary fields, and there are no subcollections or nested maps. This structure is suitable for data that doesn't change frequently and doesn't need to be related to other data.

```
// Example of a flat data structure

const db = firebase.firestore();

db.collection('products').add({

productId: 'p001',

name: 'Wireless Mouse',

price: 29.99,

stock: 100

});
```

In this example, each document in the products collection represents a single product with fields for productId, name, price, and stock.

2. Nested Data for Hierarchical Structures

FOR DATA THAT HAS A hierarchical structure, such as categories and subcategories, you can use nested documents or subcollections. This approach allows you to group related data together and retrieve it in a single query.

// Example of a nested data structure with subcollections

db.collection('categories').doc('electronics').collection('subcategories').a

name: 'Laptops',

description: 'Portable computers'

});

In this example, the categories collection contains a document for each main category, and each category document contains a subcollection of subcategories. This structure is ideal for data that requires multiple levels of categorization.

Handling Relationships Between Data Entities

FIRESTORE DOES NOT support joins, so handling relationships between data entities requires careful planning. There are two main types of relationships in Firestore: one-to-many and many-to-many. Each type requires a different approach to data modeling.

1. One-to-Many Relationships

A ONE-TO-MANY RELATIONSHIP is common in applications where a single entity is related to multiple other entities. For example, a blog application might have a one-to-many relationship between authors and posts.

There are two primary methods for modeling one-to-many relationships:

Subcollections: Each document in the parent collection contains a subcollection of related documents. This is useful when the child entities need to be grouped under the parent entity.

```
// Example of one-to-many relationship using subcollections

db.collection('authors').doc('authorId').collection('posts').add({

title: 'Firestore Data Modeling',

content: 'Content of the blog post',

published: true

});
```

References: The child documents contain a reference to the parent document. This approach is suitable when the child entities don't need to be directly nested under the parent entity but still need to maintain a relationship.

```
// Example of one-to-many relationship using references

db.collection('posts').add({

authorId: 'authorId',

title: 'Firestore Data Modeling',

content: 'Content of the blog post',

published: true
```

```
});
```

•

2. Many-to-Many Relationships

IN A MANY-TO-MANY RELATIONSHIP, both entities can have multiple relationships with each other. For example, in a social media app, users can follow multiple users, and each user can be followed by multiple users.

There are several ways to model many-to-many relationships in Firestore:

References with Arrays: Each document contains an array of references to related documents. This is useful when the number of relationships is small and manageable.

```
// Example of many-to-many relationship using references with arrays

db.collection('users').doc('userId').set({

following: ['userId1', 'userId2', 'userId3']

});
```

•

Mapping Collections: Create a separate collection to store relationships between entities. This allows for scalability and flexibility, as you can add or remove relationships without modifying the original documents.

```
// Example of many-to-many relationship using a mapping collection
```

```
db.collection('followers').add({

followerId: 'userId1',

followedId: 'userId2'

});
```

•

Optimizing Data Model for Performance

WHEN DESIGNING A DATA model in Firestore, it's important to consider performance. Here are some best practices for optimizing your data model:

1. Minimize Reads and Writes

FIRESTORE CHARGES BASED on the number of reads, writes, and deletes, so minimizing these operations can reduce costs. Use caching, denormalization, and batch writes to minimize the number of operations.

```
// Example of batch writes to minimize operations

const batch = db.batch();

const docRef1 = db.collection('products').doc('productId1');

const docRef2 = db.collection('products').doc('productId2');

batch.set(docRef1, { stock: 50 });

batch.set(docRef2, { stock: 75 });

batch.commit();
```

2. Use Indexes to Speed Up Queries

FIRESTORE AUTOMATICALLY creates indexes for simple queries, but you may need to create composite indexes for complex queries involving multiple fields. Use the Firebase Console to manage indexes and monitor query performance.

3. Leverage Offline Caching

FIRESTORE'S OFFLINE caching feature allows data to be stored locally, reducing the need for repeated reads. Enable offline persistence in your app to improve performance and enhance the user experience.

```
// Enable offline persistence

firebase.firestore().enablePersistence()

.catch((err) => {

if (err.code == 'failed-precondition') {

console.log('Offline persistence failed: multiple tabs open');

} else if (err.code == 'unimplemented') {

console.log('Offline persistence is not available');

}

});
```

Dealing with Large Datasets

FOR LARGE DATASETS, consider using Firestore's pagination and data partitioning features to manage data efficiently. Firestore supports pagination with limit() and startAfter() methods to retrieve data in chunks.

```
// Example of pagination

const firstPage = db.collection('products').orderBy('name').limit(10);

firstPage.get().then((snapshot) => {

const lastVisible = snapshot.docs[snapshot.docs.length - 1];

// Retrieve next page

db.collection('products').orderBy('name').startAfter(lastVisible).limit(10).

.then((nextSnapshot) => {

// Process the next page of results

});

});
```

Conclusion

DATA MODELING IN FIRESTORE requires a balance between flexibility and performance. By understanding Firestore's structure and employing best practices for data modeling, you can design scalable applications that meet your app's needs. Whether you are working with simple or complex data structures, Firestore provides the tools to manage and query your data effectively, enabling you to build responsive and robust applications.

Integrating Firestore with Google Cloud Datastore

INTEGRATING FIREBASE Firestore with Google Cloud Datastore opens up a range of possibilities for developers who want to leverage the benefits of both Firebase and Google Cloud Platform (GCP). Firestore and Datastore are both document-oriented NoSQL databases, but they cater to slightly different use cases. While Firestore is ideal for real-time, client-centric applications with synchronization capabilities, Datastore is designed for large-scale, server-side applications that require high durability and scalability. By understanding how to integrate these services, you can create robust, flexible, and scalable applications that span multiple platforms and use cases.

In this section, we'll explore the differences between Firestore and Datastore, discuss when and why you might integrate these services, and outline the steps to set up and manage an integration between Firestore and Datastore. We'll also delve into best practices for maintaining data consistency and optimizing performance in a hybrid environment.

Key Differences Between Firestore and Datastore

WHILE FIRESTORE AND Datastore share some similarities, there are several key differences that influence how they are used:

- **Data Model**: Both Firestore and Datastore use a NoSQL, document-oriented data model. However, Firestore organizes data into collections and documents, with support for nested subcollections. In contrast, Datastore organizes data into entities and kinds, which are more akin to a traditional table-and-row structure, though still document-based.

- **Query Capabilities**: Firestore offers a richer set of querying capabilities, such as real-time data synchronization and offline support. Datastore focuses on scalability and supports more complex, server-side querying and indexing.

- **Transactions**: Both databases support transactions, but Firestore offers client-side transactions while Datastore focuses on server-side, cross-regional transactions that are more suitable for large-scale enterprise applications.

- **Performance**: Firestore is optimized for real-time synchronization and is better suited for mobile and web applications where low latency is essential. Datastore, on the other hand, is optimized for scalability, with support for massive datasets and high throughput.

Why Integrate Firestore with Datastore?

INTEGRATING FIRESTORE and Datastore can provide a unified approach to data management across client and server environments. Here are some scenarios where integration might be beneficial:

- **Scaling Real-Time Applications**: Use Firestore for real-time features such as chat, notifications, or collaborative editing, while leveraging Datastore for large-scale data storage and complex analytics.

- **Data Archiving and Retrieval**: Use Firestore to handle real-time data that changes frequently, and archive historical data in Datastore for long-term storage and retrieval.

- **Hybrid Applications**: For applications that span both client and server environments, Firestore can be used for client-facing features while Datastore handles server-side processing and batch operations.

Setting Up Integration Between Firestore and Datastore

TO INTEGRATE FIRESTORE with Datastore, you'll need to configure both databases within the same Google Cloud Project. Here's how you can set up the integration:

Step 1: Create a Google Cloud Project

IF YOU HAVEN'T ALREADY, start by creating a Google Cloud Project in the Google Cloud Console. This project will house both Firestore and Datastore resources.

1. Go to the Google Cloud Console and sign in with your Google account.
2. Click on "Select a project" and then "New Project."
3. Enter a name for your project and select a billing account.
4. Click "Create" to set up your Google Cloud Project.

Step 2: Enable Firestore and Datastore

IN YOUR GOOGLE CLOUD Project, you need to enable both Firestore and Datastore. Note that Firestore can operate in two modes: Native mode and Datastore mode. To integrate with Datastore, select Firestore in Datastore mode.

1. In the Google Cloud Console, navigate to the Firestore section.

2. Choose Firestore in Datastore mode, which allows you to access Datastore features within Firestore.

3. Follow the on-screen instructions to enable Firestore and select your desired database location.

Step 3: Configure Firestore in Datastore Mode

FIRESTORE IN DATASTORE mode provides a unified interface that combines features from both Firestore and Datastore. To configure this mode:

1. After enabling Firestore in Datastore mode, you'll be able to use Datastore entities alongside Firestore documents.

2. Use the Google Cloud Console or the Firestore client libraries to create entities and perform operations.

3. In this mode, data is stored in Firestore but accessed through the Datastore API, allowing you to benefit from Datastore's scalability and transaction capabilities.

Interacting with Firestore and Datastore

ONCE YOUR PROJECT IS configured, you can interact with both Firestore and Datastore using client libraries or the Google Cloud Console. Here are some common operations for interacting with data in a Firestore-Datastore hybrid environment:

Creating Entities in Datastore Mode

YOU CAN CREATE ENTITIES in Firestore in Datastore mode using the Datastore client libraries. Here's an example in Node.js:

```
const { Datastore } = require('@google-cloud/datastore');

const datastore = new Datastore();
```

```javascript
const taskKey = datastore.key(['Task', 'sampleTask']);

const task = {

key: taskKey,

data: {

description: 'Buy milk',

created: new Date()

},

};

datastore.save(task)

.then(() => {

console.log(`Task ${task.key.name} created successfully.`);

})

.catch(err => {

console.error('Error creating task:', err);

});
```

In this example, we create an entity of kind Task with a description and a created timestamp. The entity is stored in Firestore using Datastore mode, leveraging Datastore's API.

Querying Entities

DATASTORE SUPPORTS complex queries, including filtering, sorting, and pagination. Here's an example of querying tasks by creation date:

```
const query = datastore.createQuery('Task').order('created', {

descending: true

});

datastore.runQuery(query)

.then(results => {

const tasks = results[0];

tasks.forEach(task => {

console.log(`Task ${task[datastore.KEY].name}:`, task);

});

})

.catch(err => {

console.error('Error running query:', err);

});
```

This query retrieves all tasks, sorted by creation date in descending order. The runQuery method executes the query and returns the results.

Using Firestore Features with Datastore Entities

ALTHOUGH FIRESTORE in Datastore mode provides limited support for Firestore-specific features like real-time updates and offline caching, you can still use Firestore's client libraries to access Datastore entities when necessary. This allows you to leverage Firestore's powerful querying capabilities while maintaining compatibility with Datastore's API.

Best Practices for Managing Data Across Firestore and Datastore

TO ENSURE OPTIMAL PERFORMANCE and data consistency when integrating Firestore with Datastore, follow these best practices:

1. Use Atomic Transactions for Consistency

FIRESTORE AND DATASTORE both support atomic transactions, allowing you to group multiple operations into a single unit. This is particularly useful when modifying multiple entities that depend on each other.

datastore.runInTransaction(async transaction => {

const taskKey = datastore.key(['Task', 'sampleTask']);

const [task] = await transaction.get(taskKey);

task.completed = true;

transaction.save({

key: taskKey,

data: task,

```
});
```

```
});
```

In this example, we use a transaction to update a task's completed status, ensuring that the operation is atomic and consistent.

2. Leverage Indexes for Complex Queries

FIRESTORE AND DATASTORE support custom indexes for complex queries involving multiple properties. Use the Google Cloud Console to configure indexes and improve query performance.

3. Optimize Data Access Patterns

IN FIRESTORE, DENORMALIZED data models work well for real-time applications, while Datastore often requires more structured data models. Design your data models based on how data is accessed and modified across both systems.

4. Implement Data Archival and Retention Policies

WHEN USING FIRESTORE for real-time data and Datastore for archival purposes, implement data archival and retention policies to manage the lifecycle of data. Periodically move historical data from Firestore to Datastore for long-term storage.

Conclusion

INTEGRATING FIRESTORE with Google Cloud Datastore allows you to combine the strengths of both databases for a wide range of application scenarios. By understanding the differences between Firestore and Datastore, and following best practices for integration, you can build scalable, efficient, and consistent data models that leverage the best of Firebase and Google Cloud Platform. This approach enables you to create versatile applications that meet the demands of both client and server environments.

Performance Optimization in Firestore Queries

OPTIMIZING FIRESTORE queries is essential for building scalable and efficient applications, especially as your data grows and your app scales to more users. Firestore is designed to handle real-time updates, but performance can be affected by how data is structured, queried, and accessed. Properly optimizing your Firestore queries ensures that your application remains fast and responsive, minimizing costs associated with reads, writes, and data storage.

This section will explore strategies and techniques for optimizing Firestore queries, including how to structure data for performance, reduce the number of reads, utilize indexing, and implement efficient querying patterns. We will also discuss how to leverage Firestore's tools for monitoring and debugging query performance.

Key Concepts for Firestore Query Optimization

BEFORE DIVING INTO optimization techniques, it's important to understand the basics of Firestore queries:

- **Shallow Queries**: Firestore queries are shallow, meaning they only retrieve documents from a single collection without automatically fetching data from subcollections.

- **Indexes**: Firestore creates automatic indexes for simple queries but requires custom indexes for more complex queries involving multiple fields. Custom indexes can significantly improve performance by reducing query latency.

- **Limits and Pagination**: Using limits and pagination helps control the number of documents retrieved in a single query, improving performance and reducing costs.

- **Document Snapshots**: Firestore queries return document snapshots, which include metadata about the documents retrieved. This metadata can be used for caching and further optimization.

Structuring Data for Query Efficiency

FIRESTORE IS A NOSQL database, which means data should be structured in a way that optimizes access patterns. Here are some key considerations for structuring data:

1. Denormalization for Fast Reads

IN FIRESTORE, DATA is often denormalized to minimize the number of queries needed to retrieve related data. While denormalization can lead to some data redundancy, it can also reduce the number of reads required to load data, resulting in faster performance.

```
// Example of denormalized data structure for a blog application

const db = firebase.firestore();

db.collection('posts').add({
```

```
title: 'Optimizing Firestore Queries',

content: 'In this post, we will explore...',

author: {

id: 'authorId123',

name: 'John Doe'

},

tags: ['optimization', 'firebase', 'queries']

});
```

In this example, the author information is embedded directly within each post document, allowing the app to retrieve all necessary data in a single read without additional queries to an authors collection.

2. Using Subcollections for Large or Related Data

SUBCOLLECTIONS ALLOW you to organize data into hierarchical structures, which can be useful for large datasets or data with complex relationships. Subcollections also enable more granular access to related data.

```
// Example of using subcollections for comments on a post

db.collection('posts').doc('postId123').collection('comments').add({

content: 'Great post!',

userId: 'userId456',

created: firebase.firestore.FieldValue.serverTimestamp()
```

```
});
```

In this structure, each post has a subcollection of comments. This allows you to retrieve a post without fetching all of its comments, and only query the comments subcollection when needed.

Minimizing Read and Write Operations

FIRESTORE CHARGES BASED on the number of reads, writes, and deletes, so minimizing these operations is crucial for cost efficiency. Here are some techniques for reducing read and write operations:

1. Batched Writes

FIRESTORE SUPPORTS batched writes, which allow you to group multiple write operations into a single transaction. Batched writes are atomic, meaning all operations within the batch succeed or fail together.

```
// Example of batched writes

const batch = db.batch();

const postRef = db.collection('posts').doc('postId123');

const commentRef = postRef.collection('comments').doc();

batch.update(postRef,                    {                    commentCount: firebase.firestore.FieldValue.increment(1) });

batch.set(commentRef, {

content: 'Another insightful comment!',

userId: 'userId789'
```

```
});

batch.commit().then(() => {

console.log('Batch write succeeded.');

});
```

In this example, both the commentCount update and the new comment creation are performed in a single batch, reducing the number of individual writes.

2. Reducing Document Reads with Caching

FIRESTORE PROVIDES an offline persistence feature that caches data locally, allowing the app to read from the cache instead of the network. This reduces the number of reads and can improve performance, especially in scenarios with frequent data access.

```
// Enable offline persistence

firebase.firestore().enablePersistence().catch((err) => {

if (err.code === 'failed-precondition') {

console.log('Persistence failed due to multiple tabs.');

} else if (err.code === 'unimplemented') {

console.log('Persistence is not available.');

}

});
```

Offline persistence caches data locally, allowing the app to serve data from the cache instead of performing a network read.

Using Indexes to Speed Up Queries

FIRESTORE AUTOMATICALLY creates indexes for simple queries. However, composite indexes must be created manually for more complex queries. Properly indexed queries can significantly reduce query latency.

1. Single-Field Indexes

FIRESTORE AUTOMATICALLY indexes individual fields in each document, making it possible to perform simple queries, such as filtering by a single field or ordering by a single field.

```
// Example of a single-field query

db.collection('posts').where('author.id',                '==',
'authorId123').get().then((querySnapshot) => {

querySnapshot.forEach((doc) => {

console.log(doc.id, ' => ', doc.data());

});

});
```

This query retrieves all posts by a specific author using an automatically generated single-field index.

2. Composite Indexes

FOR COMPLEX QUERIES involving multiple fields, such as filtering and sorting by multiple criteria, a composite index is required. You can create composite indexes using the Firebase

Console or by following the error messages that Firestore generates for queries requiring additional indexes.

```
// Example of a multi-field query that requires a composite index

db.collection('posts')

.where('tags', 'array-contains', 'optimization')

.orderBy('created', 'desc')

.get()

.then((querySnapshot) => {

querySnapshot.forEach((doc) => {

console.log(doc.id, ' => ', doc.data());

});

});
```

In this example, Firestore requires a composite index on the tags and created fields to efficiently execute the query. The Firebase Console will prompt you to create this index if it doesn't exist.

Leveraging Query Limits and Pagination

USING QUERY LIMITS and pagination allows you to control the amount of data retrieved, improving performance and reducing costs. Firestore provides limit(), startAfter(), and endBefore() methods for implementing pagination.

1. Limiting Query Results

LIMITING THE NUMBER of documents retrieved helps manage large datasets and reduces read costs. For example, you can retrieve only the first 10 posts in a collection:

```
db.collection('posts').orderBy('created',
'desc').limit(10).get().then((querySnapshot) => {

querySnapshot.forEach((doc) => {

console.log(doc.id, ' => ', doc.data());

});

});
```

This query retrieves the latest 10 posts, which is useful for displaying a limited number of items on a page.

2. Implementing Pagination

FIRESTORE SUPPORTS pagination, allowing you to retrieve data in chunks and navigate between pages. This is particularly useful for handling large datasets.

```
let lastVisibleDoc;

db.collection('posts').orderBy('created').limit(10).get().then((querySnaps
=> {

lastVisibleDoc = querySnapshot.docs[querySnapshot.docs.length
- 1];

// Get the next page
```

```
db.collection('posts').orderBy('created').startAfter(lastVisibleDoc).limit(

.then((nextQuerySnapshot) => {

nextQuerySnapshot.forEach((doc) => {

console.log(doc.id, ' => ', doc.data());

});

});

});
```

This code snippet retrieves the first 10 documents and then uses startAfter() to retrieve the next 10 documents.

Monitoring and Debugging Query Performance

FIRESTORE PROVIDES tools for monitoring query performance and identifying bottlenecks. The Firebase Console includes a Firestore usage dashboard that displays metrics such as read and write operations, storage usage, and query performance.

1. Using the Firebase Console for Monitoring

IN THE FIREBASE CONSOLE, you can access the Firestore usage dashboard to view real-time and historical data on query performance. This dashboard provides insights into the number of reads, writes, and deletes, as well as the storage used by Firestore.

2. Debugging with Firebase Profiler

FIREBASE PROFILER ALLOWS you to monitor specific Firestore queries and operations in your app. You can use the profiler to track the latency and execution time of individual queries, helping you identify areas for optimization.

Conclusion

OPTIMIZING FIRESTORE queries involves structuring data effectively, minimizing read and write operations, and leveraging indexing and pagination to improve performance. By understanding Firestore's query capabilities and following best practices for data modeling, you can build applications that are responsive, cost-effective, and capable of scaling with user demand. Regularly monitoring query performance and adjusting your data model as needed will ensure that your Firestore queries remain efficient as your app grows.

Case Study: Real-Time Data with Firestore and GCP

TO ILLUSTRATE THE REAL-world applications of Firebase Firestore and Google Cloud Platform (GCP) in managing real-time data, let's delve into a detailed case study. In this case study, we will explore the development of a collaborative document editing application that leverages Firestore for real-time data synchronization, GCP Cloud Functions for server-side processing, and various GCP tools for monitoring and optimizing performance.

This application, named "CollabDocs," allows multiple users to edit a document simultaneously. The real-time synchronization of edits, combined with a scalable backend, ensures that users can collaborate seamlessly without latency. This case study will cover the architecture, implementation, challenges, and solutions involved in building and deploying CollabDocs using Firebase and GCP.

Overview of CollabDocs Architecture

THE ARCHITECTURE OF CollabDocs is designed to support real-time data synchronization, scalability, and efficient data processing. The key components of the architecture include:

1. **Firestore**: Used as the primary data store for managing document data and synchronizing edits across clients in real time.
2. **Cloud Functions**: Used for server-side processing, such as validating document edits, handling notifications, and managing user permissions.
3. **Firebase Authentication**: Manages user authentication and access control.
4. **Google Cloud Monitoring**: Provides insights into application performance, including query latency, error rates, and resource usage.
5. **Cloud Storage**: Stores media files and other large assets associated with documents.

The combination of these tools provides a robust platform for building real-time applications that require high availability, low latency, and seamless user experiences.

Setting Up Firestore for Real-Time Data Synchronization

IN COLLABDOCS, FIRESTORE is used to store documents and synchronize edits across clients. Each document is stored as a Firestore document within a collection, and edits are tracked in real time to ensure all users see changes as they happen.

1. Data Structure for Documents and Edits

EACH DOCUMENT IS STORED as a Firestore document within the documents collection. Edits are stored in a subcollection named edits, allowing for granular tracking of changes.

```javascript
// Data structure for a document

const db = firebase.firestore();

db.collection('documents').doc('docId').set({

title: 'Project Plan',

content: 'Initial draft...',

authorId: 'userId123',

created: firebase.firestore.FieldValue.serverTimestamp()

});

// Data structure for an edit within the document

db.collection('documents').doc('docId').collection('edits').add({

editorId: 'userId456',

timestamp: firebase.firestore.FieldValue.serverTimestamp(),

changes: { line: 2, text: 'Updated text...' }

});
```

In this setup, each edit is associated with the document it modifies, and the edits subcollection enables real-time synchronization for all users editing the same document.

2. Implementing Real-Time Listeners

FIRESTORE'S REAL-TIME listeners allow clients to receive updates whenever a document or its edits are modified. This is essential for maintaining a consistent user experience across multiple devices.

```
// Real-time listener for document changes

db.collection('documents').doc('docId').onSnapshot((doc) => {

console.log('Document data:', doc.data());

});

// Real-time listener for edits within the document

db.collection('documents').doc('docId').collection('edits')

.orderBy('timestamp', 'asc')

.onSnapshot((querySnapshot) => {

querySnapshot.forEach((doc) => {

console.log('Edit data:', doc.data());

});

});
```

These listeners ensure that all users viewing or editing the document see updates immediately, reflecting changes as they occur.

Using Cloud Functions for Server-Side Processing

CLOUD FUNCTIONS ARE integral to CollabDocs for handling server-side logic, such as validating edits, sending notifications, and managing user permissions. These functions enable the app to offload processing tasks to the server, reducing client-side workload and ensuring consistent data validation.

1. Validating Edits with Cloud Functions

TO MAINTAIN DOCUMENT integrity, a Cloud Function validates each edit before it is applied. This function checks for potential conflicts, unauthorized changes, and other issues that could disrupt the editing experience.

```
const functions = require('firebase-functions');

const admin = require('firebase-admin');

admin.initializeApp();

exports.validateEdit                                    =
functions.firestore.document('documents/{docId}/edits/{editId}')

.onCreate((snap, context) => {

const edit = snap.data();

const docId = context.params.docId;

return admin.firestore().collection('documents').doc(docId).get()

.then((docSnap) => {

if (!docSnap.exists) {

throw new Error('Document does not exist');
```

```
}

const docData = docSnap.data();

// Perform validation logic here

if (edit.editorId !== docData.authorId) {

throw new Error('Unauthorized edit attempt');

}

return true; // Edit is valid

})

.catch((error) => {

console.error('Validation failed:', error);

});

});
```

This function listens for new edits in the edits subcollection, validates the edit, and ensures it adheres to predefined rules.

2. Sending Notifications on Document Changes

COLLABDOCS CAN ALSO notify users when a document is modified. A Cloud Function can send push notifications to alert users about updates or important changes.

```
exports.sendNotification                                    =
functions.firestore.document('documents/{docId}')

.onUpdate((change, context) => {
```

```
const newDocData = change.after.data();

const oldDocData = change.before.data();

if (newDocData.content !== oldDocData.content) {

// Send notification to users

console.log('Document content changed:', newDocData.content);

// Add notification logic here

}

});
```

This function triggers whenever a document is updated, allowing the app to notify users of changes in real time.

Monitoring and Optimizing Performance with GCP Tools

GOOGLE CLOUD PLATFORM offers various tools to monitor and optimize the performance of CollabDocs. Effective monitoring is essential to ensure that the application performs well as the user base grows.

1. Using Google Cloud Monitoring for Real-Time Insights

GOOGLE CLOUD MONITORING provides real-time insights into Firestore's performance, including query latency, error rates, and resource utilization. These metrics help identify potential bottlenecks and areas for optimization.

In the Google Cloud Console, you can create custom dashboards to monitor Firestore metrics and set up alerts for specific events, such as high latency or increased error rates. This allows the team to proactively address issues before they affect users.

2. Debugging with Cloud Trace and Logging

CLOUD TRACE AND CLOUD Logging are valuable tools for diagnosing issues in CollabDocs. Cloud Trace provides latency data for Firestore queries, while Cloud Logging captures detailed logs of function executions and application events.

By integrating these tools, developers can analyze Firestore query performance, identify slow operations, and investigate errors in Cloud Functions. This information is crucial for optimizing queries and resolving issues.

Managing Storage and Media Files with Cloud Storage

FOR DOCUMENTS THAT include media files, such as images or videos, Cloud Storage is used to store these assets. Cloud Storage offers scalable, secure storage with easy integration into Firestore.

1. Uploading Media Files to Cloud Storage

USERS CAN UPLOAD MEDIA files to Cloud Storage, and the file URLs are stored in Firestore documents. This separates media storage from document storage, ensuring that Firestore remains optimized for text data while Cloud Storage handles large files.

const storageRef = firebase.storage().ref();

const fileRef = storageRef.child('media/docId/fileName.jpg');

```
fileRef.put(file).then((snapshot) => {

console.log('File uploaded successfully:',
snapshot.metadata.name);

});
```

2. Managing Access Permissions for Media Files

ACCESS TO MEDIA FILES is controlled through Firebase Security Rules, ensuring that only authorized users can upload or download files. This provides an additional layer of security for user-generated content.

```
service firebase.storage {

match /b/{bucket}/o {

match /media/{docId}/{fileName} {

allow read: if request.auth != null;

allow write: if request.auth.uid == resource.data.ownerId;

}

}

}
```

Conclusion and Key Takeaways

THE COLLABDOCS CASE study demonstrates the power of integrating Firebase Firestore with Google Cloud Platform to build a robust real-time collaboration application. By leveraging Firestore for data synchronization, Cloud Functions for server-side processing, and GCP tools for monitoring and storage, CollabDocs delivers a seamless user experience.

Key takeaways from this case study include:

- **Designing for Real-Time Synchronization**: Firestore's real-time capabilities enable smooth collaboration by keeping all users in sync.

- **Server-Side Processing with Cloud Functions**: Offloading processing tasks to Cloud Functions enhances security, consistency, and scalability.

- **Monitoring and Optimization**: Utilizing GCP monitoring tools allows for proactive management of app performance, ensuring a high-quality user experience.

- **Scalable Storage Solutions**: Cloud Storage provides efficient management of large media files, keeping Firestore optimized for text data.

This approach to building CollabDocs illustrates how Firestore and GCP can be combined to create scalable, responsive, and collaborative applications that cater to a wide range of user needs and scenarios.

Chapter 5: Cloud Functions and Firebase Functions

Introduction to Firebase Cloud Functions

FIREBASE CLOUD FUNCTIONS allow developers to execute backend code in response to events triggered by Firebase features and HTTPS requests. This serverless solution leverages Google Cloud's infrastructure to handle scaling automatically, ensuring your functions can manage high traffic without additional configuration or management overhead. Firebase Cloud Functions are a cornerstone for extending Firebase capabilities, enabling the integration of custom logic to respond to events within your application seamlessly.

Firebase Cloud Functions can be written in JavaScript, TypeScript, Python, Go, and several other languages, though JavaScript is the most widely used due to its flexibility and integration with Firebase SDKs. Functions are defined in a functions folder within your Firebase project directory and are deployed to Firebase's serverless infrastructure using the Firebase CLI.

Advantages of Using Firebase Cloud Functions

1. **Scalability**: Firebase Cloud Functions automatically scale up based on demand, so your backend infrastructure grows as your user base does. This feature eliminates the need for manual intervention to manage server capacity.
2. **Serverless Management**: With Firebase Cloud Functions, there's no need to manage or provision servers. You simply write your function, deploy it, and Firebase handles the rest.

3. **Event-Driven Architecture**: Firebase Cloud Functions can be triggered by various events, such as Firestore changes, authentication events, or analytics conversions. This enables an event-driven architecture that can easily adapt to user interactions and application dynamics.

4. **Seamless Integration with Firebase and GCP**: Firebase Cloud Functions integrate directly with other Firebase services, as well as Google Cloud Platform services, enabling you to extend the functionality of your Firebase project with GCP's vast service ecosystem.

Setting Up Firebase Cloud Functions

TO GET STARTED WITH Firebase Cloud Functions, you need to have the Firebase CLI installed on your system. If you haven't installed it yet, you can do so by running the following command:

npm install -g firebase-tools

Once you have the Firebase CLI, you can initialize your Firebase project for Cloud Functions by navigating to your project directory and running:

firebase init functions

During this process, the CLI will prompt you to choose the programming language for your Cloud Functions, provide options for linting, and offer the option to install dependencies automatically. Once initialized, the CLI creates a functions folder containing essential files, such as index.js (or index.ts for TypeScript) and package.json.

Writing Your First Cloud Function

HERE'S AN EXAMPLE OF a simple HTTP-triggered function. This function returns a "Hello World" message when accessed:

```
const functions = require('firebase-functions');

exports.helloWorld = functions.https.onRequest((request, response) => {

response.send("Hello from Firebase!");

});
```

This function is structured as follows:

- **exports.helloWorld**: This exports the function as helloWorld, making it accessible as a callable HTTP endpoint.

- **functions.https.onRequest**: This specifies that the function should be triggered by an HTTP request.

- **request, response**: These are the standard parameters for handling HTTP requests and responses in Express.js, allowing you to send back data to the client.

Deploying Cloud Functions

ONCE YOU'VE WRITTEN your function, you can deploy it to Firebase's serverless infrastructure. Run the following command in your terminal:

```
firebase deploy—only functions
```

The Firebase CLI will compile, package, and deploy your functions to Google Cloud's infrastructure. After deployment, you'll receive

URLs for any HTTP functions that you can use to test and integrate them with your application.

Event-Driven Cloud Functions

BESIDES HTTP TRIGGERS, Firebase Cloud Functions can respond to various Firebase and Google Cloud events, such as:

- **Firestore Document Events**: Triggered by changes to Firestore documents.

- **Authentication Events**: Triggered by user creation or deletion events.

- **Storage Events**: Triggered by file uploads, updates, or deletions in Firebase Storage.

- **Analytics Events**: Triggered by custom or conversion events recorded by Firebase Analytics.

Example: Firestore Trigger

BELOW IS AN EXAMPLE of a Cloud Function triggered by changes to a Firestore document. This function listens for new documents added to a users collection and sends a welcome email using a third-party service like SendGrid or Mailgun.

```
const functions = require('firebase-functions');

const admin = require('firebase-admin');

admin.initializeApp();

exports.sendWelcomeEmail = functions.firestore

.document('users/{userId}')
```

```
.onCreate((snap, context) => {

const newValue = snap.data();

const email = newValue.email;

// Call email service provider here

return sendWelcomeEmail(email); // Assume sendWelcomeEmail
is a helper function

});
```

In this example:

- **admin.initializeApp**(): Initializes the Firebase Admin SDK, allowing access to other Firebase services.

- **functions.firestore.document**: Specifies a Firestore document trigger.

- **onCreate**: Listens for new document creations in the users collection.

- **sendWelcomeEmail**: Hypothetical helper function that uses an email API to send a welcome email.

Best Practices for Firebase Cloud Functions

1. **Minimize Cold Starts**: Cold starts happen when a function hasn't been invoked for a while, and the environment needs to spin up before processing the request. Keep functions lightweight to minimize cold start times.
2. **Use Environment Variables**: Avoid hard-coding sensitive data (like API keys) within your functions. Instead, use

Firebase's functions.config() to store and access environment variables securely.

3. **Optimize Function Memory and Timeout Settings**: Adjust memory and timeout settings to optimize performance and reduce costs. Firebase offers up to 2GB of memory and a maximum of 9 minutes of execution time.

4. **Monitor Function Performance**: Firebase offers comprehensive monitoring through the Firebase Console, where you can track invocations, errors, and latency. For deeper insights, integrate with Google Cloud's monitoring services.

5. **Handle Errors Gracefully**: Use try-catch blocks to handle potential errors and log them using console.error. This ensures your function fails gracefully, providing useful information for debugging.

Example of Error Handling in a Cloud Function

HERE'S A FUNCTION THAT reads from Firestore and includes error handling to ensure graceful degradation:

```
exports.getUserData = functions.https.onRequest(async (req, res) => {

try {

const userId = req.query.userId;

const doc = await admin.firestore().collection('users').doc(userId).get();

if (!doc.exists) {

throw new Error('User not found');
```

```
}

res.json(doc.data());

} catch (error) {

console.error('Error fetching user data:', error);

res.status(500).send('Internal Server Error');

}

});
```

In this example:

- **try-catch**: The function attempts to fetch a user's data from Firestore. If it fails, it catches the error and logs it, responding with a 500 status code and an error message.

- **console.error**: Logs the error for debugging purposes.

Conclusion

FIREBASE CLOUD FUNCTIONS provide a flexible, scalable, and powerful way to extend the capabilities of your Firebase applications without needing to manage backend servers. With support for various trigger types and seamless integration with both Firebase and Google Cloud services, you can build highly responsive, event-driven architectures. Following best practices and optimizing function performance can help you maintain a reliable and efficient serverless backend as your application grows.

For more advanced use cases, such as integrating with external APIs or implementing complex business logic, Firebase Cloud Functions offer the customization and scalability required to meet modern application demands.

Writing and Deploying Firebase Functions

FIREBASE FUNCTIONS are a serverless way to build backend functionality that responds to events within your Firebase app, such as changes in Firestore, user authentication events, or direct HTTP requests. Writing and deploying Firebase Functions involves coding the logic in JavaScript or TypeScript, testing it locally, and then deploying it to the Firebase serverless infrastructure using the Firebase CLI.

Setting Up Your Environment for Firebase Functions

TO BEGIN DEVELOPING Firebase Functions, ensure that you have:

1. **Firebase CLI**: Installable via npm, this tool allows you to initialize, develop, and deploy functions.
2. **Node.js**: Firebase Functions support JavaScript and TypeScript, both of which require Node.js.
3. **Firebase Project**: Set up a Firebase project and link it to your local environment using the Firebase CLI.

After ensuring these prerequisites, start by initializing your functions environment within your Firebase project directory by running:

firebase init functions

During the initialization process, the CLI will prompt you to choose between JavaScript and TypeScript, whether to install dependencies immediately, and if you want to use ESLint for code linting.

Basic Structure of Firebase Functions

ONCE INITIALIZED, THE functions folder contains several files, including:

- **index.js (or index.ts for TypeScript)**: This is the main entry file where all functions are defined and exported.

- **package.json**: Manages dependencies for your functions, such as Firebase and Express.

- **node_modules**/: Contains installed dependencies.

Below is a basic example of a Firebase Function responding to an HTTP request:

const functions = require('firebase-functions');

exports.helloWorld = functions.https.onRequest((req, res) => {

res.send("Hello from Firebase Functions!");

});

This simple function responds with "Hello from Firebase Functions!" whenever the associated HTTP endpoint is accessed.

Advanced Example: CRUD Operations with Firestore

FIREBASE FUNCTIONS allow you to perform CRUD (Create, Read, Update, Delete) operations on Firestore, which can be useful for building RESTful APIs. Below is an example of CRUD operations within Firebase Functions:

```javascript
const functions = require('firebase-functions');

const admin = require('firebase-admin');

admin.initializeApp();

exports.createUser = functions.https.onRequest(async (req, res) => {

const data = req.body;

try {

const newDoc = await admin.firestore().collection('users').add(data);

res.status(201).send(`User created with ID: ${newDoc.id}`);

} catch (error) {

res.status(500).send('Error creating user: ' + error.message);

}

});

exports.getUser = functions.https.onRequest(async (req, res) => {

const id = req.query.id;

try {

const doc = await admin.firestore().collection('users').doc(id).get();

if (!doc.exists) {
```

```
res.status(404).send('User not found');

} else {

res.status(200).json(doc.data());

}

} catch (error) {

res.status(500).send('Error retrieving user: ' + error.message);

}

});

exports.updateUser = functions.https.onRequest(async (req, res)
=> {

const id = req.query.id;

const data = req.body;

try {

await admin.firestore().collection('users').doc(id).update(data);

res.status(200).send('User updated');

} catch (error) {

res.status(500).send('Error updating user: ' + error.message);

}

});

exports.deleteUser = functions.https.onRequest(async (req, res)
=> {
```

```
const id = req.query.id;

try {

await admin.firestore().collection('users').doc(id).delete();

res.status(200).send('User deleted');

} catch (error) {

res.status(500).send('Error deleting user: ' + error.message);

}

});
```

This example includes four functions that allow for full CRUD operations on the users collection:

1. **createUser**: Creates a new user in Firestore with data from the request body.
2. **getUser**: Retrieves a user document based on an ID passed as a query parameter.
3. **updateUser**: Updates user information with new data from the request body.
4. **deleteUser**: Deletes a user document identified by an ID.

Testing Firebase Functions Locally

FIREBASE PROVIDES A local emulator that allows you to test functions before deploying them. To start the emulator, use:

```
firebase emulators:start
```

This command spins up a local environment mimicking Firebase services, allowing you to test HTTP functions, Firestore triggers, and more. Access the emulator dashboard at http://localhost:4000 to monitor function execution, view logs, and test endpoints.

Deploying Functions to Firebase

AFTER TESTING, DEPLOY your functions to Firebase's serverless infrastructure using:

firebase deploy—only functions

This command uploads your code to Firebase, and you'll receive a URL for each HTTP-triggered function. Non-HTTP functions will be automatically triggered based on events such as Firestore document changes.

Handling Middleware with Firebase Functions

FIREBASE FUNCTIONS can incorporate middleware for additional functionality. Using libraries like Express, you can build more complex HTTP endpoints, including middleware for logging, authentication, and more.

Example with Express Middleware

CONST FUNCTIONS = REQUIRE('firebase-functions');

const express = require('express');

const app = express();

app.use((req, res, next) => {

console.log(`Request URL: ${req.url}`);

next();

```
});

app.get('/hello', (req, res) => {

res.send('Hello from Express and Firebase!');

});

exports.app = functions.https.onRequest(app);
```

In this example:

- The middleware logs each request URL.

- app.get defines a route that sends a response when the /hello endpoint is accessed.

Error Handling and Logging

FIREBASE FUNCTIONS include built-in logging through console.log, console.warn, and console.error. This allows for detailed tracking of function execution, aiding in debugging and performance monitoring.

```
exports.logExample = functions.https.onRequest((req, res) => {

console.log('Log Message: Function triggered');

console.warn('Warning Message: Something to note');

console.error('Error Message: An error occurred');

res.send('Logging example');

});
```

The Firebase Console provides a view of logs, where you can filter and analyze them to troubleshoot issues.

Optimizing Firebase Functions

TO OPTIMIZE YOUR FUNCTIONS:

1. **Minimize Dependencies**: Import only required modules to reduce cold start times.
2. **Configure Memory and Timeout**: Tailor function settings based on performance needs, as higher memory can reduce cold start times but increases costs.
3. **Set Up Retry Policies**: Define retry policies for critical functions to handle failures gracefully.

Example of a Configured Function

```
EXPORTS.IMPORTANTTASK = functions.runWith({

timeoutSeconds: 300,

memory: '2GB'

}).https.onRequest((req, res) => {

res.send('Configured function');

});
```

This example sets the function's memory to 2GB and timeout to 300 seconds, providing greater resources for intensive tasks.

Deploying and Versioning

FIREBASE DEPLOYS ALL functions by default, but you can deploy specific functions using:

```
firebase deploy—only functions:functionName
```

Versioning is managed through function names, so be sure to use descriptive names and organize them within index.js for easier maintenance.

Conclusion

FIREBASE FUNCTIONS provide a powerful serverless backend for Firebase apps, allowing for scalable, event-driven logic with minimal maintenance. By leveraging Firebase's integration with Google Cloud Platform, you can extend your applications efficiently, harnessing both Firebase services and external APIs to build robust, responsive applications. As you continue to develop, remember to implement logging, optimize resources, and thoroughly test your functions in the local emulator to ensure stability and reliability in production.

Using GCP Cloud Functions for Advanced Use Cases

GOOGLE CLOUD FUNCTIONS provide a versatile and powerful serverless computing environment, enabling you to execute code in response to various events from Firebase, Google Cloud, and external services. While Firebase Cloud Functions are tailored to Firebase services, GCP Cloud Functions offer broader capabilities, including integration with a wide range of Google Cloud services and advanced configuration options. This section covers the setup, development, and deployment of GCP Cloud Functions and explores advanced use cases such as connecting to other GCP services, handling complex triggers, and working with asynchronous tasks.

Setting Up Google Cloud Functions

TO BEGIN WITH GOOGLE Cloud Functions, you need to have a Google Cloud Platform account and a Google Cloud Project configured. Follow these steps to set up your environment:

1. **Enable Cloud Functions API**: Navigate to the Google Cloud Console and enable the Cloud Functions API for your project.
2. **Install Google Cloud SDK**: The Google Cloud SDK provides tools to manage and deploy Cloud Functions. You can install it by following the instructions on the Google Cloud documentation page.
3. **Configure Authentication**: Use gcloud auth login to authenticate your environment and gcloud config set project [PROJECT_ID] to specify your project ID.

After configuring your environment, you can begin developing GCP Cloud Functions. Functions can be deployed using the Google Cloud Console, Google Cloud SDK, or Cloud Functions' HTTP API.

Creating and Deploying a GCP Cloud Function

GCP CLOUD FUNCTIONS support various languages, including JavaScript, Python, and Go. Below is an example of an HTTP-triggered GCP Cloud Function written in JavaScript:

```javascript
exports.helloWorld = (req, res) => {

res.status(200).send('Hello from Google Cloud Functions!');

};
```

To deploy this function, use the following command:

gcloud functions deploy helloWorld \

—runtime nodejs14 \

—trigger-http \

—allow-unauthenticated

In this command:

- —runtime nodejs14 specifies the runtime environment.

- —trigger-http sets an HTTP trigger for the function.

- —allow-unauthenticated makes the function publicly accessible.

Integrating Google Cloud Functions with Other GCP Services

ONE OF THE ADVANTAGES of GCP Cloud Functions is their ability to integrate with a wide array of GCP services, such as Google Cloud Storage, BigQuery, and Pub/Sub. This enables you to build complex workflows that leverage GCP's powerful data processing and storage capabilities.

Example: Triggering a Function from Google Cloud Storage

HERE'S AN EXAMPLE OF a Cloud Function that automatically resizes images uploaded to a Cloud Storage bucket:

```
const {Storage} = require('@google-cloud/storage');

const sharp = require('sharp');
```

```javascript
const storage = new Storage();

const bucketName = 'your-bucket-name';

exports.resizeImage = async (file, context) => {

const fileName = file.name;

const bucket = storage.bucket(file.bucket);

const tempFilePath = `/tmp/${fileName}`;

await bucket.file(fileName).download({destination: tempFilePath});

await sharp(tempFilePath)

.resize(200, 200)

.toFile(`/tmp/resized-${fileName}`);

await bucket.upload(`/tmp/resized-${fileName}`, {

destination: `resized/${fileName}`,

});

console.log(`Image resized and uploaded to resized/${fileName}`);

};
```

This function:

1. **Downloads** the image file from Cloud Storage to a temporary local directory.
2. **Resizes** the image using the sharp library.
3. **Uploads** the resized image back to the resized/ folder in

the Cloud Storage bucket.

To deploy this function with a Cloud Storage trigger, use the following command:

gcloud functions deploy resizeImage \

—runtime nodejs14 \

—trigger-resource=your-bucket-name \

—trigger-event=google.storage.object.finalize

Working with Pub/Sub for Event-Driven Architectures

GOOGLE CLOUD PUB/SUB allows for scalable event-driven architectures by enabling asynchronous messaging between services. You can use Pub/Sub to decouple services, integrate with microservices, and implement task queues.

Example: Processing a Pub/Sub Message

THE FOLLOWING FUNCTION is triggered by a Pub/Sub message and processes the message data:

exports.processMessage = (message, context) => {

const data = Buffer.from(message.data, 'base64').toString();

console.log(`Received message: ${data}`);

// Perform additional processing here

};

To deploy the function, specify the Pub/Sub topic trigger:

gcloud functions deploy processMessage \

—runtime nodejs14 \

—trigger-topic=your-topic-name

This setup allows you to handle messages asynchronously, which is useful for tasks that require background processing, such as data transformation, event aggregation, or sending notifications.

Advanced Use Case: Asynchronous Task Processing with Cloud Tasks

GOOGLE CLOUD TASKS enables the scheduling and execution of asynchronous tasks, which is ideal for handling operations that are resource-intensive or that should not block the main application flow. Cloud Tasks can also ensure retries for failed tasks, making it suitable for handling critical operations.

Example: Enqueuing Tasks to Cloud Tasks from a Cloud Function

HERE'S HOW YOU CAN enqueue tasks into Cloud Tasks within a Cloud Function. This function enqueues a task with a payload to a specific queue:

```javascript
const {CloudTasksClient} = require('@google-cloud/tasks');

const client = new CloudTasksClient();

exports.enqueueTask = async (req, res) => {

const project = 'your-project-id';

const queue = 'your-queue-id';
```

```javascript
const location = 'us-central1';

const url = 'https://your-function-url';

const payload = JSON.stringify({message: 'Hello, Cloud Tasks!'});

const request = {

parent: client.queuePath(project, location, queue),

task: {

httpRequest: {

httpMethod: 'POST',

url: url,

headers: {

'Content-Type': 'application/json',

},

body: Buffer.from(payload).toString('base64'),

},

},

};

const [response] = await client.createTask(request);

res.send(`Created task ${response.name}`);

};
```

Deploy this function as an HTTP-triggered function, and it can enqueue tasks to a Cloud Tasks queue, where they will be processed based on your configuration.

Security Considerations

WHEN USING GOOGLE CLOUD Functions, consider the following best practices to secure your functions:

1. **Use IAM Roles**: Assign only the necessary permissions to the service account associated with your functions.
2. **Environment Variables for Secrets**: Store sensitive information like API keys in environment variables or use Secret Manager for enhanced security.
3. **IP and Network Restrictions**: For more sensitive functions, consider restricting access to specific IP addresses or VPC networks.

Monitoring and Logging with Google Cloud Functions

GOOGLE CLOUD FUNCTIONS integrate with Google Cloud's monitoring and logging tools, such as Cloud Monitoring and Cloud Logging, providing insights into function performance and enabling you to troubleshoot issues efficiently.

Example: Accessing Logs and Monitoring

YOU CAN VIEW FUNCTION logs directly from the Google Cloud Console or via the gcloud command-line tool:

gcloud functions logs read [FUNCTION_NAME]

Additionally, you can set up alerts in Cloud Monitoring to notify you when certain thresholds are exceeded, such as memory usage or execution time. This proactive monitoring helps ensure the reliability of your functions.

Conclusion

GOOGLE CLOUD FUNCTIONS extend the flexibility of serverless computing with broader integrations and advanced use cases. By leveraging GCP Cloud Functions in combination with other GCP services, you can build scalable, event-driven applications that are both powerful and efficient. Whether you are processing real-time events from Pub/Sub, manipulating large files in Cloud Storage, or managing asynchronous tasks with Cloud Tasks, Google Cloud Functions provide a comprehensive solution for advanced cloud computing needs.

Triggering Functions with Firestore, Auth, and More

FIREBASE CLOUD FUNCTIONS allow you to trigger backend logic in response to various events within Firebase services. These event-driven triggers enable you to automate processes, enhance app functionality, and react to real-time changes without needing manual intervention. In this section, we'll explore how to set up and use different types of triggers, including those for Firestore, Authentication, Firebase Storage, and more. We'll also cover practical examples and best practices to maximize the efficiency and reliability of your triggered functions.

Types of Firebase Cloud Functions Triggers

FIREBASE CLOUD FUNCTIONS can be triggered by a variety of events within Firebase, including:

1. **Firestore Triggers**: React to changes in Firestore documents.
2. **Auth Triggers**: Respond to authentication events such as user creation or deletion.
3. **Storage Triggers**: Handle events related to file uploads, updates, and deletions in Firebase Storage.
4. **Analytics Triggers**: Enable functions based on Firebase Analytics conversion events.
5. **HTTP Triggers**: Accessible through HTTP requests, ideal for building RESTful APIs and webhooks.

Firestore Document Triggers

FIRESTORE DOCUMENT triggers enable functions to respond to changes in Firestore, such as new documents being added, updated, or deleted. These triggers are useful for maintaining derived data, updating related documents, or performing tasks based on real-time updates.

Example: Sending Notifications on Document Creation

THE FOLLOWING EXAMPLE demonstrates a Cloud Function that sends a notification whenever a new user profile is added to a Firestore profiles collection.

```
const functions = require('firebase-functions');

const admin = require('firebase-admin');
```

```javascript
admin.initializeApp();

exports.sendWelcomeNotification = functions.firestore

.document('profiles/{userId}')

.onCreate((snap, context) => {

const newValue = snap.data();

const userId = context.params.userId;

const message = {

notification: {

title: 'Welcome!',

body: `Hello ${newValue.name}, welcome to our platform!`,

},

token: newValue.fcmToken,

};

return admin.messaging().send(message)

.then(response => console.log('Successfully sent message:', response))

.catch(error => console.error('Error sending message:', error));

});
```

In this example:

- **onCreate Trigger**: The function is triggered when a new document is created in the profiles collection.

- **Firebase Cloud Messaging**: The function sends a welcome notification using Firebase Cloud Messaging, making it ideal for sending notifications based on user activities.

Authentication Triggers

AUTHENTICATION TRIGGERS allow functions to respond to Firebase Authentication events, such as when users sign up or delete their accounts. These triggers are useful for managing user data, sending welcome emails, and handling cleanup tasks when users leave.

Example: Creating User Profiles on Signup

THE FOLLOWING EXAMPLE automatically creates a user profile in Firestore when a new user registers:

```
exports.createUserProfile = functions.auth.user().onCreate((user) => {

const profileData = {

email: user.email,

displayName: user.displayName || 'Anonymous',

createdAt: admin.firestore.FieldValue.serverTimestamp(),

};

return
admin.firestore().collection('profiles').doc(user.uid).set(profileData)

.then(() => console.log('Profile created for user:', user.uid))
```

```
.catch(error => console.error('Error creating profile:', error));
```

```
});
```

Here:

- **onCreate Trigger**: Fires when a new user signs up.

- **Firestore Integration**: A new document is added to the profiles collection using the user's unique ID as the document ID.

Firebase Storage Triggers

STORAGE TRIGGERS ENABLE you to perform actions in response to file uploads, updates, and deletions in Firebase Storage. This is useful for processing images, videos, or other media files as they're uploaded by users.

Example: Image Resizing on Upload

HERE'S A FUNCTION THAT automatically resizes images to a thumbnail size whenever a new image is uploaded to the uploads directory in Firebase Storage:

```
const sharp = require('sharp');
```

```
const path = require('path');
```

```
const os = require('os');
```

```
exports.resizeImage = functions.storage.object().onFinalize(async (object) => {
```

```
const filePath = object.name;
```

```
const fileName = path.basename(filePath);

const tempFilePath = path.join(os.tmpdir(), fileName);

const bucket = admin.storage().bucket(object.bucket);

if (!filePath.startsWith('uploads/')) {

return null;

}

await bucket.file(filePath).download({ destination: tempFilePath });

await sharp(tempFilePath).resize(100, 100).toFile(tempFilePath);

const thumbFileName = `thumb_${fileName}`;

const thumbFilePath = `thumbnails/${thumbFileName}`;

await bucket.upload(tempFilePath, { destination: thumbFilePath });

return bucket.file(tempFilePath).delete();

});
```

This function:

- **onFinalize Trigger**: Fires when a new file is uploaded to Firebase Storage.

- **Image Processing**: Uses the sharp library to resize images and uploads the thumbnail to a separate folder in Storage.

Firebase Analytics Triggers

ANALYTICS TRIGGERS respond to Firebase Analytics conversion events, enabling you to act on user behaviors tracked within your app. This can be used to send targeted notifications or log events for further analysis.

Example: Triggering a Function on Conversion Event

HERE'S A FUNCTION THAT sends a promotional notification when a user completes a specific conversion event, such as making an in-app purchase:

```
exports.sendPromoOnPurchase = functions.analytics.event('purchase').onLog((event) => {

const userId = event.params.userId;

const promoMessage = {

notification: {

title: 'Thank You for Your Purchase!',

body: 'Here's a 10% off coupon on your next purchase.',

},

};

return admin.messaging().sendToDevice(userId, promoMessage)

.then(response => console.log('Promotion sent:', response))

.catch(error => console.error('Error sending promotion:', error));

});
```

In this function:

- **onLog Trigger**: Activates when a purchase event is logged in Firebase Analytics.

- **Sending Promotions**: Uses Firebase Cloud Messaging to send a targeted promotional message based on the conversion event.

HTTP Triggers

HTTP TRIGGERS ALLOW you to create webhooks or RESTful APIs, providing an interface for third-party services or direct integration with web and mobile apps. These functions can be called using standard HTTP methods like GET, POST, PUT, and DELETE.

Example: Creating a RESTful API

THE FOLLOWING EXAMPLE shows a RESTful API setup for managing a collection of books, allowing clients to create, read, update, and delete book records:

```
const express = require('express');

const app = express();

app.use(express.json());

app.post('/books', (req, res) => {

const data = req.body;

admin.firestore().collection('books').add(data)
```

```javascript
.then(docRef => res.status(201).send(`Created book with ID:
${docRef.id}`))

.catch(error => res.status(500).send('Error creating book: ' +
error.message));

});

app.get('/books/:id', (req, res) => {

const id = req.params.id;

admin.firestore().collection('books').doc(id).get()

.then(doc => {

if (!doc.exists) {

res.status(404).send('Book not found');

} else {

res.status(200).json(doc.data());

}

})

.catch(error => res.status(500).send('Error fetching book: ' +
error.message));

});

exports.api = functions.https.onRequest(app);
```

This setup:

- **Express Middleware**: Uses Express for handling routing and parsing JSON payloads.

- **CRUD Operations**: Provides endpoints for creating and fetching book records, demonstrating how Firebase Functions can support a full RESTful API.

Best Practices for Triggered Functions

1. **Use Batching**: For triggers responding to bulk actions (e.g., multiple document changes), use batched writes to reduce the number of individual requests, improving efficiency and reducing costs.
2. **Optimize Memory and Timeout Settings**: Configure function memory and timeout settings according to the workload, particularly for intensive tasks like file processing or analytics processing.
3. **Implement Error Handling**: Always include try-catch blocks and log errors to make debugging easier and ensure that functions degrade gracefully.
4. **Avoid Long-Running Processes**: For tasks that may take longer than the maximum function timeout, consider using Pub/Sub or Cloud Tasks to decouple and handle long-running tasks asynchronously.
5. **Utilize Cloud Monitoring**: Set up alerting and monitoring to track function performance and get notified of any anomalies, such as high latency or error rates.

Conclusion

TRIGGERING FIREBASE Cloud Functions using Firestore, Auth, Storage, Analytics, and HTTP provides a versatile way to respond to user actions, manage backend processes, and enhance app functionality. By combining these triggers, you can build a robust, event-driven architecture that seamlessly integrates with

Firebase and Google Cloud Platform services. With careful planning, optimization, and monitoring, you can ensure that your triggered functions are efficient, cost-effective, and capable of handling real-world demands as your application scales.

Monitoring and Debugging Cloud Functions

MONITORING AND DEBUGGING Firebase Cloud Functions are crucial tasks to ensure that your serverless backend is performing optimally, responding quickly, and operating with minimal errors. Firebase provides several tools and best practices for monitoring functions, tracking their performance, and debugging issues when they arise. In this section, we will explore various methods for logging, monitoring, and debugging Cloud Functions, including how to use Firebase and Google Cloud's integrated tools, handle errors, and optimize functions based on the insights gathered.

Logging with Firebase Functions

LOGS ARE THE MOST BASIC form of monitoring and debugging in Firebase Functions. Firebase provides built-in logging capabilities that allow you to track the behavior of your functions and identify issues during execution. You can use standard logging functions, such as console.log, console.error, and console.warn, to capture detailed information about your function's execution.

Example: Implementing Basic Logging

```
EXPORTS.PROCESSORDER                                    =
functions.https.onRequest((req, res) => {
```

```
console.log('Received order:', req.body);

try {

// Process the order

const result = processOrder(req.body);

console.log('Order processed successfully:', result);

res.status(200).send(result);

} catch (error) {

console.error('Error processing order:', error);

res.status(500).send('Internal Server Error');

}

});
```

In this example:

- **console.log**: Used to log incoming data and successful processing.

- **console.error**: Used to log errors for debugging when an exception is caught.

Accessing Logs in Firebase Console

LOGS GENERATED BY YOUR functions are accessible through the Firebase Console or the Google Cloud Console. Here's how to access them:

1. **Firebase Console**: Navigate to the Functions dashboard and select the function you wish to inspect. Here, you can

view recent invocations, execution time, memory usage, and logs.

2. **Google Cloud Console**: For more advanced log filtering, navigate to the Google Cloud Console and select **Logging** under **Operations**. You can filter logs by function name, severity, or specific keywords.

You can also access logs using the Google Cloud SDK with the following command:

gcloud functions logs read [FUNCTION_NAME]

Using Cloud Monitoring for In-Depth Analysis

FIREBASE INTEGRATES with Google Cloud Monitoring, which provides more advanced insights into your functions' performance, including metrics on latency, memory usage, and error rates. You can set up dashboards and alerts within Cloud Monitoring to track these metrics over time and receive notifications for any anomalies.

Setting Up a Monitoring Dashboard

TO SET UP A DASHBOARD for your Cloud Functions in Google Cloud Monitoring:

1. Navigate to the **Google Cloud Console** and go to **Monitoring**.

2. Under **Dashboards**, click **Create Dashboard**.

3. Add widgets for the metrics you want to monitor, such as:

○ **Execution time**: Monitors how long functions take to complete.

○ **Memory usage**: Tracks memory consumption during function execution.

○ **Error rate**: Keeps an eye on the frequency of errors in your functions.

Using these metrics, you can gain a clearer understanding of your function's behavior and identify areas where optimizations are needed.

Error Reporting and Debugging

WHEN AN ERROR OCCURS in a Firebase Function, it is essential to capture detailed information to facilitate troubleshooting. Google Cloud offers **Error Reporting**, which automatically aggregates and tracks errors in your functions, making it easier to spot patterns and prioritize fixes.

Example: Using Try-Catch for Enhanced Error Logging

IMPLEMENTING ERROR handling using try-catch blocks ensures that your function can log detailed error information without failing abruptly:

```
exports.updateUserProfile =
functions.firestore.document('users/{userId}')

.onUpdate((change, context) => {

try {

const beforeData = change.before.data();
```

```
const afterData = change.after.data();

// Simulate processing and update

console.log(`User data updated from ${JSON.stringify(beforeData)} to ${JSON.stringify(afterData)}`);

} catch (error) {

console.error('Error updating user profile:', error);

throw new functions.https.HttpsError('internal', 'Failed to update user profile');

}

});
```

In this example:

- **Error Handling**: The try-catch block ensures that errors are logged and rethrown in a structured way using HttpsError, which helps with debugging and client-side error handling.

Optimizing Cloud Functions Based on Monitoring Insights

ONCE YOU'VE MONITORED your functions and identified potential issues, the next step is to optimize them. Here are some common optimization strategies:

1. **Minimize Cold Starts**: Cold starts occur when a function is invoked after being idle, resulting in higher latency. You can reduce cold starts by:

o Increasing memory allocation (e.g., from 256 MB to 512 MB).

o Optimizing imports to avoid unnecessary libraries that increase load times.

2. **Reduce Execution Time**: Long-running functions can be costly and may indicate inefficiencies in your code. To reduce execution time:

o Optimize database queries to reduce latency.

o Use async operations and avoid blocking code.

Optimize Memory Usage: Functions that consume more memory than allocated will fail. Monitor memory usage and adjust the allocation in the function configuration as needed:

```
exports.memoryIntensiveFunction = functions.runWith({ memory: '1GB' })

.https.onRequest((req, res) => {

// Memory-intensive logic here

res.send('Function completed successfully');

});
```

3.

Setting Up Alerts for Real-Time Monitoring

ALERTS ARE USEFUL FOR detecting issues in real-time. You can set up alerts in Google Cloud Monitoring to notify you of specific events, such as high error rates or latency spikes, via email, SMS, or other channels.

To create an alert:

1. Go to **Monitoring** in the Google Cloud Console.
2. Click **Alerting** and then **Create Policy**.
3. Set the conditions for your alert, such as error rate exceeding a specific threshold.
4. Specify the notification channels for receiving alerts.

Debugging with the Google Cloud Debugger

GOOGLE CLOUD DEBUGGER allows you to inspect the state of your functions at runtime without stopping or slowing down your application. This is especially useful for pinpointing issues that are difficult to replicate in a local development environment.

To enable Cloud Debugger:

1. In the Google Cloud Console, go to **Debugger** under **Operations**.
2. Select the function you wish to debug and set breakpoints directly in the source code.

Logging Best Practices for Effective Debugging

HERE ARE SOME BEST practices for logging and debugging Cloud Functions effectively:

- **Log Verbosely During Development**: Use detailed logs during development and testing to capture as much information as possible.

- **Use Log Levels**: Use different logging levels (e.g., console.debug, console.info, console.warn, console.error) to categorize log entries and filter them easily in production.

- **Avoid Logging Sensitive Data**: Ensure that sensitive data, such as user credentials or personal information, is not logged to maintain compliance with privacy regulations.

- **Implement Structured Logging**: Use structured logging with JSON objects for logs. This approach facilitates querying and filtering logs in the Google Cloud Console.

```
console.log(JSON.stringify({

event: 'orderProcessed',

orderId: order.id,

status: 'success',

timestamp: new Date().toISOString()

}));
```

Structured logging allows you to log additional context around events and makes it easier to analyze logs using tools like BigQuery.

Conclusion

BY LEVERAGING FIREBASE'S integrated logging and monitoring tools, you can efficiently track the performance and health of your Cloud Functions. Setting up alerts, using the Google Cloud Debugger, and following logging best practices are key to ensuring that your functions operate smoothly and issues are resolved quickly. Regularly reviewing monitoring insights will help you optimize your functions to improve performance, reduce costs, and enhance user experience. With these tools and strategies, you can ensure that your Firebase backend remains reliable and responsive as your application grows.

Chapter 6: Hosting with Firebase and GCP

Firebase Hosting Basics

FIREBASE HOSTING IS a fast, secure, and reliable hosting solution designed to serve web content and assets for web apps, mobile apps, and static sites. Firebase Hosting provides a global content delivery network (CDN) backed by SSD storage, which ensures that users can access your content quickly and reliably from anywhere in the world. This service is particularly suited for web apps that need low latency and high availability.

Firebase Hosting supports multiple types of content, including HTML, CSS, JavaScript, images, and other static assets. You can also deploy dynamic content by connecting Firebase Hosting with Cloud Functions or Cloud Run, enabling server-side processing for your app. Moreover, Firebase Hosting makes it easy to set up SSL, manage custom domains, and configure caching and rewrites for more advanced web app architectures.

Key Features of Firebase Hosting

1. **Fast Deployments:** With Firebase Hosting, you can deploy your web app in seconds. Firebase Hosting uses a single command, firebase deploy, to push your latest updates to a global network of servers.
2. **Global CDN:** Firebase Hosting leverages Google's CDN, which caches your content at strategically located data centers around the world, reducing latency and improving load times.
3. **Automatic SSL:** Every Firebase Hosting site is

automatically provisioned with an SSL certificate, ensuring secure HTTPS access for your users.

4. **Custom Domain Support:** You can easily connect custom domains to Firebase Hosting, complete with free SSL and easy domain management through the Firebase Console.

5. **Zero-Downtime Deployments:** Firebase Hosting ensures that your site is always available, even while you deploy updates. New versions of your site are served immediately without affecting ongoing user sessions.

6. **Seamless Integration with Other Firebase Services:** Firebase Hosting integrates effortlessly with other Firebase services, including Firestore, Cloud Functions, and Firebase Authentication, enabling a comprehensive backend solution for your app.

Getting Started with Firebase Hosting

TO START USING FIREBASE Hosting, you'll need to create a Firebase project and initialize Firebase Hosting within your local development environment. Here's a step-by-step guide:

___

Step 1: Install the Firebase CLI

THE FIREBASE CLI (COMMAND Line Interface) is a powerful tool that enables you to interact with Firebase services directly from your terminal. To install the Firebase CLI, use the following command:

npm install -g firebase-tools

After installing, verify the installation by running:

firebase—version

This command should output the version of the Firebase CLI installed on your system.

Step 2: Login to Firebase

ONCE THE FIREBASE CLI is installed, log in to your Firebase account by running:

firebase login

This command will open a browser window where you can authenticate using your Google account. After successful authentication, you can return to the terminal to continue.

Step 3: Initialize Firebase Hosting

NAVIGATE TO THE ROOT directory of your web app project, then initialize Firebase Hosting by running:

firebase init hosting

During initialization, the Firebase CLI will prompt you to select an existing Firebase project or create a new one. Follow the prompts to configure your Hosting setup:

- **Project Setup:** Choose the Firebase project that you want to use for Hosting. If you don't have a project yet, you can create one in the Firebase Console or select the option to create a new project during initialization.

- **Public Directory:** Specify the directory that contains your app's public assets, such as public or build. This is the folder that will be deployed to Firebase Hosting.

- **Single-Page App Configuration:** If your app is a single-page application (SPA), Firebase Hosting can be configured to automatically rewrite all URLs to your index.html file.

- **Automatic Builds and Deploys:** You can choose to set up GitHub integration for automatic deploys on new commits to specific branches of your repository.

Step 4: Deploy Your App to Firebase Hosting

AFTER INITIALIZATION, you can deploy your web app using a single command:

firebase deploy—only hosting

The Firebase CLI will build your app (if configured) and deploy it to Firebase Hosting. Once the deployment is complete, the CLI will provide a URL where you can view your live site.

Configuring Firebase Hosting

FIREBASE HOSTING OFFERS several configuration options through the firebase.json file, located at the root of your project. Key settings include:

Rewrites: Used for directing specific URL patterns to Firebase Functions, Cloud Run services, or other URLs. Rewrites are useful for dynamic apps where server-side processing is required.

```
{
"hosting": {
"rewrites": [
```

```json
{
"source": "/api/**",
"function": "myFunction"
}
]
}
}
```

-

Redirects: Redirects can send visitors from one URL to another, either within your site or to an external site. This is useful for managing outdated URLs or creating vanity URLs.

json

Copy code

```json
{
"hosting": {
"redirects": [
{
"source": "/old-page",
"destination": "/new-page",
"type": 301
}
```

```
    ]
  }
}
```

•

Headers: Custom headers can be added to specific files or directories, enhancing security and performance.

```
{
"hosting": {
"headers": [
{
"source": "/images/**",
"headers": [
{
"key": "Cache-Control",
"value": "public, max-age=86400"
}
]
}
]
}
```

}

•

- **Caching:** Firebase Hosting allows you to control caching behavior using headers. Proper caching can significantly improve performance by reducing the need to re-download unchanged assets.

Custom Domains and SSL

FIREBASE HOSTING SUPPORTS custom domains, enabling you to serve your app under a personalized domain name. Adding a custom domain to your Firebase project is straightforward and includes the following steps:

1. **Add a Custom Domain:** In the Firebase Console, navigate to Hosting > Connect Domain. Follow the on-screen instructions to verify ownership of your domain.

2. **Configure DNS Records:** Firebase will provide DNS records that you need to add to your domain registrar's DNS settings. These typically include an A record and sometimes a TXT record for verification.

3. **SSL Configuration:** Firebase automatically provisions an SSL certificate for your custom domain, ensuring secure HTTPS access. You don't need to manually install or configure SSL, as Firebase manages the certificate lifecycle.

Security and Optimization

FIREBASE HOSTING AUTOMATICALLY enforces HTTPS, ensuring that all data transmitted between your users and the hosting servers is encrypted. Additionally, Firebase Hosting supports HTTP/2, which further improves performance by allowing multiple requests to be multiplexed over a single connection.

Security Rules

FIREBASE HOSTING ALSO supports security rules for file access, enabling you to control who can access specific files or directories. For example, you can restrict access to specific assets to authenticated users:

```
{

"hosting": {

"rules": {

"source": "/admin/**",

"role": "admin"

}

}

}
```

Performance Optimization

IN ADDITION TO CACHING, Firebase Hosting supports several optimization techniques, such as:

- **Compression:** Firebase Hosting automatically compresses text-based assets like HTML, CSS, and JavaScript to reduce bandwidth usage.

- **Lazy Loading:** Integrate lazy loading for images and other assets to load only when they enter the viewport, improving initial load times.

- **Minification:** Ensure that your CSS and JavaScript files are minified to reduce file size.

By leveraging these tools and techniques, Firebase Hosting can help you deliver a fast, secure, and scalable web app experience for your users.

Deploying a Web App to Firebase Hosting

DEPLOYING A WEB APP to Firebase Hosting is a straightforward process that allows developers to publish their applications to a global audience quickly. Firebase Hosting is optimized for static files like HTML, CSS, JavaScript, and assets, making it ideal for single-page applications (SPAs) and static websites. Additionally, Firebase Hosting can serve dynamic content when integrated with Firebase Cloud Functions or Cloud Run, providing flexibility to accommodate more complex architectures.

Step-by-Step Guide to Deploying a Web App

TO DEPLOY A WEB APP to Firebase Hosting, you'll first need to set up a Firebase project and configure Firebase Hosting within your project. Let's go through the deployment process step by step.

Step 1: Set Up Your Firebase Project

IF YOU HAVEN'T ALREADY created a Firebase project for your web app, you'll need to set one up. Here's how:

1. **Go to the Firebase Console:** Open the Firebase Console and log in with your Google account.
2. **Create a New Project:** Click on the "Add Project" button and follow the prompts to create a new project. Enter a project name, select your preferred region, and accept the terms of service.
3. **Enable Firebase Hosting:** Once the project is created, navigate to the Firebase Hosting section in the Firebase Console and click "Get Started."

This process links your Firebase project with Firebase Hosting, enabling you to deploy web assets from your local development environment.

Step 2: Initialize Firebase Hosting in Your Project

IN YOUR LOCAL DEVELOPMENT environment, you'll need to initialize Firebase Hosting. Navigate to your project directory, and then run the following command:

firebase init hosting

The Firebase CLI will prompt you to choose the Firebase project you want to link. If you have multiple Firebase projects, select the one you just created. Next, follow the prompts to complete the setup:

- **Public Directory:** Specify the directory where your web app's build files are located. For most projects, this might be public, build, or dist. If you're unsure, check the output directory in your app's build configuration.

- **Single-Page App Rewrite:** If your app is a single-page application, select "Yes" when prompted to configure as an SPA. This setting ensures that all URLs route to your index.html file.

- **Automatic Build and Deploy with GitHub:** You can enable this option if you want to set up continuous deployment from GitHub. This is optional but recommended for teams using GitHub for version control.

After the initialization is complete, you should see a firebase.json configuration file in your project directory, which defines your Hosting settings.

Step 3: Build Your Web App (Optional)

BEFORE DEPLOYING, MAKE sure your web app is ready for production by running a build. If you're using a JavaScript framework like React, Vue, or Angular, build the project using the appropriate command:

For React:

npm run build

For Vue:

npm run build

For Angular:

ng build—prod

This process compiles your code and optimizes it for production, outputting the files to your specified directory (e.g., build or dist). These files are then ready to be deployed to Firebase Hosting.

Step 4: Deploy to Firebase Hosting

WITH YOUR WEB APP FILES prepared, you're now ready to deploy them to Firebase Hosting. Simply run the following command:

firebase deploy—only hosting

The Firebase CLI will upload your files to Firebase Hosting and provide a unique URL for your deployed site. If you have a custom domain set up, it will also be available under that domain.

Upon successful deployment, you should see output similar to this:

✔ Deploy complete!

Project Console: https://console.firebase.google.com/project/your-project-id/hosting

Hosting URL: https://your-project-id.web.app

Step 5: Test Your Deployed Site

VISIT THE PROVIDED URL to view your live site. Verify that all pages and assets are loading correctly, and ensure that your app functions as expected. You can also test specific routes or functionalities to confirm that everything works as intended.

Advanced Firebase Hosting Features

FIREBASE HOSTING INCLUDES advanced features that allow you to manage and optimize your web app's deployment effectively. These features include custom domain support, rewrites, redirects, and cache control.

Custom Domains

YOU CAN CONNECT A CUSTOM domain to Firebase Hosting directly from the Firebase Console. Here's how:

1. **Add a Custom Domain:** In the Firebase Console, go to Hosting and click on "Connect Domain."
2. **Verify Domain Ownership:** Follow the prompts to verify ownership of your domain. Firebase will generate DNS records that you need to add to your domain registrar's settings.
3. **Configure DNS Settings:** Once verified, Firebase automatically provisions an SSL certificate for your domain. This process may take a few minutes.

After configuring your domain, Firebase will serve your site under the custom domain with HTTPS enabled.

Rewrites and Redirects

FIREBASE HOSTING SUPPORTS URL rewrites and redirects, which are useful for routing traffic and managing URL structures.

Rewrites: Use rewrites to direct traffic from one URL to another URL or service. This is particularly useful for single-page applications that require all routes to resolve to index.html. You can also rewrite requests to Firebase Cloud Functions or Cloud Run for dynamic content.

json

Copy code

{

```json
"hosting": {

"rewrites": [

{

"source": "/api/**",

"function": "app"

}

]

}

}
```

●

Redirects: Redirects send users from one URL to another and can be configured with different HTTP status codes (e.g., 301 for permanent redirects).

json

Copy code

```json
{

"hosting": {

"redirects": [

{

"source": "/old-page",

"destination": "/new-page",
```

```
"type": 301

}

]

}

}
```

•

Caching and Headers

CONTROL CACHING BEHAVIOR with custom headers to improve load times and reduce server load. Firebase Hosting supports header configuration through firebase.json:

Cache Control: You can specify caching rules for different file types. For example, to cache images for one day:

json

Copy code

```
{

"hosting": {

"headers": [

{

"source": "/images/**",

"headers": [

{
```

```
"key": "Cache-Control",

"value": "public, max-age=86400"

    }

  ]

  }

  ]

  }

}
```

●

This configuration helps minimize the number of requests to your server and enhances the user experience by serving cached assets quickly.

Rollbacks and Version Control

FIREBASE HOSTING PROVIDES easy rollback capabilities, allowing you to revert to a previous version of your site in case of errors. In the Firebase Console, you can view a history of deployments and restore any previous version with a single click. This feature is valuable for maintaining stability and quickly addressing issues.

Integrating Firebase Hosting with CI/CD

FOR TEAMS WORKING IN collaborative environments, integrating Firebase Hosting with a Continuous Integration/ Continuous Deployment (CI/CD) pipeline can automate the deployment process. Firebase Hosting supports GitHub Actions, making it easy to deploy from GitHub automatically.

To set up GitHub Actions with Firebase Hosting:

1. **Enable GitHub Integration:** In the Firebase Console, go to Hosting > GitHub and follow the prompts to link your repository.
2. **Configure GitHub Actions:** Firebase will create a .github/workflows/firebase-hosting-pull-request.yml file in your repository, which defines the deployment workflow. Customize this file to suit your CI/CD pipeline.

This setup ensures that every commit to your main branch triggers an automatic deployment to Firebase Hosting, streamlining the release process.

Summary

FIREBASE HOSTING SIMPLIFIES web app deployment with powerful features like global CDN, custom domains, SSL, rewrites, redirects, and caching. By following the steps outlined above, you can quickly deploy your web app, configure advanced settings, and manage deployments effectively. Integrating Firebase Hosting with CI/CD tools further enhances your workflow, enabling you to focus on building great experiences while Firebase handles the infrastructure.

Utilizing GCP's App Engine for Web Apps

GOOGLE CLOUD PLATFORM (GCP) offers App Engine as a platform-as-a-service (PaaS) solution for deploying and managing web applications. Unlike Firebase Hosting, which is optimized for static files and serverless backends, App Engine supports more complex and dynamic web applications, making it an ideal choice for web apps that require custom runtime environments, extensive backend services, or support for multiple programming languages.

App Engine offers both a **Standard Environment** and a **Flexible Environment**. The Standard Environment provides automatic scaling and is suitable for applications with lightweight, predictable workloads, while the Flexible Environment supports more customization and is ideal for applications with dynamic requirements or dependencies on native libraries.

Key Features of Google App Engine

1. **Support for Multiple Languages:** App Engine supports popular languages like Python, Java, Node.js, PHP, Ruby, Go, and .NET, giving developers flexibility in choosing the best tools for their applications.
2. **Automatic Scaling:** App Engine scales your application automatically based on incoming traffic, allowing your app to handle traffic spikes without manual intervention.
3. **Integrated with GCP Services:** App Engine integrates seamlessly with other GCP services, such as Cloud SQL, Firestore, and BigQuery, providing a comprehensive ecosystem for building and managing scalable applications.
4. **Custom Runtimes:** In the Flexible Environment, you can deploy applications using custom runtimes, enabling support for any language or runtime using Docker.
5. **Built-In Security and Monitoring:** App Engine offers built-in security features like SSL, identity management, and access control. It also integrates with Google Cloud's monitoring tools, such as Cloud Monitoring and Cloud

Logging, for real-time insights and alerts.

Getting Started with Google App Engine

TO DEPLOY AN APP TO App Engine, you'll first need to create a GCP project and configure your development environment. Here's a step-by-step guide to deploying a simple web app on App Engine:

Step 1: Create a GCP Project

1. **Access the Google Cloud Console:** Navigate to the Google Cloud Console and sign in with your Google account.
2. **Create a New Project:** Click on the "Select a Project" dropdown in the top navigation, then click "New Project." Enter a project name and select a billing account, if prompted.
3. **Enable Billing and APIs:** App Engine requires billing to be enabled for your GCP project. Follow the prompts to enable billing and the necessary APIs, such as App Engine API and Cloud Build API.

Step 2: Install the Google Cloud SDK

TO INTERACT WITH GCP services from your local environment, you'll need to install the Google Cloud SDK, which includes the gcloud command-line tool.

- **Download and Install:** Visit the Google Cloud SDK installation page and follow the instructions for your operating system.

Initialize the SDK: Open a terminal and run the following command to initialize the SDK:

bash

Copy code

gcloud init

- This command will prompt you to log in, select a GCP project, and configure other settings. Ensure that you select the project you created earlier.

Step 3: Write Your Application

FOR THIS EXAMPLE, WE'LL create a simple Python web application using Flask, a lightweight web framework. You can use other languages and frameworks based on your needs.

1. **Set Up the Project Directory:** Create a new directory for your app and navigate into it.

mkdir my-app-engine-app

cd my-app-engine-app

1. **Create the Application File:** Write a basic Flask application in main.py:

```
from flask import Flask

app = Flask(__name__)

@app.route('/')

def hello():
```

```python
return 'Hello, App Engine!'

if __name__ == '__main__':

app.run(host='0.0.0.0', port=8080)
```

1. **Define App Engine Configuration:** Create an app.yaml file in the root directory to configure your App Engine environment. For this example, we'll use the Python runtime in the Standard Environment:

```yaml
runtime: python39

entrypoint: python main.py

handlers:

- url: /.*

script: auto
```

The app.yaml file specifies the runtime environment, entry point, and URL handlers for your app. You can customize this file based on your application's needs, such as adding environment variables or configuring scaling options.

Step 4: Deploy to App Engine

TO DEPLOY YOUR APP, use the gcloud command-line tool. Make sure you're in the root directory of your project, then run the following command:

```
gcloud app deploy
```

The gcloud tool will prompt you to confirm deployment settings and specify a region. Choose a region that is geographically close to your users for optimal performance. After confirming, the deployment process will begin, and App Engine will handle the rest.

Once the deployment is complete, you'll receive a URL where you can access your live application. For example:

Deploying service [default] to App Engine...

Deployed service [default] to [https://your-project-id.appspot.com]

You can view your application in the Cloud Console: https://console.cloud.google.com/ appengine?project=your-project-id

Step 5: Access and Test Your App

VISIT THE URL PROVIDED by App Engine to see your deployed app in action. Test various routes and functionalities to ensure everything is working as expected. You can also monitor your app's performance in the Google Cloud Console, where you can access logs, metrics, and other monitoring tools.

Advanced Configuration Options

APP ENGINE OFFERS EXTENSIVE configuration options for customizing your app's behavior. Let's explore some of the advanced settings you can leverage:

Environment Variables

ENVIRONMENT VARIABLES are essential for securely managing sensitive data, such as API keys or database credentials. You can define environment variables in your app.yaml file:

env_variables:

MY_API_KEY: 'your-api-key'

DATABASE_URL: 'your-database-url'

To access these variables in your Python app, use the os module:

import os

api_key = os.getenv('MY_API_KEY')

Scaling Settings

APP ENGINE PROVIDES automatic scaling out-of-the-box, but you can customize scaling parameters to control costs and performance. In the Standard Environment, you can specify instance settings like max_instances and idle_timeout:

automatic_scaling:

max_instances: 5

min_idle_instances: 1

min_pending_latency: 300ms

In the Flexible Environment, you have even more control over scaling with settings like cpu, memory, and disk:

resources:

cpu: 2

memory_gb: 4

disk_size_gb: 10

Custom Domains and SSL

LIKE FIREBASE HOSTING, App Engine supports custom domains. To add a custom domain, navigate to App Engine in the Google Cloud Console, then go to Settings > Custom Domains. Follow the prompts to verify your domain ownership and configure DNS settings. App Engine will provision an SSL certificate automatically, ensuring secure HTTPS access.

Managing Services and Versions

APP ENGINE ALLOWS YOU to deploy multiple services within a single project, enabling you to break down your application into smaller, manageable microservices. Each service can have multiple versions, making it easy to roll out new updates gradually or test different versions of your app.

To deploy a new service, simply add the service attribute in your app.yaml file:

service: api

runtime: python39

entrypoint: python main.py

Deploying this file will create a new service called api that you can access independently. Similarly, you can deploy multiple versions by specifying a version name:

gcloud app deploy—version v2

Monitoring and Troubleshooting

GOOGLE CLOUD PROVIDES robust monitoring and logging tools for App Engine. You can access logs directly from the Google Cloud Console, where you can filter and search for specific entries. Additionally, Cloud Monitoring offers real-time insights into your app's performance, including CPU and memory usage, response times, and error rates.

To further enhance monitoring, you can integrate App Engine with Stackdriver, which provides advanced logging, tracing, and alerting capabilities. This is particularly useful for debugging and ensuring your app meets performance requirements.

Summary

GOOGLE APP ENGINE IS a powerful and flexible platform for deploying and managing web applications. With support for multiple languages, automatic scaling, and integration with other GCP services, App Engine enables you to build scalable and resilient apps with ease. By following the steps outlined in this section, you can deploy your web app to App Engine and take advantage of its advanced configuration options to customize, scale, and monitor your application effectively.

Setting Up Custom Domains and SSL with Firebase

FIREBASE HOSTING PROVIDES a powerful and user-friendly way to host web apps, static sites, and dynamic web content. One of the key features of Firebase Hosting is its support for custom domains, allowing you to host your web app under a personalized domain name instead of the default your-project-id.web.app or your-project-id.firebaseapp.com domain. Custom domains improve brand recognition, enhance trust, and provide a better user experience.

Firebase also simplifies the process of securing your web app with SSL (Secure Sockets Layer) certificates, automatically provisioning SSL certificates for all custom domains at no additional cost. This ensures that your website uses HTTPS, providing secure communication between your users and the server.

Benefits of Using Custom Domains

CUSTOM DOMAINS BRING numerous advantages to your web app or website, including:

1. **Branding and Professionalism:** Custom domains allow you to establish a unique and memorable web address that reflects your brand. This enhances your web presence and makes your app more recognizable.
2. **Improved SEO:** Search engines prioritize custom domains over generic subdomains when ranking search results, improving your website's visibility and discoverability.
3. **Enhanced Trust and Credibility:** Users are more likely to trust a website with a personalized domain name, as it signifies professionalism and attention to detail.
4. **Consistency Across Platforms:** By using the same domain name for your web and email services, you create a consistent user experience across multiple platforms and communication channels.

Steps to Set Up a Custom Domain in Firebase

SETTING UP A CUSTOM domain for your Firebase-hosted web app is a straightforward process. The steps include verifying domain ownership, configuring DNS settings, and securing your domain with SSL.

Step 1: Verify Domain Ownership

TO BEGIN USING A CUSTOM domain with Firebase Hosting, you need to prove that you own the domain. Follow these steps:

1. **Access the Firebase Console:** Open the Firebase Console and navigate to the Hosting section of your project.
2. **Connect a Custom Domain:** Under the Hosting tab, click on "Add Custom Domain" and enter the domain name you want to use (e.g., www.example.com).
3. **Domain Verification:** Firebase will ask you to verify domain ownership by adding a TXT record to your domain's DNS settings. This record proves that you control the domain. Firebase will generate the TXT record with specific values that you need to add to your domain registrar's DNS settings.
4. **Add the TXT Record:** Log in to your domain registrar (e.g., GoDaddy, Namecheap, Google Domains) and navigate to the DNS management section. Add the TXT record provided by Firebase. It may take a few minutes for the DNS changes to propagate.

Once the DNS changes propagate, Firebase will automatically verify domain ownership. You can check the status in the Firebase Console.

Step 2: Configure DNS Records

AFTER VERIFYING OWNERSHIP, the next step is to configure your DNS records to point your domain to Firebase Hosting. Firebase requires the following DNS records to be added to your domain:

A Records: These records map your domain to Firebase Hosting's IP addresses. Firebase provides the IP addresses, and you must add them to the DNS settings for the root domain (e.g., example.com).

Example of A records:

plaintext

Copy code

Type: A

Host: @

Value: 151.101.1.195

Value: 151.101.65.195

Value: 151.101.129.195

Value: 151.101.193.195

TTL: 3600
   1.

CNAME Record (for www subdomain): If you want to use a www subdomain (e.g., www.example.com), you need to add a CNAME record pointing to Firebase Hosting.

Example of a CNAME record:

plaintext

Copy code

Type: CNAME

Host: www

Value: ghs.googlehosted.com

TTL: 3600

1.

Once these records are added, it may take a few minutes to propagate across the DNS system. After propagation, your custom domain should be fully linked to Firebase Hosting.

Step 3: Provisioning SSL Certificates

FIREBASE HOSTING AUTOMATICALLY provisions an SSL certificate for your custom domain. This ensures that all traffic between your users and your website is encrypted, enhancing security and protecting sensitive data such as login credentials and payment information. Here's what happens behind the scenes:

- **Automatic SSL Certificate:** As soon as your custom domain is verified and DNS records are configured, Firebase requests and installs an SSL certificate for your domain from Let's Encrypt, a free and widely trusted certificate authority.

- **HTTPS by Default:** Once the SSL certificate is active, your custom domain will automatically use HTTPS. Users accessing your site over HTTP will be redirected to the HTTPS version to ensure secure communication.

You don't need to manually configure the SSL certificate or handle renewals—Firebase takes care of everything. The SSL certificate will renew automatically every 90 days, ensuring continuous security for your web app.

Step 4: Testing and Validation

AFTER CONFIGURING YOUR custom domain and SSL certificate, it's important to test your website to ensure everything is working correctly.

1. **Access Your Website via Custom Domain:** Open a browser and navigate to your custom domain (e.g., www.example.com). Ensure that the site loads correctly and that all assets (CSS, JavaScript, images) are served securely over HTTPS.
2. **Check for HTTPS:** Verify that the address bar in your browser shows the padlock icon, indicating that the SSL certificate is active and the site is secure. The URL should start with https://, not http://.
3. **Test Redirects:** Try accessing your site with both the www and non-www versions of your domain (e.g., www.example.com and example.com). Make sure they both redirect to the same site and use HTTPS.

Custom Domain Settings in firebase.json

FIREBASE ALLOWS YOU to customize your Hosting configuration through the firebase.json file, located in the root directory of your project. This file defines how Firebase should serve your content, handle redirects, and manage caching. When using a custom domain, you may want to configure the following settings:

Rewrites for Single-Page Applications (SPAs)

IF YOUR WEB APP IS a single-page application, you'll need to configure rewrites in the firebase.json file to ensure that all routes are handled by the same HTML file (typically index.html). This prevents 404 errors when users navigate to specific routes within your app.

Example of a rewrite rule for an SPA:

```
{

"hosting": {

"rewrites": [

{

"source": "**",

"destination": "/index.html"

}

]

}

}
```

This rule rewrites all incoming URLs to index.html, allowing the client-side router in your app (e.g., React Router, Vue Router) to handle navigation.

Redirects

IF YOU'RE MIGRATING your website from another hosting provider or restructuring your URL scheme, you can use Firebase's redirect feature to send users from old URLs to new ones. Redirects are especially useful for maintaining SEO and ensuring that users don't encounter broken links.

Example of a redirect rule:

```
{

"hosting": {

"redirects": [

{

"source": "/old-page",

"destination": "/new-page",

"type": 301

}

]

}

}
```

This rule redirects all requests from /old-page to /new-page with a 301 status code (permanent redirect), ensuring that search engines and browsers update their records.

Custom Headers

FIREBASE HOSTING ALSO supports custom headers, which allow you to control caching, security policies, and other HTTP header settings. Custom headers can be applied to specific file types or paths to enhance performance and security.

Example of a caching header for images:

```
{

"hosting": {

"headers": [

{

"source": "/images/**",

"headers": [

{

"key": "Cache-Control",

"value": "public, max-age=86400"

}

]

}

]

}

}
```

This rule applies a cache control header to all images, instructing browsers to cache the images for 24 hours (86400 seconds), reducing load times for repeat visitors.

Managing Multiple Domains

FIREBASE HOSTING ALLOWS you to connect multiple custom domains to a single project. This is useful if you want to support multiple brands, subdomains, or localized versions of your website (e.g., example.com, fr.example.com, blog.example.com). You can manage all connected domains from the Firebase Console.

Each domain is automatically secured with SSL, and Firebase ensures that all traffic is redirected to the correct version of your site (e.g., non-www to www, or HTTP to HTTPS).

Troubleshooting Common Issues

WHILE SETTING UP A custom domain is generally a smooth process, you may encounter some common issues:

1. **DNS Propagation Delays:** DNS changes can take time to propagate across the internet. If your custom domain doesn't work immediately after configuration, wait a few hours and check again.
2. **SSL Certificate Pending:** It may take a few minutes for Firebase to provision the SSL certificate after verifying your domain. During this time, your site may be accessible over HTTP but not HTTPS. Be patient and check back after a few minutes.
3. **Incorrect DNS Settings:** Double-check that your DNS records are configured correctly, especially the A and CNAME records. Use online tools like dnschecker.org to verify that your DNS settings have propagated correctly.

Summary

SETTING UP A CUSTOM domain and SSL with Firebase Hosting is an essential step in creating a secure and professional web presence. By following these steps, you can connect your custom domain, configure DNS records, and automatically secure your site with SSL. Firebase handles the technical details, allowing you to focus on building and optimizing your web app while benefiting from improved branding, security, and user trust.

Optimizing Hosting for Performance and Security

WHEN DEPLOYING WEB applications, performance and security are crucial considerations that directly impact user experience, search engine ranking, and data protection. Firebase Hosting offers several built-in features and configuration options that enable you to optimize your web app for speed and security. By leveraging these features, you can ensure that your app loads quickly, scales effectively, and remains secure against potential threats.

This section explores best practices and tools available in Firebase Hosting for optimizing performance and security, including caching, compression, content delivery, and security rules.

Performance Optimization Techniques

FIREBASE HOSTING IS backed by a global Content Delivery Network (CDN), which plays a significant role in improving performance by caching content close to users and reducing latency. However, there are additional strategies you can employ to further enhance your app's performance.

1. Caching Strategies

CACHING IS A CRITICAL factor in optimizing load times and reducing server load. By caching static assets like images, stylesheets, and JavaScript files, you can minimize the need to re-download these resources on subsequent visits, resulting in a faster user experience.

Firebase Hosting allows you to configure caching rules using the firebase.json file. You can define cache expiration times for different types of files to control how long they are stored in the user's browser cache.

Example of a caching configuration:

```json
{
  "hosting": {
    "headers": [
      {
        "source": "/css/**",
        "headers": [
          {
            "key": "Cache-Control",
            "value": "public, max-age=31536000, immutable"
          }
        ]
      },
      {
        "source": "/js/**",
        "headers": [
          {
            "key": "Cache-Control",
            "value": "public, max-age=31536000, immutable"
          }
        ]
```

```json
    },
    {
      "source": "/images/**",
      "headers": [
        {
          "key": "Cache-Control",
          "value": "public, max-age=86400"
        }
      ]
    }
  ]
}
```

In this example:

- CSS and JavaScript files are cached for one year (max-age=31536000) with the immutable directive, indicating that these files do not change over time.

- Images are cached for one day (max-age=86400), which provides a balance between performance and flexibility, allowing for daily updates if needed.

2. Compression with Brotli and Gzip

FIREBASE HOSTING AUTOMATICALLY compresses text-based resources (such as HTML, CSS, and JavaScript) using Brotli and Gzip, which reduces the amount of data transferred between the server and the client. Compression improves load times, especially on slower networks, by reducing the size of the files that need to be downloaded.

To ensure that your files are compressed:

- Verify that compression is enabled in your browser's developer tools.

- Confirm that all text-based resources are being delivered in a compressed format.

Firebase Hosting handles compression for you, but you can also use build tools (e.g., Webpack) to further optimize and minify your files before deployment.

3. Using Lazy Loading for Images and Resources

LAZY LOADING IS A TECHNIQUE where images and other resources are only loaded when they enter the viewport, reducing the initial load time of the page. By deferring the loading of off-screen elements, you can improve perceived performance and enhance the user experience.

To implement lazy loading, use the loading="lazy" attribute for images:

```
<img src="example-image.jpg" alt="Example" loading="lazy">
```

For other resources, consider using libraries like react-lazyload (for React) or vue-lazyload (for Vue.js) to manage lazy loading within your application framework.

4. Minifying and Bundling Resources

MINIFYING AND BUNDLING your CSS, JavaScript, and HTML files reduces file size by removing whitespace, comments, and redundant code. These optimizations are typically performed during the build process using tools like Webpack, Parcel, or Rollup.

Example configuration for minifying JavaScript with Webpack:

const TerserPlugin = require('terser-webpack-plugin');

module.exports = {

optimization: {

minimize: true,

minimizer: [new TerserPlugin()],

},

};

Bundling can also reduce the number of HTTP requests by combining multiple files into a single file. However, ensure that your bundles are not too large, as they can negate the benefits of caching and may lead to longer load times for initial visits.

5. Prefetching and Preloading Critical Resources

PREFETCHING AND PRELOADING are techniques that instruct the browser to download critical resources before they are needed, improving page load speed.

Preload: Use rel="preload" to load resources (like fonts or critical scripts) during the initial page load:

html

Copy code

```
<link rel="preload" href="/fonts/myfont.woff2" as="font" type="font/woff2" crossorigin="anonymous">
```

-

Prefetch: Use rel="prefetch" to load resources that may be needed in the near future, such as the next page or deferred JavaScript:

html

Copy code

```
<link rel="prefetch" href="/js/next-page.js">
```

-

Preloading is ideal for essential assets that impact the first contentful paint, while prefetching is useful for non-essential assets that improve navigation and subsequent page loads.

Security Best Practices

FIREBASE HOSTING OFFERS various features to enhance the security of your web app, from built-in SSL certificates to custom security rules. By implementing these security measures, you can protect your app and its users from potential threats.

1. Enforce HTTPS and SSL Certificates

FIREBASE HOSTING AUTOMATICALLY provides SSL certificates for both Firebase subdomains and custom domains, ensuring that all traffic is encrypted with HTTPS. Enforcing HTTPS is essential for protecting user data, as it prevents third parties from intercepting or tampering with the data in transit.

- **Automatic HTTPS Redirects:** Firebase Hosting enforces HTTPS by default. If users attempt to access your site over HTTP, they will be redirected to the HTTPS version automatically.

- **SSL Management:** Firebase handles SSL certificate provisioning and renewal, eliminating the need for manual certificate management.

2. Implementing HTTP Security Headers

HTTP SECURITY HEADERS provide an additional layer of security by defining how browsers should behave when handling your app. Common headers include Content-Security-Policy, Strict-Transport-Security, and X-Content-Type-Options.

Example of security headers in firebase.json:

```
{
```

```json
"hosting": {
"headers": [
{
"source": "**",
"headers": [
{
"key": "Strict-Transport-Security",
"value": "max-age=31536000; includeSubDomains"
},
{
"key": "X-Content-Type-Options",
"value": "nosniff"
},
{
"key": "X-Frame-Options",
"value": "DENY"
},
{
"key": "X-XSS-Protection",
"value": "1; mode=block"
```

```
    }

  ]

  }

]

}

}
```

These headers achieve the following:

- **Strict-Transport-Security:** Ensures that the browser only accesses the site over HTTPS.

- **X-Content-Type-Options:** Prevents MIME type sniffing, protecting against some forms of injection attacks.

- **X-Frame-Options:** Blocks the site from being embedded in iframes, preventing clickjacking attacks.

- **X-XSS-Protection:** Enables cross-site scripting (XSS) filters in the browser.

3. Configuring Content Security Policy (CSP)

A CONTENT SECURITY Policy (CSP) helps prevent cross-site scripting (XSS) attacks by restricting the sources from which content can be loaded. By specifying trusted sources for scripts, styles, and other resources, you can reduce the risk of malicious code execution.

Example CSP header:

```
{

"hosting": {

"headers": [

{

"source": "**",

"headers": [

{

"key": "Content-Security-Policy",

"value": "default-src 'self'; script-src 'self' https://apis.google.com;
style-src 'self' 'unsafe-inline';"

}

]

}

]

}

}
```

This CSP configuration allows scripts from the same origin and Google APIs, while restricting styles to self and inline styles.

4. Using Firebase Security Rules for Data Access Control

IF YOUR WEB APP INTERACTS with Firebase services like Firestore or Realtime Database, you can enforce access controls using Firebase Security Rules. Security rules allow you to define who can read or write data, ensuring that only authorized users can access sensitive information.

Example Firestore security rule:

service cloud.firestore {

match /databases/{database}/documents {

match /users/{userId} {

allow read, write: if request.auth != null && request.auth.uid == userId;

}

}

}

This rule allows authenticated users to access their own data in the users collection while preventing unauthorized access.

5. Regularly Monitor and Audit Your App

FIREBASE HOSTING INTEGRATES with Google Cloud's monitoring tools, such as Cloud Logging and Cloud Monitoring, allowing you to track your app's performance and security in real-time. Regular monitoring and auditing help identify potential issues before they impact users, ensuring your app remains reliable and secure.

To set up monitoring:

- **Enable Logging:** Use the Firebase Console to access Cloud Logging, where you can view detailed logs of user activity, errors, and access patterns.

- **Set Up Alerts:** Configure alerts in Cloud Monitoring to receive notifications about potential security threats, such as increased error rates or unusual access patterns.

Conclusion

OPTIMIZING YOUR FIREBASE Hosting environment for performance and security is essential for delivering a fast, reliable, and safe web experience. By implementing caching strategies, compression, lazy loading, and security headers, you can significantly enhance your app's performance and protect it against common threats. Firebase Hosting provides the tools and flexibility needed to build a scalable, secure, and high-performing web application that meets the demands of modern users.

Chapter 7: Storage Solutions: Firebase Storage vs. Google Cloud Storage

Introduction to Firebase Cloud Storage

FIREBASE CLOUD STORAGE is a powerful, secure, and reliable storage solution for developers who want to store and serve user-generated content, such as photos, videos, and other large files, directly within their Firebase projects. Built on top of Google Cloud Storage, Firebase Storage provides a streamlined and user-friendly way to handle file storage with real-time features and integrations that make it a go-to choice for mobile and web applications.

Key Features of Firebase Cloud Storage

FIREBASE CLOUD STORAGE offers a host of features that make it an ideal solution for handling storage in modern applications:

- **Scalability**: Firebase Storage is built on Google Cloud's infrastructure, providing scalable storage that grows with your app.

- **Reliability and Security**: Firebase Storage ensures that files are always available when needed, with strong security protocols to protect data.

- **Efficient Media Handling**: With Firebase, you can handle images, videos, and other media files efficiently, supporting various operations like resizing, cropping, and transcoding.

- **Real-time Updates**: Firebase Storage integrates seamlessly with other Firebase services, allowing for real-time updates, which is particularly useful for collaborative applications.

- **Cross-platform Compatibility**: Firebase Storage provides SDKs for various platforms, including iOS, Android, and web, enabling developers to store and retrieve files consistently across different devices.

Core Concepts of Firebase Cloud Storage

UNDERSTANDING THE CORE concepts of Firebase Cloud Storage can help you effectively manage and retrieve files in your application:

1. **Storage Buckets**: In Firebase Storage, files are organized into buckets. A bucket is essentially a container for storing data, and each project typically has a default bucket tied to it. You can create additional buckets if your project requires more organization.
2. **Object Storage**: Files in Firebase Storage are stored as objects. Each object is uniquely identified within a bucket by a file name or path, enabling efficient retrieval and organization.
3. **Security Rules**: Firebase Storage employs Firebase Security Rules, which allow you to control access to your stored files. Security rules can be tailored based on various conditions, such as user authentication status or file metadata.
4. **Access Tokens and Metadata**: Files in Firebase Storage can have associated metadata, including access tokens. These tokens are used for secure access and can be

configured to allow for specific permissions, such as read or write access.

Setting Up Firebase Storage in Your Project

TO USE FIREBASE CLOUD Storage, you first need to enable it in your Firebase project and configure the necessary settings:

1. **Enable Firebase Storage**: In the Firebase console, navigate to the "Storage" section and enable Firebase Storage for your project. By default, you will be provided with a single storage bucket.
2. **Configure Security Rules**: Firebase provides default security rules to protect your files, but it's essential to customize these rules to suit your app's requirements. For example, you may want to allow only authenticated users to upload files or restrict certain file types.
3. **Install the Firebase SDK**: To interact with Firebase Storage from your app, you need to install the Firebase SDK. For web projects, you can add the SDK via a script tag, while for mobile projects, you can use package managers like npm, CocoaPods, or Gradle.

```
// Example of initializing Firebase Storage in a web app

import { initializeApp } from "firebase/app";

import { getStorage } from "firebase/storage";

const firebaseConfig = {

apiKey: "your-api-key",

authDomain: "your-auth-domain",
```

```
projectId: "your-project-id",

storageBucket: "your-storage-bucket",

messagingSenderId: "your-messaging-sender-id",

appId: "your-app-id",

};

const app = initializeApp(firebaseConfig);

const storage = getStorage(app);
```

Uploading Files to Firebase Storage

ONCE FIREBASE STORAGE is configured, you can start uploading files. Firebase provides straightforward methods to handle file uploads, with options to monitor progress and handle errors.

Basic File Upload

HERE'S AN EXAMPLE OF uploading a file in a web application using Firebase's JavaScript SDK:

```
import { ref, uploadBytesResumable, getDownloadURL } from "firebase/storage";

// Create a reference to the file location in the storage bucket

const fileInput = document.getElementById("fileInput");

const file = fileInput.files[0];

const storageRef = ref(storage, 'uploads/' + file.name);
```

```javascript
// Create an upload task

const uploadTask = uploadBytesResumable(storageRef, file);

// Monitor the upload process

uploadTask.on(

'state_changed',

(snapshot) => {

// Observe the progress of the upload

const progress = (snapshot.bytesTransferred / snapshot.totalBytes)
* 100;

console.log('Upload is ' + progress + '% done');

},

(error) => {

// Handle errors

console.error("Upload failed:", error);

},

() => {

// Get the download URL once the upload is complete

getDownloadURL(uploadTask.snapshot.ref).then((downloadURL)
=> {

console.log('File available at', downloadURL);

});
```

```
}

);
```

In this example, the file is uploaded to the uploads folder in Firebase Storage, and the progress is monitored using the state_changed event. Once the upload is complete, you can retrieve the file's download URL to display or store it for later use.

Downloading Files from Firebase Storage

DOWNLOADING FILES FROM Firebase Storage is as simple as uploading. You can retrieve a file's download URL and use it to display the file in your app or offer it as a download.

```
import { ref, getDownloadURL } from "firebase/storage";

// Reference to the file in Firebase Storage

const fileRef = ref(storage, 'uploads/your-file.jpg');

// Get the download URL

getDownloadURL(fileRef)

.then((url) => {

console.log('File download URL:', url);

// For example, display the file in an <img> element

document.getElementById('image').src = url;

})

.catch((error) => {

console.error("Failed to retrieve file:", error);
```

```
});
```

Managing Access and Permissions

FIREBASE STORAGE PROVIDES a powerful way to control who can read or write files. Using Firebase Security Rules, you can define access control based on user properties or custom claims.

Here's an example of a simple rule that allows only authenticated users to upload files:

```
service firebase.storage {

match /b/{bucket}/o {

match /{allPaths=**} {

allow read, write: if request.auth != null;

}

}

}
```

In this rule, access to all files within the bucket is restricted to authenticated users. You can further customize these rules to allow access only to specific files or folders based on user roles or file metadata.

Integrating Firebase Storage with Google Cloud Storage

FIREBASE STORAGE IS built on Google Cloud Storage, and you can extend its functionality by directly using Google Cloud Storage for advanced features like data transfer between buckets, versioning, and lifecycle management. This integration allows for a more complex storage setup, enabling you to handle large datasets and perform background tasks such as transcoding or watermarking files.

To work with Google Cloud Storage directly, you need to configure IAM permissions in the Google Cloud Console and use the @google-cloud/storage library to interact with the storage buckets.

Conclusion

FIREBASE STORAGE PROVIDES an efficient and easy-to-use solution for handling file storage within Firebase projects, with the flexibility to scale up using Google Cloud Storage for more advanced needs. Whether you are building a simple file uploader or a complex media sharing application, Firebase Storage offers the tools needed to ensure your files are stored securely and are readily accessible.

Handling File Uploads and Downloads in Firebase

FIREBASE CLOUD STORAGE provides a simple and powerful solution for handling file uploads and downloads in real-time, making it an excellent choice for applications that involve media files, documents, and other types of user-generated content. In this section, we'll explore the process of uploading and downloading files using Firebase Storage, along with the best practices for ensuring performance, reliability, and security.

File Uploads with Firebase Storage

FIREBASE STORAGE OFFERS robust methods for uploading files. These methods are particularly useful for handling user-generated content, such as photos or videos, which can be directly uploaded from client devices. Here's a step-by-step guide to uploading files to Firebase Storage:

Step 1: Set Up Firebase Storage

TO USE FIREBASE STORAGE, make sure you have configured it in your Firebase project as described in the previous section. The Firebase Storage service will be accessible via the Firebase SDK, allowing you to perform various file operations.

Step 2: Create File References

FILE UPLOADS IN FIREBASE Storage begin by creating a reference to the target file's path in your storage bucket. Firebase Storage references are similar to file paths, which are used to uniquely identify the location where each file is stored.

```javascript
// Example in JavaScript (Web)

import { getStorage, ref } from "firebase/storage";

const storage = getStorage();

const storageRef = ref(storage, 'uploads/myFile.jpg'); // Reference to 'uploads/myFile.jpg'
```

Here, the uploads/myFile.jpg path indicates that the file will be stored in a folder called "uploads" with the name "myFile.jpg". If the folder does not exist, Firebase will automatically create it.

Step 3: Upload Files

ONCE YOU HAVE A REFERENCE to the file location, you can upload the file using the uploadBytesResumable method, which allows you to monitor the upload process and handle progress updates.

```
import { uploadBytesResumable, getDownloadURL } from "firebase/storage";

const file = document.getElementById("fileInput").files[0];

const uploadTask = uploadBytesResumable(storageRef, file);

// Listen for state changes, errors, and completion of the upload.

uploadTask.on(

'state_changed',

(snapshot) => {

// Observe the progress of the upload

const progress = (snapshot.bytesTransferred / snapshot.totalBytes) * 100;

console.log('Upload is ' + progress + '% done');

},

(error) => {

// Handle any errors that occur during the upload process

console.error("Upload failed:", error);

},
```

```
() => {

// Handle successful upload and retrieve the file's download URL

getDownloadURL(uploadTask.snapshot.ref).then((downloadURL)
=> {

console.log('File available at', downloadURL);

});

}

);
```

This code provides real-time updates on the upload progress and handles potential errors during the upload process. Once the upload is complete, it retrieves the file's download URL, which can be used to access the file.

Step 4: Handle File Uploads on Mobile (Android and iOS)

FIREBASE STORAGE ALSO provides SDKs for mobile platforms, enabling seamless file uploads directly from Android and iOS devices. Here's an example of how to handle file uploads on Android using Kotlin:

```
import com.google.firebase.storage.FirebaseStorage

import com.google.firebase.storage.StorageReference

val storage = FirebaseStorage.getInstance()

val storageRef: StorageReference = storage.reference.child("uploads/myFile.jpg")

val file = Uri.fromFile(File("path/to/file"))
```

```
val uploadTask = storageRef.putFile(file)

uploadTask.addOnFailureListener {

// Handle unsuccessful uploads

}.addOnSuccessListener {

// File uploaded successfully

}
```

This code example shows how to use the Firebase Storage SDK on Android to upload a file and manage the upload status with success and failure listeners.

File Downloads with Firebase Storage

AFTER FILES HAVE BEEN uploaded to Firebase Storage, you can easily retrieve them by downloading them back to the client. Firebase Storage supports multiple methods for downloading files, depending on the type of file and its intended use.

Step 1: Create a Reference to the File

TO DOWNLOAD A FILE, you first need to create a reference to its location in Firebase Storage. This is similar to the upload process and helps identify the file in the storage bucket.

```
// Reference to an existing file

const fileRef = ref(storage, 'uploads/myFile.jpg');
```

Step 2: Retrieve the File's Download URL

ONCE YOU HAVE A REFERENCE to the file, you can retrieve its download URL using the getDownloadURL method. This URL can be used to display or link to the file within your application.

```
getDownloadURL(fileRef)

.then((url) => {

console.log('File download URL:', url);

// Example: set the URL as the src of an <img> element

document.getElementById('image').src = url;

})

.catch((error) => {

console.error("Failed to retrieve file:", error);

});
```

By obtaining the download URL, you can embed or share the file within your application. If the file is an image or video, you can display it directly in an HTML element or provide the URL for user download.

Step 3: Downloading Files in Android and iOS

FIREBASE STORAGE'S mobile SDKs also support downloading files in a platform-native manner. Here's how you can retrieve a file's download URL on Android:

```
fileRef.downloadUrl.addOnSuccessListener { uri ->

val downloadUrl = uri.toString()

println("File download URL: $downloadUrl")

}.addOnFailureListener { exception ->

println("Error: ${exception.message}")

}
```

This example retrieves the download URL for an existing file in Firebase Storage and handles both success and error cases with listeners.

Handling Large Files and Error Management

WHEN DEALING WITH LARGE files, Firebase Storage provides options for resuming uploads that were interrupted due to network issues or other errors. Using uploadBytesResumable allows for automatic retry and resume, which ensures that your files are uploaded successfully even if the connection is unstable.

Additionally, error handling is crucial to provide a seamless user experience. Here are some common error codes and their meanings in Firebase Storage:

- **storage/unauthorized**: The user is not authorized to perform the action.

- **storage/canceled**: The user canceled the upload/download operation.

- **storage/unknown**: An unknown error occurred.

You can handle these errors by providing informative messages to the user and implementing retry mechanisms when appropriate.

Security Considerations for File Uploads and Downloads

TO ENSURE THAT FILES are securely uploaded and downloaded, it is essential to configure Firebase Storage Security Rules. These rules allow you to specify who can access your storage bucket and under what conditions.

For example, you may want to restrict uploads to authenticated users only:

```
service firebase.storage {

match /b/{bucket}/o {

match /uploads/{allPaths=**} {

allow read, write: if request.auth != null;

}

}

}
```

This rule restricts both read and write access to authenticated users, helping to prevent unauthorized access to your files.

Firebase Storage Best Practices

FOLLOWING BEST PRACTICES when working with Firebase Storage will help ensure that your file handling is both efficient and secure. Here are some key best practices:

1. **Use Compression for Media Files**: To reduce storage and bandwidth usage, compress images and videos before uploading.
2. **Implement File Type Validation**: Validate file types on the client-side to prevent unwanted files from being uploaded.
3. **Leverage Caching for Downloads**: If your app frequently accesses certain files, consider caching them to reduce repeated downloads.
4. **Monitor Storage Usage**: Regularly monitor your storage usage and clean up unused files to manage costs effectively.

Conclusion

HANDLING FILE UPLOADS and downloads in Firebase Storage is straightforward and provides robust features that cater to a wide range of applications. By following best practices and securing your storage with Firebase Security Rules, you can effectively manage user-generated content in a reliable, scalable, and secure manner.

Integration with Google Cloud Storage Buckets

INTEGRATING FIREBASE Storage with Google Cloud Storage (GCS) provides developers with enhanced flexibility and scalability, enabling them to take advantage of advanced Google Cloud features within their Firebase projects. Google Cloud Storage, being the underlying infrastructure of Firebase Storage, offers a variety of storage classes, data transfer options, and lifecycle management capabilities that are especially useful for larger or more complex projects.

This section will cover how to set up and configure Google Cloud Storage in conjunction with Firebase, leverage its features, and implement best practices for integrating Firebase Storage with Google Cloud Storage for advanced file management needs.

Benefits of Integrating Firebase Storage with Google Cloud Storage

BEFORE DIVING INTO the integration process, it's essential to understand the benefits of leveraging Google Cloud Storage alongside Firebase Storage:

- **Scalability and Cost-Effectiveness**: Google Cloud Storage supports a range of storage classes such as Standard, Nearline, Coldline, and Archive, which allow you to optimize costs based on data access frequency and durability requirements.

- **Lifecycle Management**: GCS provides lifecycle management policies, enabling automatic data migration across storage classes based on pre-defined rules, which helps in reducing costs over time.

- **Enhanced Security and Access Control**: With Google Cloud Storage, you can configure Identity and Access Management (IAM) roles for fine-grained access control, enabling more sophisticated security configurations.

- **Advanced Data Management**: Google Cloud Storage supports object versioning, which allows you to maintain and access multiple versions of a file, and provides tools for large-scale data transfer and retention policies.

Setting Up Google Cloud Storage in Firebase

TO START USING GOOGLE Cloud Storage with Firebase, you need to link your Firebase project with Google Cloud. This process involves enabling necessary APIs, creating storage buckets, and configuring access permissions.

Step 1: Enable Google Cloud Storage API

1. Go to the Google Cloud Console.
2. Select your Firebase project from the project selector.
3. Navigate to **APIs & Services > Library**.
4. Search for "Google Cloud Storage" and enable the API for your project.

ENABLING THIS API ALLOWS your Firebase project to interact with Google Cloud Storage and manage storage buckets programmatically.

Step 2: Create a Google Cloud Storage Bucket

FIREBASE PROJECTS AUTOMATICALLY come with a default storage bucket. However, you can create additional buckets directly from the Google Cloud Console for specific storage needs. To create a new bucket:

1. In the Google Cloud Console, go to **Storage > Browser**.
2. Click **Create bucket**.
3. Specify a unique name for the bucket. This name must be globally unique across Google Cloud.
4. Choose the appropriate **location type** (Region, Multi-region, or Dual-region) based on where your users are located.

5. Select a **storage class** (Standard, Nearline, Coldline, or Archive) based on your expected access patterns and cost preferences.
6. Set up **access control**. Choose between Uniform (recommended) or Fine-grained access control depending on your security needs.
7. Review your settings and create the bucket.

Step 3: Configure IAM Permissions

CONFIGURING IDENTITY and Access Management (IAM) roles is crucial for securing your Google Cloud Storage bucket. To integrate with Firebase, ensure that your Firebase project has the appropriate permissions to access the bucket:

1. In the Google Cloud Console, navigate to **IAM & Admin > IAM**.
2. Click **Add** to grant permissions to a specific member or service account.
3. Select **Firebase Admin SDK** or specify the email associated with your Firebase project's service account.
4. Assign roles such as **Storage Admin** or **Storage Object Viewer**, depending on the level of access required.

These permissions allow Firebase to read from and write to Google Cloud Storage buckets, making them accessible from your Firebase application.

Accessing Google Cloud Storage Buckets from Firebase

ONCE YOUR BUCKET IS set up and permissions are configured, you can access it from within your Firebase application using the Firebase Admin SDK. This SDK provides server-side access to Google Cloud resources, including storage buckets.

```
// Example in Node.js

const admin = require('firebase-admin');

const { Storage } = require('@google-cloud/storage');

// Initialize Firebase Admin SDK

admin.initializeApp({

storageBucket: 'your-bucket-name.appspot.com',

});

// Create a Google Cloud Storage instance

const storage = new Storage();

const bucket = storage.bucket('your-bucket-name');

// Upload a file to Google Cloud Storage

const filePath = './local/path/to/your-file.jpg';

bucket.upload(filePath, { destination: 'remote/path/in-bucket.jpg'
})

.then(() => {

console.log('File uploaded to Google Cloud Storage');

})

.catch(err => {

console.error('Error uploading file:', err);
```

```
});
```

This code demonstrates how to initialize the Firebase Admin SDK and interact with a Google Cloud Storage bucket. You can upload files directly from your server or cloud functions and store them in your GCS bucket.

Working with Storage Classes and Lifecycle Policies

GOOGLE CLOUD STORAGE offers multiple storage classes to optimize costs based on data access frequency. These classes include:

1. **Standard**: Suitable for frequently accessed data.
2. **Nearline**: Ideal for data accessed less than once a month.
3. **Coldline**: Suitable for data accessed less than once a year.
4. **Archive**: Best for long-term storage of infrequently accessed data.

You can set lifecycle policies to automatically transition objects between storage classes, delete old versions, or remove objects based on custom conditions.

Configuring Lifecycle Policies

TO CONFIGURE LIFECYCLE policies for your bucket:

1. In the Google Cloud Console, go to **Storage > Browser**.
2. Select your bucket, then go to the **Lifecycle** tab.
3. Click **Add rule**, then choose actions such as **Delete** or **Set storage class**.
4. Define conditions like object age or the number of newer versions available.
5. Save the rule to apply it to your bucket.

These policies enable you to automate data management and control costs effectively.

Object Versioning in Google Cloud Storage

OBJECT VERSIONING ALLOWS you to maintain multiple versions of an object in your bucket, which is useful for tracking changes or recovering previous versions. To enable versioning:

1. In the Google Cloud Console, go to **Storage > Browser**.
2. Select your bucket and navigate to **Configuration**.
3. Enable **Object versioning** under the bucket settings.

Once enabled, each time you overwrite an object, GCS preserves the previous version. You can list all versions and restore or delete specific versions as needed.

```
// Example: Listing object versions in a bucket

bucket.getFiles({ versions: true })

.then(([files]) => {

files.forEach(file => {

console.log(`Name: ${file.name}, Generation: ${file.generation}`);

});

})

.catch(err => {

console.error('Error listing files:', err);

});
```

Transferring Data Between Firebase Storage and Google Cloud Storage

FIREBASE STORAGE SUPPORTS transferring data between Firebase and Google Cloud Storage buckets, making it easy to move files as your needs evolve. You can automate these transfers using Google Cloud's **Transfer Service** or by writing custom code to handle data migration.

Using Google Cloud Storage Transfer Service

THE TRANSFER SERVICE provides a simple way to schedule and manage data transfers between buckets or from on-premises storage systems:

1. Go to the Google Cloud Console and navigate to **Transfer Service**.
2. Click **Create Transfer Job** and select the source and destination buckets.
3. Configure settings such as transfer frequency, filters, and notifications.
4. Review and start the transfer job.

This service is ideal for large-scale migrations or recurring transfers between storage locations.

Securing Data with IAM and Access Control Lists (ACLs)

BEYOND FIREBASE STORAGE Rules, Google Cloud Storage allows additional security configurations through IAM and Access Control Lists (ACLs). These controls allow you to manage access at an object level, defining who can view, edit, or delete specific files.

- **IAM**: Use IAM roles to manage access at the bucket level, applying permissions to all objects within the bucket.

- **ACLs**: Use ACLs for finer control over individual objects, granting specific users or groups access to particular files.

```
// Example: Setting an ACL for a file

const file = bucket.file('remote/path/in-bucket.jpg');

file.acl.add({

entity: 'user-email@example.com',

role: 'READER',

}).then(() => {

console.log('ACL updated for user');

}).catch(err => {

console.error('Error updating ACL:', err);

});
```

Conclusion

INTEGRATING FIREBASE Storage with Google Cloud Storage extends the capabilities of your Firebase project by providing access to advanced storage features, scalability, and enhanced security options. By leveraging GCS alongside Firebase, you can optimize your application's data storage, handle complex data workflows, and reduce costs over time through efficient data management and lifecycle policies.

Managing Access and Permissions

MANAGING ACCESS AND permissions in Firebase Storage is crucial for ensuring the security and proper control of data within your application. Firebase provides flexible and robust options for controlling who can access or modify files stored in Firebase Storage, using Firebase Security Rules. Additionally, when integrating with Google Cloud Storage, Identity and Access Management (IAM) roles and Access Control Lists (ACLs) offer further granularity. This section will cover best practices for managing access, creating effective permissions policies, and securing data in Firebase Storage and Google Cloud Storage.

Firebase Storage Security Rules

FIREBASE SECURITY RULES allow you to control access to your storage bucket and files based on conditions such as authentication status, file metadata, or user attributes. By default, Firebase Storage is configured with restrictive rules, but you can customize them to suit the specific needs of your application.

Basic Structure of Firebase Storage Security Rules

FIREBASE STORAGE SECURITY Rules follow a JSON-like syntax. They define conditions for accessing files within a storage bucket, specifying read and write permissions.

Here is a basic example of Firebase Security Rules:

```
service firebase.storage {

match /b/{bucket}/o {

match /{allPaths=**} {
```

```
allow read, write: if request.auth != null;

      }

    }

}
```

In this example, only authenticated users are allowed to read and write to any file in the storage bucket. The request.auth != null condition ensures that users must be logged in to access files.

Common Conditions for Firebase Storage Rules

YOU CAN DEFINE VARIOUS conditions in Firebase Security Rules to control access based on different attributes:

1. **User Authentication**: Require users to be authenticated before accessing certain files.
2. **File Path**: Restrict access based on the file path, allowing different permissions for different folders.
3. **User ID**: Grant access only to specific users by checking the user's UID against the file owner metadata.
4. **File Metadata**: Use custom metadata to define access controls, such as allowing access only if the user's role matches a certain value.

Example: Role-Based Access Control

```
SERVICE FIREBASE.STORAGE {

match /b/{bucket}/o {

match /user_uploads/{userId}/{allPaths=**} {
```

```
allow read, write: if request.auth.uid == userId &&
request.auth.token.role == 'editor';

}

}

}
```

In this rule, access to files within the user_uploads directory is limited to authenticated users whose UID matches the userId path parameter and who have an editor role.

Advanced Security Practices for Firebase Storage

IMPLEMENTING ADVANCED security practices in Firebase Storage can help protect your data from unauthorized access and ensure compliance with data protection regulations.

1. Restrict Access Based on Time of Day or Date

YOU CAN CONFIGURE RULES that allow or deny access based on the current date or time. This is useful for applications that need to restrict access during certain periods.

```
allow read: if request.time < timestamp.date(2024, 12, 31);
```

This rule allows read access only until December 31, 2024. After this date, the access is automatically revoked.

2. Limit Access to Specific File Types

YOU MAY WANT TO RESTRICT file uploads to certain types, such as images or PDFs. This can be done by checking the file's metadata.

allow write: if request.resource.contentType.matches('image/.*');

This rule only allows files of type image/* to be uploaded, restricting access to other file types.

3. Implement Quotas for User Uploads

TO PREVENT USERS FROM consuming excessive storage, you can set up a quota system by tracking the number of files or total storage usage per user.

allow write: if get(/databases/(default)/documents/users/$(request.auth.uid)).data.totalStorageUsed < 10485760;

In this example, the rule checks the user's document in Firestore and only allows uploads if the totalStorageUsed is below 10 MB.

Using IAM for Google Cloud Storage Integration

FOR MORE ADVANCED CONTROL over storage permissions, especially when working with Google Cloud Storage directly, IAM roles provide fine-grained access control at the bucket level.

IAM Roles for Google Cloud Storage

GOOGLE CLOUD STORAGE offers several predefined IAM roles that can be assigned to users or service accounts:

- **Storage Admin**: Full control over objects and bucket configurations.

- **Storage Object Admin**: Full control over objects within a bucket but no control over bucket settings.

- **Storage Object Viewer**: Read-only access to objects.

- **Storage Object Creator**: Allows uploading objects but no permission to delete.

To assign IAM roles:

1. Go to the Google Cloud Console and navigate to **IAM & Admin > IAM**.
2. Click **Add** to assign a role to a user or service account.
3. Select the role that fits your requirements (e.g., Storage Object Viewer).
4. Save the changes to update permissions.

Custom IAM Roles

IF PREDEFINED ROLES do not fit your specific use case, Google Cloud allows you to create custom IAM roles with specific permissions.

1. In the Google Cloud Console, go to **IAM & Admin > Roles**.
2. Click **Create Role** and define permissions, such as storage.objects.get for read access or storage.objects.delete for delete access.
3. Assign this role to users or service accounts as needed.

Custom IAM roles provide the flexibility to tailor permissions based on precise needs, offering enhanced security and control.

Managing Access with Access Control Lists (ACLs)

ACCESS CONTROL LISTS (ACLs) offer an additional layer of control over individual objects in Google Cloud Storage. While

IAM operates at the bucket level, ACLs provide object-level permissions.

Setting ACLs on Google Cloud Storage Objects

ACLS CAN BE MANAGED through the Google Cloud Console or via the command line. Each ACL consists of an entity (user, group, domain, etc.) and a role (READER, WRITER, OWNER).

Example using the Google Cloud CLI:

gsutil acl ch -u user@example.com:READER gs://your-bucket-name/your-file-name

This command grants read access to user@example.com for the specified file.

Best Practices for Access and Permission Management

HERE ARE SOME BEST practices to ensure robust access control in Firebase Storage and Google Cloud Storage:

1. **Principle of Least Privilege**: Assign only the permissions necessary for users to perform their tasks. Avoid giving full access unless required.
2. **Regular Audits**: Periodically review IAM roles, ACLs, and Security Rules to ensure they are up-to-date and follow security best practices.
3. **Use Groups for IAM Roles**: Instead of assigning roles to individual users, use groups to manage permissions at scale, making it easier to update and maintain.
4. **Monitor Access Logs**: Enable logging in Google Cloud Storage to monitor access and identify any unauthorized

attempts. These logs can be integrated with Cloud Audit Logs for detailed tracking.

5. **Automate Security Scans**: Use Firebase and Google Cloud tools to automate security scans and detect misconfigurations or overly permissive rules.

Conclusion

BY EFFECTIVELY MANAGING access and permissions in Firebase Storage and Google Cloud Storage, you can secure your application's data and maintain control over who has access to it. Whether through Firebase Security Rules, IAM roles, or ACLs, understanding and implementing these tools ensures that your data is protected and that your storage resources are utilized responsibly. Regular reviews and adherence to security best practices further strengthen the overall integrity of your application's data handling procedures.

Comparing Storage Solutions: When to Use Firebase or GCP

CHOOSING BETWEEN FIREBASE Storage and Google Cloud Storage (GCP) depends on various factors, including your application's requirements, budget, scalability needs, and data management preferences. While Firebase Storage provides a simpler and more integrated solution with Firebase services, Google Cloud Storage offers advanced storage classes, lifecycle policies, and fine-grained access controls suitable for large-scale applications. This section will compare both solutions in detail, highlighting their strengths and suitable use cases to help you make an informed decision.

Firebase Storage Overview

FIREBASE STORAGE IS specifically designed for quick and easy integration with Firebase applications, providing a seamless experience for developers working on mobile and web apps. Key features of Firebase Storage include:

1. **Real-Time Synchronization**: Firebase Storage integrates directly with Firebase Realtime Database and Firestore, making it ideal for applications that require real-time updates.
2. **Simple Security Rules**: Firebase Security Rules allow for straightforward access control based on user authentication and request parameters.
3. **Cross-Platform SDKs**: Firebase Storage provides native SDKs for iOS, Android, and Web, simplifying the process of handling media uploads and downloads across platforms.
4. **Optimized for User-Generated Content**: Firebase Storage is well-suited for apps dealing with user-generated content, such as photos and videos, where rapid uploads and easy access are crucial.

Despite its ease of use, Firebase Storage has certain limitations, particularly regarding advanced data management, scalability, and custom access controls. These are areas where Google Cloud Storage shines.

Google Cloud Storage Overview

GOOGLE CLOUD STORAGE is a powerful, flexible, and scalable object storage service, designed for enterprises and large-scale applications. It provides a range of storage classes, extensive data lifecycle management capabilities, and granular access controls through IAM and ACLs. Key features of Google Cloud Storage include:

1. **Multiple Storage Classes**: Google Cloud Storage offers Standard, Nearline, Coldline, and Archive storage classes, allowing for cost optimization based on data access frequency.
2. **Lifecycle Management**: GCS provides advanced lifecycle policies that can automatically transition data between storage classes or delete data based on custom rules.
3. **Detailed Access Controls**: With IAM and ACLs, GCS supports detailed access permissions at both bucket and object levels, offering fine-grained control over who can view, modify, or delete data.
4. **Scalability and Performance**: GCS is built for handling large datasets and offers high performance, making it suitable for data-intensive applications like media streaming or big data analytics.

Google Cloud Storage is ideal for applications with complex data management needs, requiring high durability and availability, as well as specific compliance or regulatory requirements.

Use Cases for Firebase Storage

FIREBASE STORAGE IS generally more suitable for applications that prioritize ease of use, integration with Firebase services, and real-time file handling. Here are some common scenarios where Firebase Storage excels:

1. Social Media and Content-Sharing Apps

FIREBASE STORAGE IS a natural fit for social media and content-sharing apps, where users frequently upload and access photos, videos, and other media. The real-time capabilities of Firebase allow for seamless content synchronization, while Firebase Authentication and Security Rules provide simple yet effective access control.

2. Mobile and Web Apps with Real-Time Requirements

APPS THAT REQUIRE REAL-time updates—such as chat applications, collaborative tools, or live streaming services—can benefit from Firebase Storage's real-time integration with other Firebase products. Firebase's ease of setup and integration across platforms make it ideal for rapidly developing cross-platform applications.

3. Small to Medium-Sized Applications

FIREBASE STORAGE IS well-suited for small to medium-sized applications that do not require extensive data management or advanced storage features. Its integration with Firebase Realtime Database and Firestore helps streamline development and reduce time to market.

Use Cases for Google Cloud Storage

GOOGLE CLOUD STORAGE offers a more robust solution for applications with high storage demands, complex data requirements, or specific compliance needs. Here are scenarios where GCS is more appropriate:

1. Data-Intensive Applications and Big Data Analytics

GOOGLE CLOUD STORAGE is designed to handle massive datasets, making it ideal for applications involved in big data analytics, machine learning, or data warehousing. With high durability and availability, GCS can store vast amounts of data across multiple regions, ensuring minimal latency and high performance.

2. Enterprise-Level Applications with Compliance Requirements

FOR APPLICATIONS THAT need to adhere to strict regulatory or compliance requirements—such as healthcare, finance, or government applications—Google Cloud Storage offers features like object versioning, detailed access logs, and compliance certifications (e.g., HIPAA, GDPR). These features help organizations maintain data integrity and comply with industry regulations.

3. Archival and Long-Term Storage

GOOGLE CLOUD STORAGE'S Archive and Coldline classes provide cost-effective solutions for long-term storage and data archiving. Organizations that need to retain large volumes of data for compliance or historical purposes can leverage these classes to minimize storage costs while ensuring data is readily available when needed.

Comparing Costs: Firebase Storage vs. Google Cloud Storage

THE COST STRUCTURE of Firebase Storage is straightforward, charging based on the amount of data stored, bandwidth used, and download operations. However, Google Cloud Storage offers a more flexible pricing model, with different rates depending on the storage class and additional features like data retrieval and operations.

Firebase Storage Pricing

FIREBASE STORAGE PRICING is simple, based on:

1. **Data Storage**: Charged per GB stored per month.
2. **Data Transfer**: Outbound data transfer is charged per GB. Inbound data transfer is free within the same Firebase region.
3. **Operations**: Uploads, downloads, and delete operations are priced based on the number of operations.

Firebase Storage is generally cost-effective for small to medium-sized applications with modest storage needs.

Google Cloud Storage Pricing

GOOGLE CLOUD STORAGE pricing varies by storage class and operation type:

1. **Storage Classes**: Standard storage is priced higher for frequently accessed data, while Nearline, Coldline, and Archive offer lower costs for less frequently accessed data.
2. **Data Retrieval and Transfer**: GCS charges for data

retrieval from Nearline, Coldline, and Archive storage classes. Additionally, cross-region transfers incur extra costs.

3. **Operations**: GCS charges for operations like PUT, GET, and LIST based on the storage class and the number of operations.

Due to the different storage classes, GCS provides more flexibility and cost-saving options for applications with varying access patterns and data retention needs.

Integration with Firebase and Google Cloud Services

BOTH FIREBASE STORAGE and Google Cloud Storage integrate seamlessly with other Google services, though they offer different levels of flexibility and functionality.

Firebase Storage Integration

FIREBASE STORAGE IS tightly integrated with Firebase services like Firebase Authentication, Firestore, and Realtime Database. This makes it ideal for applications already using Firebase services, as it provides an out-of-the-box solution that requires minimal configuration.

Google Cloud Storage Integration

GOOGLE CLOUD STORAGE integrates with a broader set of Google Cloud services, such as BigQuery, Google Dataflow, and Google AI Platform. These integrations make it suitable for complex workflows involving data processing, analytics, or machine learning. GCS also supports Transfer Service for automating data movement and Storage Transfer Service for importing data from on-premises systems or other cloud providers.

Choosing the Right Solution for Your Application

HERE ARE SOME GUIDING principles to help decide between Firebase Storage and Google Cloud Storage:

1. Consider Firebase Storage if:

○ You need real-time file handling and synchronization.

○ You are building a mobile or web app with Firebase and require seamless integration with Firebase services.

○ Your application involves user-generated content and doesn't require advanced data management features.

2. Consider Google Cloud Storage if:

○ You need scalability to handle large datasets and have complex data retention requirements.

○ Your application needs advanced security features, compliance certifications, or detailed access control through IAM.

○ You are working with data-intensive processes, such as big data analytics or machine learning, and require integration with Google Cloud's data and AI services.

Conclusion

BOTH FIREBASE STORAGE and Google Cloud Storage offer robust solutions for storing and managing files in the cloud, though they cater to different use cases. Firebase Storage provides simplicity and real-time capabilities that are ideal for mobile and web applications with Firebase. On the other hand, Google Cloud Storage offers a more advanced and scalable platform suitable for enterprise-level applications, big data projects, and long-term data storage. By understanding the strengths and limitations of each service, you can select the storage solution that best aligns with your application's goals and technical requirements.

Chapter 8: Analytics, Monitoring, and Performance

Firebase Analytics Overview

IN THIS SECTION, WE will explore Firebase Analytics, which provides powerful insights into app usage, user engagement, and user behavior. Firebase Analytics is a free, unlimited analytics solution specifically tailored for mobile applications. It helps developers understand their audience and improve their applications accordingly. Firebase Analytics integrates seamlessly with other Firebase services and Google products, providing a holistic view of an application's performance.

Firebase Analytics is based on events, which track user interactions within your app. Events can include anything from app opens, in-app purchases, screen views, or custom-defined actions. Firebase Analytics automatically captures a set of events (e.g., first open, user engagement) and also allows developers to define their own custom events.

1. Setting Up Firebase Analytics

TO START USING FIREBASE Analytics, you must first add Firebase to your app. The setup process varies slightly depending on whether you're developing an Android or iOS app.

1. Add Firebase to Your App:

○ Go to the Firebase Console, create a new project or select an existing one, and click "Add App."

○ Download the google-services.json file for Android or GoogleService-Info.plist file for iOS.

○ Integrate the downloaded file into your app by following the setup instructions provided by Firebase.

2. **Add Firebase SDK for Analytics**:

For Android, add the Analytics SDK to your build.gradle file:

implementation 'com.google.firebase:firebase-analytics'

For iOS, add the Analytics SDK to your Podfile:

pod 'Firebase/Analytics'

○ Sync your project to include the SDK.

3. **Initialize Firebase in Your Application**:

For Android, initialize Firebase in your app's onCreate method:

FirebaseAnalytics firebaseAnalytics = FirebaseAnalytics.getInstance(this);

For iOS, initialize Firebase in your app delegate:

FirebaseApp.configure()

Once Firebase Analytics is set up, the SDK automatically logs some common events like app installs, in-app purchases, and user engagement.

2. Logging Custom Events

FIREBASE ANALYTICS allows for custom event logging. Custom events can capture specific interactions users have within your app. For example, if you have a feature that allows users to save articles, you might log a custom event when a user saves an article.

Here's how you can log a custom event:

Android Example:

```
Bundle params = new Bundle();

params.putString("article_id", "12345");

params.putString("article_title", "Firebase Analytics Guide");

firebaseAnalytics.logEvent("save_article", params);
```

iOS Example:

```
let params: [String: Any] = ["article_id": "12345", "article_title": "Firebase Analytics Guide"]

Analytics.logEvent("save_article", parameters: params)
```

Firebase Analytics also lets you define up to 25 user properties, which are attributes that describe segments of your user base, such as language preference or geographic region.

3. Using Firebase Analytics Data

FIREBASE ANALYTICS provides detailed reports in the Firebase Console, where you can view data on various metrics such as user demographics, behavior, and events. The key metrics include:

- **Active Users**: Shows the number of users currently active in your app.

- **Retention**: Measures how often users return to your app over a certain period.

- **Engagement**: Tracks the duration and frequency of user sessions.

Firebase Analytics also integrates with Google BigQuery, allowing for more in-depth data analysis. You can export your analytics data to BigQuery and use SQL-like queries to extract insights or visualize data.

4. Event Parameters and Custom Dimensions

TO GAIN MORE INSIGHTS, Firebase Analytics allows you to attach parameters to events, which add context to the events being logged. For instance, when logging an event like "purchase," you might include parameters such as item name, item ID, and price. Parameters can be numeric or string values and can help filter and break down event reports.

Android Example with Parameters:

Bundle params = new Bundle();

params.putString(FirebaseAnalytics.Param.ITEM_ID, "id123");

params.putString(FirebaseAnalytics.Param.ITEM_NAME, "Shoe");

params.putDouble(FirebaseAnalytics.Param.PRICE, 59.99);

firebaseAnalytics.logEvent(FirebaseAnalytics.Event.PURCHASE, params);

iOS Example with Parameters:

let params: [String: Any] = [

AnalyticsParameterItemID: "id123",

AnalyticsParameterItemName: "Shoe",

AnalyticsParameterPrice: 59.99

]

Analytics.logEvent(AnalyticsEventPurchase, parameters: params)

5. Integrating Firebase Analytics with Google Analytics for Additional Insights

FIREBASE ANALYTICS can also be integrated with Google Analytics for enhanced web analytics capabilities. This integration allows you to measure user interactions across both app and web platforms and offers access to Google's advanced analytics tools.

To enable this integration, navigate to the Firebase Console under the Analytics settings and select "Link to Google Analytics." From there, follow the prompts to complete the connection.

6. Tracking Conversions and User Funnels

FIREBASE ANALYTICS enables conversion tracking, which allows you to track specific user actions that are critical to your business. Conversions can include actions like completing a purchase, signing up, or reaching a particular screen in the app.

1. **Define Conversions**: Go to the Firebase Console, navigate to the Analytics section, and select "Conversions." Here, you can mark events as conversions.
2. **Creating User Funnels**: Funnels help visualize user journeys within your app, from acquisition to engagement

and retention. By analyzing user funnels, you can identify drop-off points and optimize the user experience to improve conversion rates.

Firebase provides a dedicated "Funnels" tab where you can define and track these steps, giving insight into the effectiveness of different parts of your app.

7. Best Practices for Firebase Analytics

- **Focus on Key Events**: Limit the number of custom events to the most impactful ones to avoid overwhelming the analytics dashboard.

- **Use Meaningful Event Names and Parameters**: Ensure event names and parameters are intuitive, as this helps with maintaining the clarity of data.

- **Regularly Review and Adjust Events**: As your app evolves, review the relevance of events and parameters and adjust them as necessary.

- **Leverage Google Tag Manager for Dynamic Events**: For apps that frequently add or change features, using Google Tag Manager can simplify event management.

FIREBASE ANALYTICS is a powerful tool for gaining insights into user behaviors, enabling data-driven decision-making. The integration with Firebase's suite of tools and Google Cloud services provides a robust platform for monitoring app performance and driving growth.

Using Google Analytics with Firebase

IN THIS SECTION, WE will delve into the integration of Google Analytics with Firebase, exploring how it provides additional insights into user behavior, app performance, and engagement across multiple platforms. By leveraging Google Analytics, developers can gain a comprehensive view of their users and make data-driven decisions to improve app performance.

Firebase Analytics and Google Analytics are seamlessly integrated, allowing you to view app data alongside web data, track conversions across platforms, and utilize advanced Google Analytics features like enhanced measurement, conversion tracking, and audience segmentation.

1. Setting Up Google Analytics in Firebase

TO BEGIN USING GOOGLE Analytics with Firebase, you first need to link your Firebase project with a Google Analytics account. If you have set up Firebase Analytics during the Firebase project creation, this integration might already be active. However, if it's not, you can easily link it by following these steps:

1. **Link Firebase to Google Analytics:**

   o In the Firebase Console, select your project.

   o Go to the **Project Settings** and navigate to the **Integrations** tab.

   o Under Google Analytics, click **Link** and follow the prompts to connect an existing Google Analytics account or create a new one.

2. **Configure Enhanced Measurement:**

○ After linking, you can enable enhanced measurement, which automatically tracks events such as page views, scrolls, outbound clicks, site search, and video engagement.

○ In Google Analytics, navigate to **Admin > Property > Data Streams**, select your app, and toggle **Enhanced Measurement** on.

3. Enabling Google Signals:

○ Google Signals enables cross-device reporting and user demographics and interests reporting.

○ To activate it, go to **Admin > Property Settings > Data Collection** and turn on Google Signals for your app.

2. Understanding Data Streams in Google Analytics

DATA STREAMS ARE SOURCES of data from your application, such as iOS apps, Android apps, or websites, which are then analyzed in Google Analytics. Once your Firebase project is linked, a data stream for your app will automatically be created.

1. View Data Streams:

○ In Google Analytics, navigate to **Admin > Property > Data Streams** to see the list of connected data streams.

○ Each stream has a unique Measurement ID (for web) or Stream ID (for app) that ensures data flows correctly into Google Analytics.

2. Adjust Stream Settings:

◦ You can configure settings for each stream to control what data is collected and processed.

◦ In each data stream, you can adjust configurations like **User-ID tracking** and **Enhanced Measurement** options.

3. Utilizing Google Analytics Reports

GOOGLE ANALYTICS OFFERS several types of reports that provide insights into user behavior, acquisition channels, and user engagement. These reports can be accessed through the **Google Analytics Dashboard** and are divided into several sections:

1. **Realtime Reports**:

◦ Realtime reports give you a live view of the users currently interacting with your app, showing the number of users, active screens, and geographic locations in real-time.

◦ To access Realtime reports, go to **Realtime** in the Google Analytics Dashboard.

2. **User Acquisition Reports**:

◦ These reports show where your users come from, breaking down data by traffic sources like organic search, social media, or referral traffic.

◦ In Google Analytics, navigate to **Acquisition > User Acquisition** to view these reports.

3. **User Engagement Reports**:

○ Engagement reports provide insights into user interactions with the app, including metrics like session duration, screen views, and events.

○ Access these reports under **Engagement** to get a clear view of how users interact with different parts of your app.

4. Monetization Reports:

○ For apps with in-app purchases, subscriptions, or ad revenue, Monetization reports help track these transactions.

○ These reports are available under **Monetization**, where you can analyze revenue data, including purchases, ad revenue, and average revenue per user (ARPU).

5. User Retention Reports:

○ Retention reports help track how well you're retaining users over time, showing metrics like new user retention and returning user retention.

○ To view retention metrics, go to **Retention** under the Google Analytics Dashboard.

4. Tracking Conversions Across Platforms

CONVERSION TRACKING in Google Analytics is crucial for measuring important user actions such as purchases, sign-ups, or form submissions. Google Analytics allows you to define and track conversions across web and mobile platforms, providing a unified view of user behavior.

1. **Setting Up Conversion Events**:

○ In the Google Analytics Console, navigate to **Events** and find the event you want to mark as a conversion.

○ Toggle on **Mark as Conversion** to track this event as a conversion.

2. **Creating Custom Conversion Goals**:

○ To set up custom goals, navigate to **Conversions > Goals > New Goal** in Google Analytics.

○ Define a goal based on specific events or actions, such as time on site, pages per session, or a particular funnel step.

3. **Attribution Reporting**:

○ Attribution reports provide insight into which marketing channels contributed to a conversion, giving you a better understanding of the customer journey.

○ Access Attribution reports under **Advertising > Attribution** and configure the attribution model that suits your business goals, such as last-click, first-click, or data-driven attribution.

5. Advanced User Segmentation with Google Analytics

GOOGLE ANALYTICS ALLOWS you to create advanced segments to analyze specific user groups based on characteristics, behaviors, or user properties. These segments help you understand diverse user cohorts and optimize your app experience for different audiences.

1. Creating a User Segment:

○ In Google Analytics, go to any report and click on **Add Segment** at the top.

○ Define the criteria for your segment, such as user demographics, technology (device, OS), or behavior (frequency, actions taken).

2. Using Audience Builder:

○ The Audience Builder tool allows you to create more complex audience definitions based on multiple conditions.

○ Access this tool under **Audience Definitions** in the **Admin** section to create or modify audiences for targeted insights.

3. Applying Segments to Reports:

○ Once a segment is created, you can apply it to reports for detailed analysis.

○ Segments can also be exported to Google Ads for targeted advertising.

6. Integrating Google Analytics with Firebase for Data Export

FIREBASE'S INTEGRATION with Google BigQuery enables exporting raw event data from Google Analytics for in-depth analysis. You can query and analyze the data using SQL or visualize it with data visualization tools like Google Data Studio.

1. **Linking BigQuery with Firebase**:

   ○ In the Firebase Console, navigate to **Project Settings > Integrations**, and enable **BigQuery**.

   ○ This will automatically export Firebase Analytics and Google Analytics data to BigQuery on a daily basis.

2. **Querying Data in BigQuery**:

   ○ With BigQuery, you can run SQL-like queries to extract insights from your data.

For example, to find the most popular events over the last 30 days, you could run a query like:

SELECT event_name, COUNT(event_name) as count

FROM `project_id.dataset_id.events_*`

WHERE _TABLE_SUFFIX BETWEEN '20230101' AND '20230131'

GROUP BY event_name

ORDER BY count DESC

3. **Visualizing Data with Google Data Studio**:

○ Google Data Studio connects directly to BigQuery, allowing you to create dashboards and reports based on your data.

○ To set up a report, link your BigQuery project to Data Studio and select the desired data tables.

○

7. Best Practices for Using Google Analytics with Firebase

● **Consolidate Data for Cross-Platform Insights**: Ensure all data streams are accurately linked to enable a unified view of user interactions across app and web platforms.

● **Use Enhanced Measurement for Automatic Event Tracking**: Enable Enhanced Measurement to reduce the need for custom coding and simplify data collection.

● **Regularly Review User Privacy Settings**: As data privacy regulations evolve, review and update your data collection and user consent settings to stay compliant.

● **Optimize Conversion Tracking**: Focus on the key events that represent your primary business goals, and ensure they are properly marked as conversions.

● **Leverage Advanced Audience Segmentation**: Use segments to understand different user behaviors and tailor the app experience to diverse user groups.

INTEGRATING GOOGLE Analytics with Firebase provides powerful tools for tracking, analyzing, and improving app performance, ultimately enabling developers to make informed decisions and create more engaging user experiences.

Monitoring Performance with Firebase Performance Monitoring

FIREBASE PERFORMANCE Monitoring is a powerful tool for gaining real-time insights into the performance of your application, helping you identify and resolve issues that impact user experience. This service allows you to monitor app performance, track user experience metrics, and optimize for smoother, faster, and more reliable apps. By using Performance Monitoring, developers can collect and analyze data related to app startup time, network latency, and screen rendering, among other factors.

This section will explore how to set up Firebase Performance Monitoring, review and interpret performance metrics, and implement best practices to ensure an optimal user experience.

1. Setting Up Firebase Performance Monitoring

TO GET STARTED WITH Firebase Performance Monitoring, you need to add the Performance Monitoring SDK to your app and set up the necessary configurations in the Firebase Console.

1. Add the Firebase Performance Monitoring SDK:

For Android, add the following dependency in your build.gradle file:

```
implementation 'com.google.firebase:firebase-perf'
```

For iOS, add the Performance Monitoring pod to your Podfile:

ruby

pod 'Firebase/Performance'

2. **Initialize Performance Monitoring**:

For Android, initialize the SDK in your app's onCreate method:

FirebasePerformance.getInstance().setPerformanceCollectionEnabled(tr

For iOS, ensure Firebase is initialized in your AppDelegate:

FirebaseApp.configure()

o

3. **Verify Performance Monitoring Installation**:

o Once set up, launch your app and go to the Firebase Console under **Performance** to confirm that data is being received. Initial data may take a few minutes to appear.

2. Understanding Firebase Performance Monitoring Metrics

FIREBASE PERFORMANCE Monitoring collects various metrics, each providing insight into different aspects of your app's performance. The key metrics include:

1. **App Startup Time**:

o This measures how long it takes for your app to become responsive after launch. High startup times can deter users, so optimizing this metric is crucial.

2. Screen Rendering Performance:

o This metric monitors the frame rate and identifies screens with low FPS, which indicates laggy or janky user experiences. Slow rendering can occur due to complex UI layouts or inefficient image processing.

3. Network Latency and Success Rates:

o Firebase tracks the latency and success rate of network requests, helping you identify slow or failing requests. This can be critical for apps relying heavily on real-time data or API calls.

4. Custom Traces:

o You can define custom traces to monitor specific processes in your app, such as loading a list of items or processing user input. Custom traces allow for granular analysis of specific areas impacting performance.

3. Using Custom Traces to Monitor Specific Tasks

FIREBASE PERFORMANCE Monitoring offers built-in traces for monitoring app startup and network requests, but you can also define custom traces to capture specific app interactions.

1. Creating a Custom Trace:

o A custom trace marks the beginning and end of an operation you want to monitor, like fetching data or completing an in-app purchase.

```
Trace myTrace = FirebasePerformance.getInstance().newTrace("fetch_data");

myTrace.start();

// Code to fetch data

myTrace.stop();
```

For iOS:

```
let trace = Performance.startTrace(name: "fetch_data")

// Code to fetch data

trace?.stop()
```

2. **Adding Metrics to Custom Traces:**

o You can add custom metrics to traces to measure specific aspects like item counts or retries.

For Android:

```
myTrace.putMetric("item_count", itemCount);
```

For iOS:

```
trace?.incrementMetric("item_count", by: itemCount)
```

3. **Analyzing Custom Trace Data:**

○ Once your traces are live, they will appear in the Firebase Console under **Performance Monitoring > Traces**. Here, you can view the average duration, count, and specific metrics of each trace, helping you pinpoint performance issues.

4. Analyzing Network Performance with Firebase

NETWORK REQUESTS ARE often a bottleneck in mobile app performance. Firebase Performance Monitoring tracks network calls and provides insights into latency, payload size, and success rates.

1. **Viewing Network Request Data**:

○ In the Firebase Console, go to **Performance Monitoring > Network Requests**. Here, you'll see a list of all network requests with metrics like average response time, payload size, and error rate.

2. **Optimizing Network Requests**:

○ Review requests with high latency or low success rates. Some best practices include:

▪ **Caching**: Reduce repeated requests by caching static data.

▪ **Compression**: Use data compression to minimize payload sizes.

▪ **Batching Requests**: Combine multiple requests into a single batch to reduce network overhead.

3. **Monitoring Real-Time Network Issues**:

○ Firebase provides real-time alerts for network issues. You can configure alerts for requests that exceed specific latency thresholds or have a high failure rate, enabling quick response to performance degradation.

5. Using Firebase's Remote Config with Performance Monitoring

FIREBASE REMOTE CONFIG is a service that lets you change app behavior and appearance without requiring users to download an app update. This feature can be combined with Performance Monitoring to fine-tune settings that impact performance.

1. A/B Testing with Remote Config:

○ Conduct A/B tests to evaluate different configurations and determine which provides better performance. For example, you can test different image resolutions or animation speeds to find the optimal balance between quality and speed.

2. Dynamic Configuration for Different User Segments:

○ Use Remote Config to adjust app performance for different user segments, such as high-speed vs. low-speed network users. This can improve user experience by tailoring app behavior to network conditions.

3. Monitoring the Impact of Remote Config Changes:

○ After implementing changes, use Firebase Performance Monitoring to track their impact on app performance metrics and ensure improvements align with user expectations.

6. Understanding Firebase Performance Monitoring Alerts

FIREBASE ALLOWS YOU to set up alerts for performance issues, enabling proactive management of app quality. Alerts can be configured based on thresholds for specific metrics like app startup time, network latency, and custom trace durations.

1. **Configuring Alerts**:

○ Go to **Performance Monitoring > Alerts** in the Firebase Console, where you can set up email or Slack notifications for specific metrics.

○ Define thresholds, such as startup time exceeding 2 seconds or network latency over 500 ms, to trigger alerts when performance dips below acceptable levels.

2. **Using Slack or Email Integrations**:

○ Integrate with Slack or other tools to receive instant notifications. This allows you to respond to issues as soon as they arise, reducing the impact on users.

3. **Prioritizing Alerts**:

○ Not all alerts are equally critical. Use Firebase's alert priority settings to categorize alerts based on their impact. High-priority alerts can be for issues directly impacting user experience, while low-priority alerts might be for less noticeable delays.

7. Best Practices for Firebase Performance Monitoring

TO MAXIMIZE THE EFFECTIVENESS of Firebase Performance Monitoring, consider implementing the following best practices:

1. Regularly Review Performance Data:

○ Consistent monitoring helps detect trends and identify recurring issues. Regularly review metrics like app startup time, screen rendering, and network latency to stay informed.

2. Use Custom Traces Wisely:

○ Focus on key user flows and resource-intensive processes. Overuse of custom traces can lead to unnecessary overhead and complicate data analysis.

3. Analyze Network Dependencies:

○ Review dependencies for third-party APIs and services. Slow third-party services can degrade app performance, so consider alternatives or optimizations if certain services are consistently slow.

4. Optimize for Low-End Devices and Slow Networks:

○ Test your app on a variety of devices and network conditions. Firebase Performance Monitoring provides insights on device and network type, helping you understand and optimize for users with limited resources.

5. Set Realistic Performance Goals:

○ Define and monitor realistic performance goals for your app. Striving for immediate perfection can lead to over-optimization, but setting attainable benchmarks can guide incremental improvements over time.

Firebase Performance Monitoring offers a comprehensive suite of tools for tracking and optimizing mobile app performance. By following these steps and best practices, developers can proactively identify issues, improve user experience, and build more robust, high-quality applications.

Leveraging Google Cloud's Monitoring Tools

GOOGLE CLOUD'S MONITORING tools provide advanced insights into your Firebase app's backend performance, offering powerful observability for both cloud infrastructure and application-specific metrics. By using these tools in conjunction with Firebase, you can achieve a deeper understanding of how your backend services perform, identify issues early, and optimize for stability and reliability.

This section will cover setting up Google Cloud Monitoring, utilizing key features like metrics and dashboards, and integrating Google Cloud's alerting capabilities. Additionally, we'll explore how to correlate Firebase and Google Cloud metrics to gain a comprehensive view of your app's performance.

1. Setting Up Google Cloud Monitoring

GOOGLE CLOUD MONITORING, previously known as Stackdriver Monitoring, is a flexible service that allows you to monitor cloud resources and applications. To get started with Google Cloud Monitoring, you need to enable it for your Google Cloud project and configure it to collect and display metrics.

1. **Enable Google Cloud Monitoring**:

○ In the Google Cloud Console, navigate to **Monitoring** and select **Enable** if it's not already active for your project.

○ Grant necessary permissions, such as the Monitoring Viewer or Monitoring Editor roles, to users who need access.

2. **Link Firebase to Google Cloud Monitoring**:

○ Google Cloud Monitoring automatically collects metrics from services within your Google Cloud project, including those used by Firebase.

○ Confirm that Firebase services are listed under **Resources > Metrics Explorer** in the Google Cloud Console.

3. **Install Monitoring Agents (Optional)**:

○ If you use custom virtual machines (VMs) or other Google Cloud resources, you can install Monitoring Agents on those resources to collect more granular metrics.

○ Install the agent on your VMs by following the steps provided in the Google Cloud Monitoring documentation.

2. Exploring Metrics in Google Cloud Monitoring

GOOGLE CLOUD MONITORING provides numerous predefined metrics and allows you to define custom metrics to track application-specific data. Key metrics categories include instance health, resource utilization, and Firebase-specific metrics like Firestore latency or Authentication response times.

1. **Using Metrics Explorer**:

   o In the Monitoring dashboard, navigate to **Metrics Explorer** to view a list of available metrics.

   o You can search for specific Firebase metrics like firestore.googleapis.com/operation_latency or firebaseauth.googleapis.com/authentication_attempts.

2. **Creating Custom Metrics**:

   o Custom metrics allow you to monitor specific aspects of your application that are not covered by default metrics.

To create a custom metric, use the Cloud Monitoring API to define the metric type and send data points. An example API request to create a custom metric in Python:

python

```python
from google.cloud import monitoring_v3

client = monitoring_v3.MetricServiceClient()

project_name = f"projects/{project_id}"

descriptor = monitoring_v3.MetricDescriptor()
```

```
descriptor.type = "custom.googleapis.com/my_custom_metric"

descriptor.metric_kind                                    =
monitoring_v3.MetricDescriptor.MetricKind.GAUGE

descriptor.value_type                                     =
monitoring_v3.MetricDescriptor.ValueType.INT64

descriptor.description = "This is a custom metric for specific
Firebase events."

client.create_metric_descriptor(name=project_name,
metric_descriptor=descriptor)
```

o

3. Monitoring Firebase-Specific Metrics:

o Google Cloud Monitoring automatically collects a set of Firebase-specific metrics, which are available under the firebase.googleapis.com namespace.

o Use Metrics Explorer to visualize metrics like Firestore read/write latencies, Authentication success/failure rates, and Storage usage.

3. Creating Custom Dashboards for Performance Visualization

CUSTOM DASHBOARDS ALLOW you to visualize key metrics in one place, making it easy to monitor app performance at a glance. Google Cloud Monitoring provides an intuitive interface for creating dashboards that can display multiple charts and data visualizations.

1. Building a Custom Dashboard:

○ In the Monitoring Console, go to **Dashboards** and select **Create Dashboard**.

○ Add charts by choosing metrics, defining aggregation settings, and customizing the appearance. For instance, you might create a dashboard showing Firestore latency, Authentication success rates, and Cloud Function execution times.

2. **Configuring Time Series Data**:

○ For each metric, you can select the aggregation type (e.g., average, maximum) and time interval (e.g., last hour, last 24 hours).

○ Use filters to display specific metric attributes, such as region or instance type, which helps you analyze performance based on different environments.

3. **Adding Custom Widgets**:

○ Google Cloud Monitoring offers widgets like line charts, heatmaps, and distribution graphs.

○ Use these widgets to customize how your data is visualized. For example, a heatmap can be used to identify regional performance issues with Firestore or Authentication.

4. Implementing Alerts for Proactive Monitoring

GOOGLE CLOUD MONITORING'S alerting capabilities enable proactive monitoring by notifying you when metrics reach certain thresholds. Setting up alerts helps detect performance issues early, allowing you to address them before they impact users.

1. **Creating Alerting Policies**:

○ Go to **Alerting** in the Monitoring Console and select **Create Policy**.

○ Choose the metric you want to monitor and set conditions for the alert, such as Firestore latency exceeding 200 ms or Authentication failure rates over 5%.

○ Define notification channels (e.g., email, SMS, or Slack) and assign the alert to those channels.

2. **Using Multi-Condition Alerts**:

○ Combine multiple conditions in a single alert to monitor complex scenarios. For example, you might trigger an alert if both Firestore latency is high and error rates are above a certain threshold.

○ This allows for more precise alerting, reducing false positives and ensuring alerts are actionable.

3. **Customizing Alert Frequency and Thresholds**:

○ Adjust alert thresholds based on your app's tolerance for latency or error rates. For critical services, set tighter thresholds for faster response.

○ Define the frequency of alerts (e.g., every minute or every five minutes) to balance timely notifications with avoiding alert fatigue.

5. Integrating Google Cloud Logging for Enhanced Observability

GOOGLE CLOUD LOGGING, formerly Stackdriver Logging, provides a centralized logging solution that integrates seamlessly with Google Cloud Monitoring. It offers detailed logs for Firebase services, allowing you to correlate log data with performance metrics.

1. Enabling Cloud Logging:

○ In the Google Cloud Console, go to **Logging** and ensure it's enabled for your project. Logging is automatically enabled for many Google Cloud services.

○ For Firebase functions, Cloud Logging collects logs by default, so you can start viewing them immediately in the Logging Console.

2. Viewing and Querying Logs:

○ Use the **Logs Explorer** to search for specific log entries by filtering based on criteria such as resource type, severity, or timestamp.

○ Query logs to find details about specific errors or warnings. For instance, you might search for all error logs related to Firestore writes.

3. Setting Up Log-Based Alerts:

○ Log-based alerts notify you based on specific log patterns. For example, if you're monitoring for a recurring error, set up a log-based alert to notify you when it appears.

○ Go to **Logging > Logs-based metrics**, create a new metric based on your query, and then use that metric in an alerting policy.

6. Best Practices for Using Google Cloud Monitoring with Firebase

MAXIMIZING THE BENEFITS of Google Cloud Monitoring requires a strategic approach to configuring metrics, dashboards, and alerts. Consider these best practices to enhance your Firebase app's observability:

1. Identify Critical Metrics and Set Baselines:

○ Determine which metrics are essential for your app's performance. Set baselines for these metrics to understand normal performance and identify deviations.

2. Combine Firebase and Cloud Metrics for Holistic Insights:

○ By correlating Firebase-specific metrics (like Authentication latency) with Google Cloud infrastructure metrics (like CPU utilization), you can diagnose issues more effectively.

3. Leverage Historical Data for Trend Analysis:

○ Use historical data to identify trends and forecast potential issues. Google Cloud Monitoring retains data for up to 24 months, enabling long-term analysis.

4. Utilize Automated Reporting:

○ Set up automated reports that compile key metrics and deliver them on a regular basis. This helps stakeholders stay informed and allows you to track improvements over time.

5. Optimize Alerts to Avoid Alert Fatigue:

○ Carefully configure alerts to minimize unnecessary notifications. Ensure that alerts are actionable and focus on high-impact metrics that correlate directly with user experience.

Google Cloud's Monitoring tools, when combined with Firebase, provide a robust solution for maintaining and improving app performance. By implementing these tools and best practices, you can proactively manage your application's health, deliver a better user experience, and respond swiftly to issues as they arise.

Ensuring App Reliability and Performance with Firebase & GCP

ENSURING THE RELIABILITY and performance of an application is crucial for user satisfaction and retention. By leveraging Firebase and Google Cloud Platform (GCP), developers can create highly resilient applications that are optimized for speed, scalability, and stability. This section explores various strategies and best practices for maintaining app reliability and performance through Firebase services, GCP tools, and proactive monitoring.

1. Designing for Scalability and High Availability

BUILDING SCALABLE AND highly available applications requires thoughtful architecture that can accommodate growth and withstand failures. Firebase and GCP provide tools and services that support both horizontal and vertical scaling while ensuring minimal downtime.

1. **Using Firebase Realtime Database and Firestore for Scalability**:

○ Firebase Realtime Database and Firestore are designed for scalability. Firestore, in particular, offers automatic scaling to handle thousands of concurrent connections.

○ Use Firestore's **collection-group queries** and **composite indexes** to optimize data access patterns, which helps in maintaining performance as your app scales.

2. **Implementing Load Balancing with Google Cloud Load Balancer**:

○ Google Cloud Load Balancer distributes incoming traffic across multiple instances, ensuring no single instance is overwhelmed. It also provides global reach with anycast IP addresses.

○ To set up load balancing, go to **Google Cloud Console > Load Balancing**, create a new load balancer, and specify backend services (e.g., App Engine instances, Cloud Functions) to distribute traffic.

3. **Leveraging Firebase Hosting's Global CDN**:

○ Firebase Hosting uses a global content delivery network (CDN) that automatically caches and delivers content from servers close to your users, reducing latency and improving load times.

o Ensure you configure caching headers properly in Firebase Hosting to control how long content is cached, which enhances performance without compromising content freshness.

2. Implementing Caching and Data Optimization

EFFECTIVE CACHING STRATEGIES can significantly reduce the load on backend services and improve response times. Firebase and GCP offer various caching solutions tailored to different types of data and application architectures.

1. Using Firebase Cache-Control for Static Content:

o Firebase Hosting allows you to set cache control headers for static assets such as images, CSS, and JavaScript files. This reduces the number of requests to the server by allowing the browser to cache frequently used resources.

Configure firebase.json to set custom caching rules:

```
{

"hosting": {

"headers": [

{

"source": "/static/**",

"headers": [
```

```
{

"key": "Cache-Control",

"value": "public, max-age=31536000"

}

]

}

]

}

}
```

○

2. Implementing In-Memory Caching with Memorystore:

○ Google Cloud Memorystore provides managed Redis and Memcached services that enable in-memory caching, ideal for caching frequently accessed data such as user sessions or app configuration.

○ To set up Memorystore, go to **Google Cloud Console > Memorystore** and select Redis or Memcached, depending on your caching needs.

3. Optimizing Firestore Queries for Performance:

○ Firestore automatically indexes all data, but complex queries can sometimes benefit from custom indexes. Use the Firebase Console's **Indexes** tab to define specific indexes for high-traffic queries.

o Avoid expensive operations like **in** or **array-contains-any** in queries if they are frequently used, as these can increase latency due to the complexity of data retrieval.

3. Monitoring and Automating Performance with Cloud Functions

AUTOMATION PLAYS A key role in maintaining reliability. By automating certain tasks using Firebase Cloud Functions and Google Cloud Functions, you can ensure that your application is always optimized and any issues are addressed promptly.

1. **Using Cloud Functions for Automated Data Processing:**

o Firebase Cloud Functions can automate data processing tasks such as cleaning up old records, resizing images, or sending notifications. This ensures that your app remains responsive and performant.

For example, a function that deletes inactive user data after 30 days:

```
CONST FUNCTIONS = REQUIRE('firebase-functions');

const admin = require('firebase-admin');

admin.initializeApp();

exports.cleanUpInactiveUsers = functions.pubsub.schedule('every 24 hours').onRun(async (context) => {
```

```
const usersRef = admin.firestore().collection('users');

const inactiveUsers = await usersRef.where('lastActive', '<=',
Date.now() - 2592000000).get();

inactiveUsers.forEach(async (doc) => {

await doc.ref.delete();

});

});
```

2. Setting Up Auto-Scaling for Cloud Functions:

○ Cloud Functions automatically scale up when there is an increase in demand, and scale down when the demand decreases, helping maintain performance during traffic spikes without incurring unnecessary costs.

○ Use GCP's **Concurrency** settings to control the number of requests handled by a single instance of your function, balancing cost and performance.

3. Scheduling Routine Maintenance with Cloud Scheduler:

○ Google Cloud Scheduler can trigger tasks like database backups, log cleanup, or system checks at specified intervals, ensuring your app remains optimized.

○ Set up a scheduled task in **Google Cloud Console > Cloud Scheduler** and configure it to invoke a Cloud Function that performs the desired maintenance task.

4. Ensuring Data Security and Compliance

DATA SECURITY IS PARAMOUNT, especially for applications handling sensitive user information. Firebase and GCP offer robust tools for securing data and ensuring compliance with industry regulations.

1. Enforcing Data Encryption:

○ Firebase automatically encrypts data at rest and in transit. For additional control, GCP offers **Customer-Managed Encryption Keys (CMEK)**, allowing you to manage your own encryption keys for data stored in Google Cloud services.

○ To enable CMEK for a Cloud Storage bucket, navigate to **Storage > Settings** in the Google Cloud Console, and specify a Cloud KMS key.

2. Implementing Fine-Grained Access Control with Firebase Security Rules:

○ Firebase Security Rules allow you to define granular access controls for Firestore, Realtime Database, and Storage. Use these rules to restrict data access based on user authentication status or custom user attributes.

Example of a Firestore security rule that allows read access only to authenticated users:

```firebase
service cloud.firestore {

match /databases/{database}/documents {
```

```
match /users/{userId} {

allow read: if request.auth != null && request.auth.uid == userId;

}

}

}
```

○

3. Conducting Regular Security Audits with GCP Security Command Center:

○ Google Cloud's Security Command Center provides visibility into the security state of your cloud assets and helps identify vulnerabilities or misconfigurations.

○ To use the Security Command Center, enable it in the **Google Cloud Console** and review findings regularly, such as policy violations or network vulnerabilities.

5. Implementing Continuous Integration and Deployment (CI/CD)

CONTINUOUS INTEGRATION and Continuous Deployment (CI/CD) automate the build, testing, and deployment processes, ensuring new code changes are reliably and efficiently pushed to production. Firebase and GCP offer tools and integrations that facilitate robust CI/CD pipelines.

1. Setting Up a CI/CD Pipeline with Cloud Build:

○ Google Cloud Build provides a serverless CI/CD platform that integrates with repositories like GitHub or Bitbucket. Use it to automate building, testing, and deploying code.

Create a cloudbuild.yaml file to define the build steps for your Firebase app:

steps:

- name: 'gcr.io/cloud-builders/npm'

args: ['install']

- name: 'gcr.io/cloud-builders/npm'

args: ['run', 'build']

- name: 'gcr.io/cloud-builders/firebase'

args: ['deploy', '—token=${FIREBASE_TOKEN}']

o

2. **Using Firebase Hosting Preview Channels for Safe Deployment**:

o Preview Channels in Firebase Hosting let you test changes in a staging environment before deploying to production. This helps catch issues early in the deployment process.

Deploy to a preview channel by running:

bash

Copy code

firebase hosting:channel:deploy preview-channel-name

○

3. Automating Rollbacks and Error Monitoring with Cloud Functions:

○ Use Firebase Cloud Functions to automate rollback procedures when issues are detected in production. Integrate with Firebase Crashlytics to monitor errors and trigger rollback functions if critical issues arise.

○ This ensures that issues are quickly mitigated, reducing the impact on users.

6. Utilizing Google Cloud's Observability Tools for Real-Time Insights

GCP'S OBSERVABILITY suite, including Cloud Monitoring, Cloud Logging, and Error Reporting, offers real-time insights into the health of your application, enabling you to maintain high reliability and performance.

1. Configuring Dashboards for Real-Time Monitoring:

○ Set up real-time dashboards in Google Cloud Monitoring to view key metrics such as request latency, error rates, and resource utilization at a glance.

2. Setting Up Error Reporting for Firebase and GCP Services:

○ Google Cloud Error Reporting aggregates errors across Firebase and GCP services, providing a centralized view of issues and stack traces. This accelerates troubleshooting and enhances reliability.

○ Access Error Reporting in the Google Cloud Console, and configure alerts for high-severity errors.

3. **Using Tracing for End-to-End Request Monitoring**:

○ Cloud Trace helps you track the path of requests across various services, allowing you to identify bottlenecks and optimize performance.

○ Enable tracing in your app by installing the Cloud Trace SDK, and visualize request latency in the Trace Console.

By following these practices and leveraging Firebase and GCP's comprehensive suite of tools, you can build and maintain high-performing, reliable applications that meet user expectations and provide a seamless experience.

Chapter 9: Machine Learning with Firebase and GCP

Introduction to Firebase ML Kit

FIREBASE ML KIT IS a powerful suite of machine learning tools provided by Google that allows developers to implement machine learning capabilities directly into their mobile applications. It is designed to be easy to integrate with Firebase and is especially useful for mobile developers who want to add machine learning without having to build complex ML models from scratch. Firebase ML Kit provides a range of pre-trained models for common tasks such as image labeling, text recognition, and language translation, while also allowing developers to deploy their own custom models.

Firebase ML Kit's capabilities include:

- **Image Labeling**: Automatically identifies objects, places, and actions within images.

- **Text Recognition**: Detects and extracts text from images, supporting multiple languages.

- **Face Detection**: Recognizes and analyzes faces in images, useful for apps with facial features like filters.

- **Barcode Scanning**: Reads and interprets standard barcodes from a range of formats.

- **Landmark Recognition**: Identifies famous landmarks in images, providing contextual information.

- **Language Identification and Translation**: Recognizes and translates over 50 languages, useful for apps with global reach.

Firebase ML Kit integrates seamlessly with Firebase Authentication, Firestore, and other Firebase services, making it easy to build apps with advanced features that enhance user experience. Additionally, Firebase ML Kit supports custom TensorFlow Lite models, allowing developers to bring their own machine learning models into the Firebase ecosystem.

Getting Started with Firebase ML Kit

TO BEGIN USING FIREBASE ML Kit, you first need to set up a Firebase project and integrate ML Kit into your application. Here is a step-by-step guide on how to get started:

1. **Create a Firebase Project**:

○ Go to the Firebase Console.

○ Click on "Add Project" and follow the prompts to create a new project.

○ Once created, go to the "Project Settings" and download the google-services.json file for Android or GoogleService-Info.plist for iOS.

2. **Add Firebase ML Kit to Your App**:

In your app-level build.gradle file, add the Firebase ML Kit dependencies. For example, to include image labeling and text recognition, you would add:

implementation 'com.google.firebase:firebase-ml-vision:24.0.3' implementation 'com.google.firebase:firebase-ml-vision-image-label-model:20.0.7'

○

○ Sync your project to ensure the dependencies are correctly integrated.

3. Initialize Firebase in Your App:

In your application's main activity, initialize Firebase by adding the following code:

FirebaseApp.initializeApp(this);

○

Implementing Image Labeling

ONE OF THE MOST POPULAR features of Firebase ML Kit is image labeling, which allows you to automatically identify objects within images. Here's how to implement it:

1. Prepare the Image:

To label an image, you first need to prepare it. Firebase ML Kit accepts FirebaseVisionImage objects, which can be created from a Bitmap, ByteBuffer, or Media.Image.

FirebaseVisionImage image = FirebaseVisionImage.fromBitmap(bitmap);

○

2. Set Up the Image Labeler:

Next, create an instance of FirebaseVisionImageLabeler and configure any options. You can use either the default labeler or a custom model:

```
FirebaseVisionImageLabeler labeler = FirebaseVision.getInstance().getOnDeviceImageLabeler();
```

o

3. Process the Image:

Pass the image to the labeler and add a success listener to handle the results:

```
labeler.processImage(image)

.addOnSuccessListener(new
OnSuccessListener<List<FirebaseVisionImageLabel>>() {

@Override

public void onSuccess(List<FirebaseVisionImageLabel> labels) {

for (FirebaseVisionImageLabel label : labels) {

String text = label.getText();

float confidence = label.getConfidence();

Log.d("ImageLabel", "Label: " + text + ", Confidence: " + confidence);

}

}

})
```

```
.addOnFailureListener(new OnFailureListener() {

@Override

public void onFailure(@NonNull Exception e) {

Log.e("ImageLabel", "Error: " + e.getMessage());

}

});
```

○

Using Custom ML Models

IN ADDITION TO THE built-in models, Firebase ML Kit allows developers to deploy and run custom models. This is particularly useful when you have a specific use case that is not covered by Firebase's pre-trained models. Here is how you can integrate a custom TensorFlow Lite model into your app:

1. Upload the Model to Firebase:

○ In the Firebase Console, navigate to the "ML Kit" section and select "Custom" under "Models".

○ Upload your TensorFlow Lite model (.tflite file), provide a name for the model, and configure any download options.

2. Download and Load the Model in Your App:

Add the Firebase ML Model dependency:

implementation 'com.google.firebase:firebase-ml-model-interpreter:22.0.4'

○

○ Initialize the model with FirebaseCustomLocalModel or FirebaseCustomRemoteModel, depending on whether the model is stored locally or remotely.

3. **Configure Input and Output Options**:

Define the input and output data types for the model:

FirebaseModelInputOutputOptions inputOutputOptions =

new FirebaseModelInputOutputOptions.Builder()

.setInputFormat(0, FirebaseModelDataType.FLOAT32, new int[]{1, 224, 224, 3})

.setOutputFormat(0, FirebaseModelDataType.FLOAT32, new int[]{1, 1000})

.build();

○

4. **Run the Model**:

Use the FirebaseModelInterpreter to process data with the model:

FirebaseModelInterpreter interpreter = FirebaseModelInterpreter.getInstance();

interpreter.run(input, inputOutputOptions)

```java
.addOnSuccessListener(new
OnSuccessListener<FirebaseModelOutputs>() {

@Override

public void onSuccess(FirebaseModelOutputs result) {

float[][] output = result.getOutput(0);

// Process the output as needed

}

})

.addOnFailureListener(new OnFailureListener() {

@Override

public void onFailure(@NonNull Exception e) {

Log.e("CustomModel", "Error: " + e.getMessage());

}

});
```

o

Advantages of Firebase ML Kit in Mobile Apps

FIREBASE ML KIT SIMPLIFIES the integration of machine learning into mobile applications. With on-device capabilities, you can ensure faster processing times and better user privacy, as data does not need to be sent to the cloud. Additionally, Firebase ML Kit's tight integration with Firebase services like Authentication, Firestore, and Hosting allows you to build comprehensive, intelligent apps that scale seamlessly.

By combining Firebase ML Kit with Google Cloud Platform services like AutoML and BigQuery, developers can create even more powerful applications that leverage the full potential of cloud computing and machine learning.

Custom Machine Learning Models in Firebase

FIREBASE ML KIT PROVIDES a streamlined approach to deploying custom machine learning models on mobile devices, allowing developers to leverage the power of machine learning without requiring deep expertise in AI. With Firebase ML Kit, you can deploy custom TensorFlow Lite models that are specifically trained to meet the unique needs of your app. This flexibility is essential for developers who need to go beyond the capabilities of Firebase's pre-trained models, enabling the creation of tailored experiences for users.

Benefits of Custom Models in Firebase

DEPLOYING CUSTOM MODELS offers several advantages:

- **Personalized User Experience**: You can create models that are specifically trained on your data, which can improve the accuracy and relevance of predictions for your users.

- **On-Device Processing**: Custom models run directly on the device, resulting in faster response times and preserving user privacy, as data does not need to be sent to the cloud.

- **Integration with Firebase Services**: Firebase ML Kit's custom model capabilities seamlessly integrate with other Firebase services, such as Firestore, Authentication, and Hosting.

Building a Custom Model with TensorFlow Lite

TO GET STARTED WITH a custom TensorFlow Lite model, you'll first need to build and convert a model using TensorFlow or any other compatible framework. Here, we'll go through the process of creating a basic image classification model, converting it to TensorFlow Lite, and deploying it with Firebase ML Kit.

Step 1: Train a Model with TensorFlow

FOR SIMPLICITY, WE'LL use a pre-trained model available in TensorFlow and fine-tune it with custom data. Let's use TensorFlow's MobileNet model, which is well-suited for mobile devices due to its compact size and efficiency.

Here's a basic code example for training and exporting a model using TensorFlow:

```python
import tensorflow as tf

from tensorflow.keras.applications import MobileNetV2

from tensorflow.keras.layers import Dense, GlobalAveragePooling2D

from tensorflow.keras.models import Model

# Load MobileNetV2 with pre-trained weights

base_model = MobileNetV2(weights='imagenet', include_top=False, input_shape=(224, 224, 3))

# Freeze the base model layers
```

```python
for layer in base_model.layers:

layer.trainable = False

# Add custom classification layers

x = base_model.output

x = GlobalAveragePooling2D()(x)

x = Dense(1024, activation='relu')(x)

predictions = Dense(10, activation='softmax')(x)

# Define the full model

model = Model(inputs=base_model.input, outputs=predictions)

# Compile the model

model.compile(optimizer='adam', loss='categorical_crossentropy',
metrics=['accuracy'])

# Train the model (assuming X_train, y_train are prepared)

model.fit(X_train, y_train, epochs=5, batch_size=32)
```

Once the model is trained, export it to the TensorFlow Lite format:

```python
# Convert the model to TensorFlow Lite format

converter = tf.lite.TFLiteConverter.from_keras_model(model)

tflite_model = converter.convert()

# Save the TensorFlow Lite model

with open('model.tflite', 'wb') as f:

f.write(tflite_model)
```

Step 2: Upload the Model to Firebase

AFTER CONVERTING THE model to TensorFlow Lite, you need to upload it to Firebase. Follow these steps:

1. Go to the Firebase Console.
2. Navigate to the "ML Kit" section and click on "Custom".
3. Upload your TensorFlow Lite model file (model.tflite).
4. Configure the model settings, such as specifying whether the model should be downloaded automatically or on demand.

Once uploaded, Firebase will manage the distribution of the model to your app users, ensuring that they receive the latest version of the model when available.

Step 3: Integrate the Model into Your App

TO USE THE CUSTOM MODEL in your app, you need to integrate Firebase ML Kit's model downloading API. Here's an example of how to set up and use a custom model in an Android application:

Add Firebase Dependencies: In your build.gradle file, add the required dependencies for Firebase ML Kit and Firebase Model:

implementation 'com.google.firebase:firebase-ml-model-interpreter:22.0.4'

1.

Load the Custom Model: In your app's code, configure Firebase to load the custom model:

```java
FirebaseCustomRemoteModel remoteModel = new
FirebaseCustomRemoteModel.Builder("your_model_name").build();

FirebaseModelDownloadConditions conditions = new
FirebaseModelDownloadConditions.Builder()

.requireWifi()

.build();

FirebaseModelManager.getInstance().download(remoteModel,
conditions)

.addOnSuccessListener(new OnSuccessListener<Void>() {

@Override

public void onSuccess(Void v) {

Log.d("CustomModel", "Model downloaded successfully");

}

})

.addOnFailureListener(new OnFailureListener() {

@Override

public void onFailure(@NonNull Exception e) {

Log.e("CustomModel", "Model download failed: " +
e.getMessage());

}
});
```
   1.

Configure the Input and Output for the Model: Define the input and output shape of the model using Firebase's FirebaseModelInputOutputOptions:

FirebaseModelInputOutputOptions inputOutputOptions =

new FirebaseModelInputOutputOptions.Builder()

.setInputFormat(0, FirebaseModelDataType.FLOAT32, new int[]{1, 224, 224, 3})

.setOutputFormat(0, FirebaseModelDataType.FLOAT32, new int[]{1, 10})

.build();
   1.

Prepare the Input Data and Run the Model:

// Assuming bitmap is the image to be classified

ByteBuffer inputBuffer = ByteBuffer.allocateDirect(4 * 224 * 224 * 3);

inputBuffer.put(bitmapToByteArray(bitmap));

FirebaseModelInputs inputs = new FirebaseModelInputs.Builder()

.add(inputBuffer)

.build();

FirebaseModelInterpreter.getInstance(remoteModel)

.run(inputs, inputOutputOptions)

```java
.addOnSuccessListener(new
OnSuccessListener<FirebaseModelOutputs>() {

@Override

public void onSuccess(FirebaseModelOutputs result) {

float[][] output = result.getOutput(0);

// Handle the model output

}

})

.addOnFailureListener(new OnFailureListener() {

@Override

public void onFailure(@NonNull Exception e) {

Log.e("CustomModel", "Model run failed: " + e.getMessage());

}

});
```

   1.

The bitmapToByteArray function should convert your image into a ByteBuffer format suitable for the model's input. Here's a basic example of how you can create such a function:

```java
private ByteBuffer bitmapToByteArray(Bitmap bitmap) {

ByteBuffer byteBuffer = ByteBuffer.allocateDirect(4 * 224 * 224 * 3);

bitmap = Bitmap.createScaledBitmap(bitmap, 224, 224, true);
```

```
int[] pixels = new int[224 * 224];

bitmap.getPixels(pixels, 0, 224, 0, 0, 224, 224);

for (int pixel : pixels) {

byteBuffer.putFloat((((pixel >> 16) & 0xFF) / 255.0f);

byteBuffer.putFloat((((pixel >> 8) & 0xFF) / 255.0f);

byteBuffer.putFloat(((pixel & 0xFF) / 255.0f);

}

return byteBuffer;

}
```

This function resizes the bitmap and extracts pixel data in the RGB format, storing it in a ByteBuffer that matches the model's expected input.

Managing Custom Model Updates

FIREBASE ML KIT'S CUSTOM model feature allows you to manage and update models effortlessly. When a new model version is available, you can upload it to the Firebase Console, and Firebase will handle versioning and distribution to the app users. Firebase also supports conditional model downloads, so you can specify that models should only be updated over Wi-Fi to avoid excessive data usage.

By using custom machine learning models with Firebase ML Kit, you gain control over the AI capabilities of your application, tailoring models to fit specific requirements and enhance the overall user experience.

Integrating GCP AI and Machine Learning Services

GOOGLE CLOUD PLATFORM (GCP) offers a suite of powerful AI and machine learning services that can enhance Firebase applications with advanced capabilities, from natural language processing to computer vision. By leveraging these services, developers can go beyond Firebase ML Kit's built-in functionalities, accessing the full range of Google's AI expertise through services like AutoML, Cloud Vision, and Cloud Natural Language.

Integrating GCP AI services into Firebase apps opens the door to scalable, production-ready AI that is ideal for applications requiring high performance and reliability. Here, we'll explore various GCP AI services and demonstrate how to integrate them with Firebase to build intelligent applications.

Using AutoML for Custom Model Training

GOOGLE AUTOML PROVIDES an accessible way to create custom machine learning models without requiring deep expertise in data science. With AutoML, you can upload datasets, and Google Cloud will automatically train a custom model optimized for your specific use case. This is particularly useful for tasks like image classification, object detection, and natural language processing.

Step 1: Prepare and Upload Your Dataset

TO BEGIN, YOU NEED a labeled dataset appropriate for your use case. For example, if you're building an image classifier, gather a set of images organized into folders by category. Once your dataset is ready:

1. Go to the Google Cloud Console.
2. Navigate to the AutoML section and select the service that fits your needs (e.g., Vision for images, Natural Language for text).
3. Create a new dataset and upload your labeled data. For image data, you can directly upload images or use Google Cloud Storage for large datasets.

Step 2: Train the Model with AutoML

AFTER UPLOADING YOUR data, you can start training your model. Google Cloud AutoML automatically chooses the best algorithms and parameters based on your dataset:

1. Select the "Train New Model" option.
2. Configure training settings, such as the amount of data to be used and the model's complexity.
3. Start the training process. AutoML will handle the entire model-building pipeline, including feature extraction, model selection, and hyperparameter tuning.

Training can take anywhere from a few minutes to several hours, depending on the complexity and size of your dataset. Once training is complete, AutoML provides a summary of model performance, including accuracy metrics and confusion matrices, to help you evaluate its effectiveness.

Step 3: Deploy the Model to Firebase

ONCE YOUR MODEL IS trained, you can deploy it and integrate it with your Firebase app. AutoML allows you to export your model as a TensorFlow Lite model or use it as an API hosted on GCP.

For TensorFlow Lite:

- Download the model file from the AutoML interface.

- Upload the model to Firebase ML Kit using the Custom Model feature, as described in Section 9.2.

For API deployment:

- Deploy the model on GCP to enable REST API access.

- Use Firebase Cloud Functions to call the AutoML API from your Firebase app.

Here's an example of a Firebase Cloud Function that calls an AutoML model hosted on GCP:

```
const functions = require('firebase-functions');

const {PredictionServiceClient} = require('@google-cloud/automl').v1;

const client = new PredictionServiceClient();

exports.predictImageCategory = functions.https.onRequest(async (req, res) => {

const projectId = 'your-project-id';
```

```
const modelId = 'your-model-id';

const filePath = req.query.filePath;

const [response] = await client.predict({

name: client.modelPath(projectId, 'us-central1', modelId),

payload: {

image: {

imageBytes: fs.readFileSync(filePath).toString('base64'),

},

},

});

res.json(response);

});
```

Leveraging Google Cloud Vision for Image Analysis

GOOGLE CLOUD VISION offers advanced image analysis capabilities, including facial detection, label detection, landmark recognition, and OCR (optical character recognition). You can integrate Cloud Vision into your Firebase app to enhance its image-processing features.

Step 1: Set Up Cloud Vision API

1. In the Google Cloud Console, enable the Cloud Vision API for your project.
2. Generate an API key and store it securely in Firebase,

using Firebase's environment configuration or Firestore for easy access.

Step 2: Integrate Cloud Vision into Your Firebase App

USE FIREBASE CLOUD Functions to call the Cloud Vision API. Here's an example of how to detect labels in an image:

```
const vision = require('@google-cloud/vision');

const client = new vision.ImageAnnotatorClient();

exports.detectLabels = functions.https.onRequest(async (req, res) => {

const filePath = req.query.filePath;

const [result] = await client.labelDetection(filePath);

const labels = result.labelAnnotations;

labels.forEach(label => console.log(label.description));

res.json(labels);

});
```

The function detectLabels takes an image file path as a query parameter, sends the image to the Cloud Vision API, and returns the detected labels as a JSON response. This can be further integrated with Firebase Firestore or Realtime Database to store and display labels within your app.

Utilizing Cloud Natural Language for Text Processing

GOOGLE CLOUD NATURAL Language provides tools for analyzing and understanding text. You can use it for sentiment analysis, entity recognition, and syntactic analysis, making it ideal for apps that handle user reviews, feedback, or any text-based content.

Step 1: Enable Cloud Natural Language API

IN THE GOOGLE CLOUD Console, enable the Cloud Natural Language API, then generate an API key and securely store it.

Step 2: Analyze Text with Firebase Cloud Functions

HERE'S AN EXAMPLE OF how to perform sentiment analysis on a piece of text:

```
const language = require('@google-cloud/language');

const client = new language.LanguageServiceClient();

exports.analyzeSentiment = functions.https.onRequest(async (req, res) => {

const text = req.query.text;

const [result] = await client.analyzeSentiment({document: {content: text, type: 'PLAIN_TEXT'}});

const sentiment = result.documentSentiment;

res.json({score: sentiment.score, magnitude: sentiment.magnitude});
```

```
});
```

This function analyzes the sentiment of the text passed in the query parameter. The response includes a score and magnitude, where the score indicates positivity or negativity, and the magnitude reflects the intensity of the sentiment.

Building a Unified Experience with GCP AI and Firebase

BY COMBINING FIREBASE and GCP's AI capabilities, you can create robust and intelligent applications that cater to diverse needs. Here's a high-level architecture for a Firebase app that uses multiple GCP AI services:

1. **Image Upload**: Users upload images via the Firebase app, which are stored in Firebase Storage.
2. **Label Detection with Cloud Vision**: A Firebase Cloud Function triggers the Cloud Vision API, retrieving labels and saving them to Firestore.
3. **Sentiment Analysis on User Comments**: User comments are analyzed using the Natural Language API, with sentiment scores stored in Firestore.
4. **AutoML Custom Model for Product Recommendations**: An AutoML model provides product recommendations based on user preferences, accessed via Cloud Functions.

This setup enables a seamless AI-powered user experience, with Firebase handling data storage, user authentication, and real-time updates, while GCP provides advanced AI processing.

Managing API Costs and Performance

USING GCP AI SERVICES alongside Firebase introduces additional considerations for managing API usage and costs. Google Cloud offers tools like Cloud Monitoring and Budget Alerts to help you keep track of costs associated with API calls. Additionally, you can optimize performance by:

- **Caching Results**: For frequently accessed data, store results in Firestore or Realtime Database.

- **Batch Processing**: Group multiple requests into a single API call, when possible, to minimize API usage.

- **Efficient Resource Use**: Use Firebase Functions to limit concurrent executions and prevent excessive API usage during high-traffic periods.

By monitoring and optimizing usage, you can provide advanced AI capabilities while maintaining cost efficiency.

In summary, GCP's AI services complement Firebase by offering scalable, production-ready machine learning capabilities that extend beyond Firebase ML Kit. Whether it's through AutoML for custom models, Cloud Vision for image analysis, or Cloud Natural Language for text processing, integrating these tools can significantly enhance the functionality and intelligence of Firebase apps.

Building Smart Applications with Firebase and GCP AI

BUILDING INTELLIGENT applications that can understand, interpret, and respond to user interactions requires the integration of advanced AI and machine learning services. Firebase, combined with Google Cloud Platform (GCP), provides a robust infrastructure for creating these smart applications. Firebase offers core app development tools like authentication, storage, and real-time databases, while GCP adds advanced AI capabilities such as AutoML, Cloud Vision, and Natural Language Processing. Together, they form a powerful ecosystem for developing intelligent, data-driven applications.

This section explores how to architect smart applications using Firebase and GCP AI services, detailing the essential components and strategies to make your app responsive and adaptive to user needs.

Designing a Smart App Architecture

THE FIRST STEP IN BUILDING a smart application is to design an architecture that effectively combines Firebase and GCP services. This involves selecting the right services for data storage, processing, and machine learning, while ensuring that these components are seamlessly integrated.

Key Components of a Smart App Architecture

1. **Firebase Authentication**: Securely authenticate users and manage user identity, with support for various sign-in methods, including email, Google, and social logins.
2. **Firestore or Realtime Database**: Store and sync user data in real-time, enabling responsive and interactive experiences.
3. **Firebase Storage**: Store and serve user-generated content, such as images or videos, with scalable cloud storage.
4. **GCP AI Services**: Use services like AutoML for custom

model training, Cloud Vision for image analysis, and Natural Language Processing for text analysis to add intelligence to the app.

5. **Firebase Cloud Functions**: Implement server-side logic to handle data processing, trigger AI services, and maintain a secure environment for backend operations.

6. **Firebase Analytics and Performance Monitoring**: Track user behavior, app performance, and optimize the app based on usage patterns.

THESE COMPONENTS WORK together to form a backend infrastructure that is scalable, secure, and capable of delivering intelligent responses in real-time.

Step-by-Step: Creating a Smart Image Processing App

TO ILLUSTRATE THE PROCESS of building a smart app, let's walk through an example application that uses image processing and analysis features. The app allows users to upload images, identifies objects within those images using GCP Cloud Vision, and provides relevant information back to the user.

Step 1: Set Up Firebase and GCP Projects

1. **Create a Firebase Project**: Go to the Firebase Console, add a new project, and configure Firebase Authentication, Firestore, and Storage.

2. **Set Up a GCP Project**: In the Google Cloud Console, create a project linked to your Firebase project, and enable the Cloud Vision API.

3. **Link Firebase to GCP**: In Firebase Console, go to "Project Settings" > "Integrations" and link the Firebase

project to the GCP project.

Step 2: Implement Image Upload with Firebase Storage

SET UP AN INTERFACE in your app where users can upload images. When an image is uploaded, store it in Firebase Storage. Here's an example of how to handle image uploads in an Android app:

```
// Assume imageUri is the URI of the selected image

StorageReference storageRef = FirebaseStorage.getInstance().getReference();

StorageReference imageRef = storageRef.child("images/" + UUID.randomUUID().toString());

imageRef.putFile(imageUri)

.addOnSuccessListener(taskSnapshot -> imageRef.getDownloadUrl()

.addOnSuccessListener(uri -> {

String imageUrl = uri.toString();

// Save imageUrl in Firestore or send it to Cloud Functions

}))

.addOnFailureListener(e -> Log.e("UploadError", "Failed to upload image: " + e.getMessage()));
```

This code uploads an image to Firebase Storage and retrieves the download URL, which can then be passed to other services or stored in Firestore.

Step 3: Analyze Uploaded Images with Cloud Vision

USE FIREBASE CLOUD Functions to invoke the Cloud Vision API on the uploaded image. This step involves setting up a Cloud Function that triggers whenever an image is uploaded to Firebase Storage.

Here's an example Cloud Function that processes an image with Cloud Vision:

```
const functions = require('firebase-functions');

const vision = require('@google-cloud/vision');

const admin = require('firebase-admin');

admin.initializeApp();

const visionClient = new vision.ImageAnnotatorClient();

exports.analyzeImage = functions.storage.object().onFinalize(async (object) => {

const filePath = object.name;

const bucketName = object.bucket;

const [result] = await visionClient.labelDetection(`gs://${bucketName}/${filePath}`);

const labels = result.labelAnnotations.map(label => label.description);

await admin.firestore().collection('images').add({

filePath: filePath,

labels: labels,
```

timestamp: admin.firestore.FieldValue.serverTimestamp()

});

console.log('Image labels:', labels);

});

This function listens for image uploads in Firebase Storage, sends the image to Cloud Vision, and saves the identified labels to Firestore.

Step 4: Display Image Labels in the App

AFTER PROCESSING THE image, retrieve the labels from Firestore and display them in the app's interface. Here's an example using Firestore on the client side:

FirebaseFirestore db = FirebaseFirestore.getInstance();

db.collection("images").document(imageId)

.get()

.addOnSuccessListener(documentSnapshot -> {

if (documentSnapshot.exists()) {

List<String> labels = (List<String>) documentSnapshot.get("labels");

// Display labels to the user

}

})

```
.addOnFailureListener(e -> Log.e("FirestoreError", "Failed to fetch
labels: " + e.getMessage()));
```

This snippet retrieves the labels associated with an image from Firestore, which can then be displayed in the app's user interface.

Using AutoML for Custom Classification

FOR MORE SPECIFIC USE cases, such as identifying products or categorizing images based on custom data, use Google AutoML to create a custom model. Here's how to implement AutoML into your app:

1. **Train a Custom Model**: Go to the AutoML section in Google Cloud Console, upload your dataset, and train a custom model.
2. **Deploy the Model**: After training, deploy the model as a REST API.
3. **Integrate the AutoML API with Firebase Cloud Functions**: Call the AutoML API from within Firebase Cloud Functions to classify images based on your custom model.

Here's an example of how to call the AutoML model in a Cloud Function:

```
const { PredictionServiceClient } = require('@google-cloud/automl').v1;

const client = new PredictionServiceClient();

exports.classifyCustomImage = functions.https.onRequest(async (req, res) => {

const projectId = 'your-project-id';
```

```
const modelId = 'your-model-id';

const imageContent = req.body.image; // Assume image is sent in
base64 format

const payload = {

image: { imageBytes: imageContent }

};

const [response] = await client.predict({

name: client.modelPath(projectId, 'us-central1', modelId),

payload: payload

});

const results = response.payload.map(label => label.displayName);

res.json({ labels: results });

});
```

Adding Natural Language Processing for User-Generated Content

TO ENHANCE YOUR APP'S interactivity, add Natural Language Processing (NLP) features that analyze user-generated content, such as comments or reviews. Google Cloud Natural Language can perform sentiment analysis, entity recognition, and syntax analysis.

Example: Sentiment Analysis on User Comments

HERE'S HOW TO USE GOOGLE Cloud Natural Language for sentiment analysis:

1. **Enable the Cloud Natural Language API** in Google Cloud Console.

Set Up a Cloud Function to analyze sentiment in user comments:

```
const language = require('@google-cloud/language');

const languageClient = new language.LanguageServiceClient();

exports.analyzeCommentSentiment = functions.https.onRequest(async (req, res) => {

const text = req.body.text;

const document = {

content: text,

type: 'PLAIN_TEXT'

};

const [result] = await languageClient.analyzeSentiment({ document });

const sentiment = result.documentSentiment;

res.json({ score: sentiment.score, magnitude: sentiment.magnitude });

});
```

1.

2. **Store Results in Firestore** and display them in the app's interface to provide feedback to users on the sentiment of their comments.

Optimizing and Monitoring App Performance

FIREBASE PERFORMANCE Monitoring and GCP's Cloud Monitoring tools can help track app performance, diagnose bottlenecks, and ensure a smooth user experience. Regularly monitor and optimize the following aspects:

- **Latency of Cloud Functions**: Measure and minimize the response time of Cloud Functions, particularly those that call external APIs.

- **Resource Usage**: Monitor API call usage, and set budgets in Google Cloud Console to control costs.

- **App Stability**: Use Firebase Crashlytics to identify and resolve issues, ensuring high app reliability.

Conclusion

BUILDING A SMART APPLICATION with Firebase and GCP AI services enables you to deliver advanced, user-centric features powered by artificial intelligence. This integration provides robust backend support and scalable AI capabilities, making it possible to create interactive and intelligent apps that adapt to user needs in real-time. By leveraging Firebase's development tools alongside GCP's AI offerings, you can build applications that not only meet but exceed user expectations.

Case Study: AI-Driven Mobile App Using Firebase and GCP

THIS CASE STUDY EXPLORES the development of an AI-driven mobile application utilizing Firebase and Google Cloud Platform (GCP) services. The app is designed to help users identify plant species by analyzing images uploaded from their mobile devices. By combining Firebase's app development and backend services with GCP's advanced machine learning tools, the app provides real-time, accurate plant identification, along with insights into the characteristics and care requirements of each plant.

Overview of the Application

THE APPLICATION OFFERS the following core features:

- **Image Upload and Processing**: Users can upload photos of plants for identification. The images are stored in Firebase Storage and analyzed using GCP's Cloud Vision and AutoML services.

- **Real-Time Identification and Feedback**: Leveraging AutoML for a custom-trained model, the app identifies plant species and provides relevant information in real-time.

- **Data Storage and Retrieval**: Firebase Firestore stores user data, including previously identified plants, user notes, and preferences.

- **User Authentication**: Firebase Authentication enables secure access to the app with various sign-in options.

● **Insights and Analytics**: Firebase Analytics tracks user interactions, providing insights into app usage patterns and popular plant species.

Architecture and Workflow

THE APP'S ARCHITECTURE consists of the following components:

1. **Frontend (Mobile Application)**: The mobile app, built with React Native, provides an interface for users to upload images, view identification results, and explore plant details.
2. **Firebase Backend**: Firebase handles user authentication, image storage, and real-time database management.
3. **GCP AI Services**: Cloud Vision API performs initial image analysis, while a custom AutoML model is used for specific plant identification.
4. **Cloud Functions**: Firebase Cloud Functions act as the glue, linking Firebase services to GCP AI services, managing workflows, and handling asynchronous tasks.

Workflow Steps

1. **Image Upload**: Users take a photo of a plant, which is uploaded to Firebase Storage.
2. **Cloud Function Trigger**: An image upload triggers a Firebase Cloud Function, which retrieves the image and sends it to Cloud Vision for general analysis.
3. **Initial Processing with Cloud Vision**: Cloud Vision API analyzes the image and returns general labels, such as "plant" or "leaf," confirming that the image is suitable for further processing.

4. **Custom Identification with AutoML**: If the image is confirmed as a plant, the Cloud Function sends it to AutoML, which is trained on a dataset of plant species to provide detailed identification.
5. **Results Storage and Notification**: Identification results are stored in Firestore, and the user receives a notification with the results.
6. **Display Results and Insights**: The app displays the plant name, characteristics, care instructions, and a record in the user's history.

Implementing the App with Firebase and GCP AI

Step 1: Set Up Firebase Services

1. **Firebase Project Creation**: Create a project in Firebase Console, enabling Firebase Authentication, Firestore, and Storage.

2. **Authentication Configuration**: Set up Firebase Authentication to support sign-in methods such as Google Sign-In, email, and anonymous authentication.

3. **Firestore Database Setup**: Define Firestore collections to store user data and plant identification results. Here's a basic schema:

○ users: Stores user profile data, preferences, and identification history.

○ plants: Stores plant data, including species, care tips, and scientific names.

○ identifications: Stores each identification request, linking to user IDs and including image URLs and identification results.

4. **Storage Setup**: Create a Firebase Storage bucket to handle image uploads.

Step 2: Configure Cloud Vision and AutoML

1. **Enable Cloud Vision API**: In the Google Cloud Console, enable the Cloud Vision API and generate an API key.
2. **AutoML Dataset Preparation**: Prepare a labeled dataset of plant species images and upload it to AutoML Vision. Train a custom model that recognizes common plants and provides species-level identification.
3. **AutoML Model Deployment**: Deploy the trained AutoML model and note the model ID for API access.

Step 3: Implement Cloud Functions for Image Processing

USE FIREBASE CLOUD Functions to link Firebase Storage with GCP AI services. Below is an example function that handles the image upload and invokes Cloud Vision and AutoML:

```
const functions = require('firebase-functions');

const vision = require('@google-cloud/vision');

const {PredictionServiceClient} = require('@google-cloud/automl').v1;

const admin = require('firebase-admin');
```

```javascript
admin.initializeApp();

const visionClient = new vision.ImageAnnotatorClient();

const predictionClient = new PredictionServiceClient();

exports.identifyPlant                                    =
functions.storage.object().onFinalize(async (object) => {

const filePath = object.name;

const bucket = object.bucket;

const imageUri = `gs://${bucket}/${filePath}`;

// Step 1: Initial Analysis with Cloud Vision

const              [visionResult]              =              await
visionClient.labelDetection(imageUri);

const labels = visionResult.labelAnnotations.map(label =>
label.description);

if (!labels.includes('plant')) {

console.log('Image does not contain a plant');

return null;

}

// Step 2: Custom Identification with AutoML

const projectId = 'your-project-id';

const modelId = 'your-automl-model-id';

const [automlResult] = await predictionClient.predict({
```

```
    name:    predictionClient.modelPath(projectId,    'us-central1',
modelId),

    payload: { image: { imageUri: imageUri } }

  });

  const plant = automlResult.payload[0].displayName;

  const confidence = automlResult.payload[0].classification.score;

  // Step 3: Save Results to Firestore

  await admin.firestore().collection('identifications').add({

    plant: plant,

    confidence: confidence,

    timestamp: admin.firestore.FieldValue.serverTimestamp(),

    imageUrl: imageUri,

    user: object.metadata.userId

  });

  console.log(`Identified    plant:    ${plant}    with    confidence
${confidence}`);

});
```

This function uses Cloud Vision to confirm that the image contains a plant, then invokes AutoML for detailed species identification. The results are stored in Firestore for access within the app.

Step 4: Building the Mobile Interface

THE MOBILE APP INTERFACE, built with React Native, allows users to upload images and view results. Here's a basic example of how to upload images to Firebase Storage from the app:

```
import storage from '@react-native-firebase/storage';

import firestore from '@react-native-firebase/firestore';

const uploadImage = async (uri, userId) => {

const filename = uri.substring(uri.lastIndexOf('/') + 1);

const storageRef = storage().ref(`plants/${filename}`);

await storageRef.putFile(uri);

const downloadURL = await storageRef.getDownloadURL();

await firestore().collection('uploads').add({

imageUrl: downloadURL,

userId: userId,

timestamp: firestore.FieldValue.serverTimestamp()

});

console.log('Image uploaded successfully');

};
```

This function uploads an image to Firebase Storage and stores the download URL in Firestore.

Leveraging Firebase Analytics for Insights

FIREBASE ANALYTICS allows you to track user interactions and understand how they use the app. For example, you can track which plant species are identified most frequently or how often users return to the app. This data can be useful for refining the app and understanding user behavior.

Tracking Key Events

SET UP EVENT TRACKING to capture actions like image uploads, successful identifications, and app opens. Here's how you might implement event tracking in React Native:

import analytics from '@react-native-firebase/analytics';

const logUploadEvent = async (species, confidence) => {

await analytics().logEvent('plant_identified', {

species: species,

confidence: confidence

});

console.log('Identification event logged');

};

This event logs details of each plant identification, which you can later analyze to improve the app.

Optimizing for Performance and Scalability

TO ENSURE THE APP PERFORMS well under high traffic, implement optimization techniques such as:

- **Using Firebase Realtime Database or Firestore for efficient data retrieval**, with indexing for fast lookups.

- **Leveraging Firestore's offline capabilities** to provide a seamless experience even when users are offline.

- **Batching image processing tasks** in Cloud Functions to handle multiple concurrent requests efficiently.

- **Monitoring resource usage** with GCP's Cloud Monitoring tools and setting budgets to control costs.

Conclusion

THIS CASE STUDY DEMONSTRATES how to build a sophisticated, AI-driven mobile app using Firebase and GCP AI services. By combining Firebase's backend tools with GCP's powerful machine learning capabilities, you can create responsive, intelligent applications that deliver real-time insights and a personalized experience for users. Whether for plant identification or other use cases, Firebase and GCP provide the flexibility, scalability, and tools necessary to build smart applications that meet the demands of modern users.

Chapter 10: Best Practices for Firebase and GCP Integration

Efficient Resource Management in Firebase and GCP

EFFICIENT RESOURCE management is essential for optimizing performance, reducing costs, and ensuring the scalability of your Firebase and GCP projects. In this section, we'll explore best practices for managing resources effectively across Firebase and GCP. We'll cover project organization, resource grouping, billing optimization, monitoring, and automation techniques. By following these practices, you can maintain a well-organized and cost-effective infrastructure while maximizing the potential of Firebase and GCP services.

1. Organizing Projects and Resources

WHEN WORKING WITH FIREBASE and GCP, it's crucial to keep your projects and resources organized. By setting up a clear organizational structure from the start, you can streamline management and avoid potential confusion as your project scales. Here are some strategies for organizing projects and resources effectively:

- **Use Descriptive Naming Conventions**: Clearly label projects, resources, and components using names that indicate their purpose, environment (development, staging, production), and team or department responsible. For example, a Firestore database for the production environment could be named prod-firestore-db, while a Firebase project for testing might be called test-firebase-app.

• **Leverage Google Cloud Resource Hierarchy**: GCP provides a resource hierarchy that includes organizations, folders, and projects. Utilize this structure to organize your resources based on business units, teams, or project types. For example, you could create folders for each department (e.g., Marketing, Engineering) and subfolders for specific projects or environments within those departments.

• **Use Labels for Easy Filtering**: Labels are key-value pairs that you can attach to resources for identification and organization. Apply labels like environment:production or team:frontend to resources, making it easier to filter and manage them across Firebase and GCP. These labels are also useful when generating reports or visualizing resource usage.

• **Implement Separate Projects for Different Environments**: Keeping development, staging, and production environments in separate projects can help mitigate risks and streamline testing and deployment. This separation allows you to isolate environments and apply specific access controls, budgets, and monitoring policies to each environment.

2. Managing Budgets and Billing

EFFECTIVE BUDGET MANAGEMENT is critical to avoid unexpected costs and to make the most of your resources. Firebase and GCP provide several tools and features that help you track and control your spending:

- **Set Up Budget Alerts**: In Google Cloud Console, you can set up budgets and configure alerts to notify you when spending reaches a specified threshold. This way, you can proactively manage costs and avoid overspending. For example, you can configure alerts to notify you when you reach 50%, 80%, or 100% of your monthly budget.

- **Enable Cost Management Dashboards**: GCP provides cost management dashboards that offer insights into spending patterns, cost trends, and resource usage. Use these dashboards to analyze your spending, identify cost-saving opportunities, and allocate resources more efficiently.

- **Use Firebase Spark Plan for Development**: For early-stage development or testing, consider using Firebase's Spark Plan, which offers free-tier services for many Firebase features. This plan allows you to test and build without incurring charges. As you move to production, you can switch to a paid plan to accommodate larger resource needs.

- **Analyze Cost Reports Regularly**: Regularly review cost reports to understand how your resources are being used and where costs are incurred. This analysis can reveal areas where resources are underutilized or over-provisioned, allowing you to adjust accordingly. GCP offers detailed reports, and you can filter by services, projects, or labels for deeper insights.

- **Automate Resource Shutdown for Cost Control**: Set up automation scripts to shut down non-essential resources during off-peak hours. For example, you can configure Google Cloud Functions to automatically disable development servers outside of business hours, reducing costs associated with idle resources.

3. Monitoring and Logging

MONITORING AND LOGGING are essential for maintaining the health of your applications, ensuring performance, and troubleshooting issues. Firebase and GCP offer a variety of tools to facilitate monitoring and logging across your infrastructure:

- **Use Firebase Crashlytics for Crash Reporting**: Firebase Crashlytics is a powerful tool for monitoring app crashes and understanding their causes. Integrate Crashlytics into your mobile apps to automatically capture crash data, prioritize issues, and resolve problems quickly.

- **Enable Google Cloud Monitoring**: Google Cloud Monitoring provides a comprehensive suite of tools for monitoring the health and performance of your resources. Set up dashboards, create alerts, and view metrics for services like Firestore, Cloud Functions, and more. Use predefined or custom metrics to gain insights into resource utilization and application performance.

- **Leverage Firebase Performance Monitoring for Real-Time Insights**: Firebase Performance Monitoring tracks key metrics such as app startup time, network latency, and resource loading times. This real-time data helps you identify performance bottlenecks and optimize your app's responsiveness.

• **Centralize Logs with Google Cloud Logging**: Google Cloud Logging allows you to aggregate and manage logs from various services in a single place. Configure logging for Firebase services and GCP resources, and use log-based metrics to trigger alerts or automate responses to specific conditions.

• **Set Up Alerting for Critical Issues**: Configure alert policies for critical events, such as high error rates, latency spikes, or unexpected cost increases. Alerts can be sent to email, Slack, or other communication channels, enabling you to respond to issues quickly and minimize their impact.

4. Implementing Access Controls and Security

SECURITY IS A TOP PRIORITY when working with cloud services. Firebase and GCP offer several tools and features to secure your resources and protect sensitive data:

• **Use IAM Roles and Permissions**: Google Cloud Identity and Access Management (IAM) allows you to define roles and assign permissions to users, groups, or service accounts. Implement the principle of least privilege by granting only the necessary permissions for each role, reducing the risk of unauthorized access.

• **Enable Firebase App Check for API Protection**: Firebase App Check helps protect your backend resources from abuse by verifying that requests come from your app. Enable App Check to validate API requests and ensure they originate from authenticated sources, preventing unauthorized access.

• **Configure Firebase Authentication and Security Rules**: Use Firebase Authentication to manage user access and Firebase Security Rules to enforce data access policies. For example, you can write rules to allow only authenticated users to access specific Firestore collections or to restrict access based on user roles.

• **Encrypt Data at Rest and in Transit**: GCP offers encryption for data at rest by default, but you can also manage your own encryption keys using Google Cloud Key Management Service (KMS). Ensure data is encrypted in transit by using HTTPS for all communication between your app and Firebase or GCP services.

• **Monitor IAM Activity with Cloud Audit Logs**: Cloud Audit Logs provide a detailed record of IAM activity, such as login attempts, resource access, and permission changes. Regularly review these logs to detect unusual behavior and ensure compliance with security policies.

5. Automating Deployment and CI/CD Pipelines

AUTOMATING DEPLOYMENT and continuous integration/ continuous delivery (CI/CD) pipelines can significantly improve your development workflow and reduce manual errors. Firebase and GCP offer several tools and integrations to streamline these processes:

- **Set Up Firebase Hosting with GitHub Integration**: Firebase Hosting supports GitHub integration, allowing you to automatically deploy web apps when changes are pushed to your repository. Set up this integration to automate deployment workflows and ensure consistency across environments.

- **Use Cloud Build for CI/CD Pipelines**: Google Cloud Build is a fully managed CI/CD platform that enables you to build, test, and deploy applications on GCP. Configure Cloud Build to automate testing and deployment tasks, such as building Docker images, deploying to App Engine, or triggering Firebase Functions.

- **Incorporate Automated Testing with Firebase Test Lab**: Firebase Test Lab provides a cloud-based infrastructure for testing mobile apps on various devices and configurations. Integrate Test Lab into your CI/CD pipeline to automate testing, identify issues early, and improve app quality.

- **Deploy Configurations as Code with Terraform**: Use Terraform to manage and deploy GCP infrastructure as code. This approach allows you to version control your infrastructure, automate deployments, and apply changes consistently across environments.

- **Monitor Deployment Health with Google Cloud Operations**: After deployment, monitor the health of your application with Google Cloud Operations. Set up automated monitoring and alerting to detect issues in real-time, such as failed deployments or performance degradation, ensuring timely responses to any disruptions.

By following these best practices for resource management, security, and automation, you can optimize your Firebase and GCP projects for performance, scalability, and cost-efficiency. Implementing these strategies will help you build a robust and resilient infrastructure that can adapt to changing demands and evolving project requirements.

Security Best Practices for Firebase and GCP Applications

SECURITY IS A CRITICAL aspect of any application, and Firebase and Google Cloud Platform (GCP) provide a robust set of tools to protect your applications, data, and users. This section explores essential security practices that you should implement when working with Firebase and GCP. We'll cover authentication, access control, data protection, and vulnerability management, as well as best practices for securing backend services, APIs, and sensitive data.

1. Securing User Authentication and Identity Management

MANAGING USER IDENTITIES securely is a cornerstone of application security. Firebase Authentication simplifies identity management while offering various methods to protect user accounts:

Implement Multi-Factor Authentication (MFA): MFA adds an extra layer of security by requiring users to verify their identity through an additional factor beyond their password. Firebase

Authentication supports MFA with SMS-based verification, and you can configure this as an optional or mandatory step for your users. For example:

```
const auth = firebase.auth();

auth.signInWithPhoneNumber(phoneNumber, appVerifier)

.then((confirmationResult) => {

// Prompt user to enter the verification code

}).catch((error) => {

console.error("Error during sign-in:", error);

});
```

●

Enable Email Verification: Requiring email verification can prevent unauthorized access and spam. Firebase Authentication allows you to send email verification links to users upon registration. This ensures that only users with valid email addresses can access your application.

```
auth.currentUser.sendEmailVerification()

.then(() => {

console.log("Verification email sent.");

}).catch((error) => {

console.error("Error sending verification email:", error);

});
```

-

  - **Utilize Identity Platform for Advanced Identity Management**: For more complex use cases, consider leveraging Identity Platform (a managed identity service on GCP) for enhanced security features, such as single sign-on (SSO), federated identity management, and advanced logging capabilities.

2. Managing Access Control with IAM and Firebase Security Rules

ACCESS CONTROL IS FUNDAMENTAL to restricting unauthorized access and enforcing security policies within your applications. Firebase and GCP provide various access control mechanisms to help you define and enforce security policies:

Define IAM Roles and Permissions: Google Cloud IAM allows you to assign roles to users, groups, and service accounts based on the principle of least privilege. Carefully define roles to grant the minimum necessary permissions. For example, you can create a custom role with specific permissions to access Firestore but restrict access to Cloud Storage.

json

Copy code

```
{

"roleId": "custom.firestoreViewer",

"includedPermissions": [

"datastore.entities.get",
```

"datastore.entities.list"

]

}

•

Implement Firebase Security Rules for Data Access: Firebase Security Rules control access to Firestore, Realtime Database, and Storage. These rules are evaluated at the request level, providing fine-grained control over data access based on the user's authentication status and data context. For example, the following rule restricts access to Firestore documents based on the user's UID:

```
SERVICE CLOUD.FIRESTORE {

match /databases/{database}/documents {

match /users/{userId} {

allow read, write: if request.auth != null && request.auth.uid == userId;

}

}

}
```

•

- **Audit IAM Policies Regularly**: Regularly review and audit IAM policies and Firebase Security Rules to ensure they adhere to your security requirements. Remove any unused permissions or roles and check for overly permissive policies that may pose security risks.

3. Data Protection and Encryption

PROTECTING SENSITIVE data is essential for maintaining user trust and complying with data protection regulations. Firebase and GCP offer robust encryption and data protection features to safeguard data at rest and in transit:

- **Enable Server-Side Encryption**: GCP automatically encrypts data at rest, but you can also manage encryption keys using Google Cloud Key Management Service (KMS) for greater control. This allows you to rotate, disable, or destroy keys as needed to comply with security policies.

- **Use HTTPS for Data in Transit**: Ensure that all data transmitted between your app, Firebase, and GCP services is encrypted using HTTPS. Firebase Hosting automatically provides HTTPS for all hosted content, and you can enforce HTTPS for other services by configuring Firebase Security Rules and GCP load balancers.

Encrypt Sensitive Data Before Storing: For additional protection, consider encrypting sensitive data on the client side before storing it in Firestore or Cloud Storage. You can use encryption libraries to encrypt data with a key that is only accessible within the client environment. Here's an example using the Web Crypto API:

```
const encryptData = async (data, key) => {
```

```
const encodedData = new TextEncoder().encode(data);

const encryptedData = await crypto.subtle.encrypt(

{ name: "AES-GCM", iv: iv },

key,

encodedData

);

return encryptedData;

};
```

-

- **Anonymize or Pseudonymize Personal Data**: To reduce the risk associated with data breaches, anonymize or pseudonymize personally identifiable information (PII) before storing it. Techniques like hashing, tokenization, and pseudonymization can help you obscure data and comply with privacy regulations.

4. Securing Backend Services and APIs

PROTECTING BACKEND services and APIs is critical for preventing unauthorized access, data leaks, and denial-of-service attacks. Firebase and GCP offer tools for securing your backend infrastructure:

- **Use Firebase App Check to Validate API Requests**: Firebase App Check ensures that only requests from your verified app can access your Firebase backend services. Enable App Check for services like Firestore,

Realtime Database, and Cloud Functions to prevent unauthorized access.

• **Limit API Access with Google Cloud Endpoints**: Google Cloud Endpoints provides API management and security features, such as rate limiting, API keys, and authentication. Use Cloud Endpoints to secure GCP APIs and control access based on user roles and permissions.

• **Implement Quotas and Rate Limiting**: Quotas and rate limiting help protect your backend services from abuse and prevent excessive resource consumption. Configure Firebase and GCP quotas to restrict usage and avoid spikes in traffic that could impact service availability.

• **Monitor and Mitigate DDoS Attacks**: Use Google Cloud Armor to protect your backend services from distributed denial-of-service (DDoS) attacks. Cloud Armor provides customizable security policies to filter incoming traffic based on IP addresses, geolocation, and other factors.

5. Regularly Testing and Updating Security Measures

MAINTAINING SECURITY requires ongoing vigilance, testing, and updates. Incorporate regular security assessments and best practices into your development process:

• **Conduct Regular Security Audits and Vulnerability Scans**: Perform regular security audits and vulnerability scans on your Firebase and GCP infrastructure to identify potential risks. Use tools like Firebase Test Lab for testing mobile app security and Google Cloud Security Command Center for GCP threat detection and analysis.

● **Apply Security Patches and Updates**: Stay informed about security updates and patches for Firebase and GCP services. Apply updates promptly to mitigate vulnerabilities and ensure your infrastructure is protected against emerging threats.

● **Use Penetration Testing to Identify Weaknesses**: Conduct penetration testing to simulate attacks on your application and identify potential security weaknesses. GCP's Vulnerability Management service provides resources and guidance for conducting effective penetration tests.

● **Implement Continuous Security Monitoring**: Leverage Google Cloud's security monitoring tools to track security events in real-time. Set up alerts for suspicious activities, such as unauthorized access attempts or unusual data access patterns, to respond quickly to potential threats.

● **Train Your Development Team on Security Best Practices**: Security is a shared responsibility, and training your development team on security best practices can help reduce the risk of vulnerabilities. Encourage practices like secure coding, regular code reviews, and adherence to security policies.

By following these security best practices, you can protect your Firebase and GCP applications from unauthorized access, data breaches, and other security threats. Implementing robust authentication, access control, encryption, and regular security assessments will help you maintain a secure and trustworthy application environment for your users.

Scaling Applications Seamlessly

SCALING APPLICATIONS is a fundamental aspect of ensuring performance and reliability as user demand grows. Firebase and Google Cloud Platform (GCP) offer a suite of tools and services that make scaling both manageable and cost-effective. This section covers the principles and strategies necessary for seamless scaling, including infrastructure planning, optimizing databases, handling traffic spikes, leveraging serverless computing, and automating scaling processes.

1. Understanding Horizontal vs. Vertical Scaling

SCALING CAN BE CATEGORIZED into two main approaches: horizontal scaling (scaling out) and vertical scaling (scaling up). Understanding the difference between these methods is crucial for making informed decisions about scaling strategies:

- **Horizontal Scaling**: This approach involves adding more instances or nodes to distribute the load across multiple machines. Firebase and GCP services, like Google Cloud Functions and Firestore, are inherently designed for horizontal scaling, allowing you to handle increased traffic without changing the infrastructure's complexity.

- **Vertical Scaling**: Vertical scaling refers to increasing the capacity of an individual instance or node, such as upgrading to a machine with more CPU, RAM, or storage. While vertical scaling can be effective for certain workloads, it has limitations and may lead to diminishing returns. Firebase generally supports horizontal scaling, but GCP services like Google Compute Engine can be scaled vertically if needed.

- **Choosing the Right Approach**: In most cases, horizontal scaling is preferable due to its flexibility and potential to handle larger workloads. However, vertical scaling can be useful for stateful applications or scenarios where minimizing latency is critical.

2. Planning for Scalability in Firebase and GCP

PROPER PLANNING IS essential to ensure scalability. By designing with scalability in mind from the beginning, you can avoid bottlenecks and accommodate growth with minimal disruptions:

- **Design with Microservices Architecture**: Breaking your application into smaller, independent services allows you to scale specific components without affecting the entire system. For example, you could separate authentication, data processing, and notification services into individual Firebase Cloud Functions or GCP Cloud Run services, scaling each independently based on demand.

Use a Global Load Balancer: Google Cloud Load Balancer provides a global, managed load-balancing solution that distributes traffic across multiple instances and regions. By setting up a load balancer, you can ensure high availability and reduce latency by directing users to the nearest server.

- name: my-load-balancer

type: global

backend_service: my-backend-service

●

- **Plan for Data Partitioning and Sharding**: For large-scale applications, consider partitioning or sharding your databases to distribute the load. Firestore, for example, is optimized for high-scale workloads, but you can further improve performance by designing your data schema to minimize hotspots. Use composite indexes and query optimizations to improve query performance.

3. Optimizing Databases for Scalability

DATABASES ARE OFTEN a key bottleneck in scaling applications. Firebase Firestore and other GCP databases offer features that enable efficient data management and scalable operations:

- **Use Firestore's Serverless Architecture**: Firestore automatically scales based on the number of requests, making it an excellent choice for applications with fluctuating workloads. Firestore's serverless nature eliminates the need to provision servers, and it can handle high throughput with sub-second latency.

- **Implement Data Caching**: Caching frequently accessed data can reduce database load and improve response times. Use Firebase's in-memory caching or integrate with services like Redis on GCP to store transient data. Implementing a caching layer helps alleviate pressure on the database and speeds up data retrieval.

Leverage Firestore's Batched Writes and Transactions: For operations that involve multiple reads or writes, use batched writes or transactions to optimize performance. Firestore transactions allow you to perform atomic operations on multiple documents, ensuring data consistency while minimizing the number of round trips.

```javascript
const db = firebase.firestore();

const batch = db.batch();

const docRef1 = db.collection('users').doc('user1');

const docRef2 = db.collection('users').doc('user2');

batch.update(docRef1, { online: true });

batch.update(docRef2, { online: false });

batch.commit().then(() => {

console.log("Batch write completed");

});
```

-

- **Optimize Query Performance with Indexes**: Firestore supports both single-field and composite indexes. By indexing frequently queried fields, you can significantly improve query performance. Monitor and analyze query execution times using Firebase Performance Monitoring to identify queries that need optimization.

4. Handling Traffic Spikes with Auto-Scaling

TRAFFIC SPIKES CAN occur due to events like marketing campaigns, seasonal peaks, or sudden surges in user activity. Auto-scaling allows your application to automatically adjust to these fluctuations:

- **Use Cloud Functions for Serverless Scaling**: Firebase Cloud Functions automatically scale based on the number of incoming requests, making them ideal for handling unpredictable workloads. By offloading tasks to Cloud Functions, you can distribute the load and avoid overwhelming your backend services.

Configure Compute Engine Auto-Scaling: For services running on Google Compute Engine, you can enable auto-scaling to automatically add or remove VM instances based on CPU utilization, memory usage, or other custom metrics. This helps maintain performance and reduce costs by adjusting resources in real-time.

resources:

- type: compute.googleapis.com/InstanceGroupManager

properties:

autoScalingPolicy:

minNumReplicas: 1

maxNumReplicas: 10

coolDownPeriodSec: 60

cpuUtilization:

utilizationTarget: 0.6

●

- **Implement Queue-Based Load Management**: For tasks that can be processed asynchronously, use Pub/Sub and Cloud Tasks to manage workloads. By offloading tasks to a queue, you can control the rate at which tasks are processed, allowing your system to handle high loads without being overwhelmed.

5. Leveraging Serverless Computing for Scalability

SERVERLESS COMPUTING abstracts away the underlying infrastructure, allowing you to focus on application logic while scaling automatically to meet demand. Firebase and GCP offer several serverless solutions that can help you scale effortlessly:

- **Deploy Stateless Services with Cloud Run**: Cloud Run is a fully managed compute environment that supports containers. It scales automatically and can handle stateless workloads, such as microservices or API endpoints, which makes it ideal for applications with unpredictable traffic.

- **Use Firebase Hosting for Web Applications**: Firebase Hosting provides a global content delivery network (CDN) that caches and serves static content, such as HTML, CSS, and JavaScript, with low latency. By leveraging Firebase Hosting, you can scale your web application globally without worrying about infrastructure management.

- **Combine Cloud Functions with Cloud Pub/Sub**: For event-driven architectures, use Cloud Functions in combination with Cloud Pub/Sub to handle asynchronous tasks and scale based on events. Pub/Sub provides reliable message delivery and enables you to build loosely coupled systems that can scale independently.

6. Automating Scaling with Infrastructure as Code (IaC)

INFRASTRUCTURE AS CODE (IaC) allows you to automate and version control your scaling infrastructure. By defining resources and configurations in code, you can replicate, modify, and manage your infrastructure more efficiently:

Use Terraform for Declarative Infrastructure Management: Terraform is a popular IaC tool that enables you to define and provision GCP resources using a declarative syntax. By storing infrastructure definitions in version control, you can easily replicate and scale your environment across regions or accounts.

```
resource "google_compute_instance" "web_server" {

name = "web-server"

machine_type = "e2-medium"
```

```
...

}
```

●

- **Automate Deployment with Cloud Deployment Manager**: Google Cloud Deployment Manager allows you to define and deploy GCP resources using YAML configuration files. Use Deployment Manager to automate scaling, manage configurations, and ensure consistency across environments.

- **Integrate CI/CD Pipelines for Automated Scaling Adjustments**: Set up CI/CD pipelines with Cloud Build to automate deployment processes, such as adding new instances or adjusting auto-scaling settings. By incorporating automated testing and monitoring, you can ensure that your scaling adjustments are effective and do not introduce regressions.

7. Monitoring and Observability for Scalable Applications

MONITORING AND OBSERVABILITY are essential for managing scalable applications. Firebase and GCP provide various tools to track performance metrics, detect anomalies, and optimize scaling configurations:

- **Use Google Cloud Monitoring for Real-Time Insights**: Google Cloud Monitoring collects metrics from your infrastructure and provides alerts based on custom thresholds. Set up dashboards to monitor CPU usage, memory consumption, and request latency, and configure alerts to notify you of any unusual activity.

- **Implement Log-Based Metrics with Cloud Logging**: Cloud Logging enables you to create metrics based on log data. Use these metrics to trigger scaling actions or generate alerts. For example, you can create a metric based on error logs to detect when an application component is experiencing issues and scale resources accordingly.

- **Monitor User Experience with Firebase Performance Monitoring**: Firebase Performance Monitoring provides insights into app performance from the user's perspective. Track metrics like app startup time, network latency, and screen rendering times to identify areas for optimization.

- **Analyze Metrics with BigQuery for In-Depth Insights**: Export monitoring data to BigQuery to perform advanced analytics and identify long-term trends. This allows you to make data-driven decisions about scaling strategies and optimize resource allocation.

By adopting these scaling best practices, you can build applications that handle large volumes of traffic seamlessly, maintain performance during peak times, and scale efficiently as demand fluctuates. Leveraging the built-in scalability of Firebase and GCP, combined with effective planning, automation, and monitoring, ensures that your applications are resilient, cost-effective, and capable of supporting a growing user base.

CI/CD Pipelines for Firebase and GCP Projects

CONTINUOUS INTEGRATION and Continuous Deployment (CI/CD) pipelines are essential for modern development workflows, enabling rapid iteration, automated testing, and streamlined deployment processes. Firebase and Google Cloud Platform (GCP) offer a robust set of tools and services for implementing CI/CD pipelines that support both development and production environments. In this section, we will explore how to build and optimize CI/CD pipelines for Firebase and GCP, covering automated builds, testing, deployment strategies, and best practices for efficient pipeline management.

1. Understanding CI/CD Pipelines

A CI/CD PIPELINE IS a series of automated steps that manage the development, testing, and deployment of code changes. The primary goals of CI/CD pipelines are to ensure code quality, reduce manual effort, and enable rapid deployment with minimal risk.

- **Continuous Integration (CI)**: CI is the process of automatically integrating code changes into a shared repository multiple times a day. This typically includes running automated tests to catch issues early, maintaining code quality, and merging changes without disrupting the main codebase.

- **Continuous Deployment (CD)**: CD involves automatically deploying code changes to production or staging environments after successful integration and testing. This ensures that new features, bug fixes, and updates reach users as quickly as possible.

● **Benefits of CI/CD Pipelines**: Implementing CI/CD pipelines accelerates development cycles, reduces time to market, and ensures that code changes are thoroughly tested and deployed with minimal risk. Automation also reduces the potential for human error and provides a repeatable process that can scale with your team.

2. Setting Up CI/CD Pipelines with Firebase and Cloud Build

FIREBASE INTEGRATES seamlessly with Google Cloud Build, a fully managed CI/CD service that automates builds, tests, and deployments. Here's how to set up a CI/CD pipeline with Firebase and Cloud Build:

Step 1: Set Up Cloud Build: Start by enabling Cloud Build in your GCP project. You can configure Cloud Build to trigger pipelines based on code changes in a Git repository, such as GitHub, Bitbucket, or Google Cloud Source Repositories.

steps:

- name: 'gcr.io/cloud-builders/npm'

args: ['install']

- name: 'gcr.io/cloud-builders/npm'

args: ['test']

- name: 'gcr.io/cloud-builders/gcloud'

args: ['firebase', 'deploy', '—only', 'hosting']

● The above configuration defines a basic Cloud Build pipeline that installs dependencies, runs tests, and deploys a Firebase project.

● **Step 2: Configure Build Triggers**: Set up triggers to automatically initiate builds based on specific events, such as commits to the main branch. This ensures that all code changes are tested and deployed without manual intervention.

● **Step 3: Use Firebase CLI for Deployment**: Integrate the Firebase CLI into your Cloud Build pipeline to deploy Firebase services, such as Firestore, Authentication, and Hosting. You can specify which Firebase features to deploy using the—only flag.

● **Step 4: Set Up Environment Variables**: Use Cloud Build's environment variables to store sensitive information, such as API keys, and environment-specific configurations. This keeps your pipeline secure and ensures consistent deployments across environments.

3. Automated Testing in CI/CD Pipelines

AUTOMATED TESTING IS a crucial component of CI/CD pipelines, as it ensures code quality and prevents issues from reaching production. Firebase and GCP provide several tools for implementing automated testing in your pipelines:

Unit Testing with Firebase and Jest: Jest is a popular testing framework for JavaScript that you can use to write and run unit tests. By including Jest in your pipeline, you can automatically verify that individual functions work as expected.

```
TEST('SHOULD ADD TWO numbers', () => {

expect(add(1, 2)).toBe(3);

});
```

-

Integration Testing with Firebase Emulator Suite: Firebase Emulator Suite provides a local environment for testing Firebase products, such as Firestore, Authentication, and Functions. By running tests against the emulator, you can verify how different Firebase components interact without affecting live data.

```
firebase emulators:start—only firestore,functions
```

-

End-to-End Testing with Firebase Test Lab: Firebase Test Lab offers a cloud-based infrastructure for running tests on real devices. You can integrate Test Lab into your CI/CD pipeline to perform end-to-end testing for mobile apps, ensuring that they work as expected on different devices and operating systems.

```
steps:

- name: 'gcr.io/cloud-builders/gcloud'

args: ['firebase', 'test', 'android', 'run', '—app', 'app.apk', '—device-ids', 'Nexus6P']
```

-

4. Deployment Strategies

WHEN DEPLOYING CODE to production, it's essential to minimize downtime and ensure a smooth user experience. Several deployment strategies can help you achieve this:

- **Blue-Green Deployment**: This strategy involves maintaining two identical environments (blue and green) where only one is live at a time. You deploy changes to the idle environment, test them, and then switch traffic to the new environment. Firebase Hosting supports this by allowing you to deploy to multiple environments and switch traffic using rewrite rules.

- **Rolling Deployment**: Rolling deployments involve gradually replacing instances with new versions of the application. While Firebase Functions and Hosting are serverless, you can use rolling deployments with GCP services like Compute Engine by configuring instance groups and load balancers to manage the rollout.

Canary Deployment: Canary deployments release new changes to a small subset of users before deploying them to the entire user base. By using Firebase Remote Config or Cloud Run traffic splitting, you can control the percentage of traffic routed to the new version and monitor for issues before a full rollout.

yaml

Copy code

spec:

template:

spec:

containers:

- image: gcr.io/my-project/my-app:canary

●

5. Managing Pipeline Security

SECURITY IS A CRITICAL aspect of CI/CD pipelines, as they handle sensitive information and directly impact production environments. Here are some best practices for securing your pipelines:

- **Use IAM to Control Access**: Apply the principle of least privilege by granting the minimum necessary permissions to users and service accounts. Use Google Cloud IAM to define roles and restrict access to CI/CD resources, such as Cloud Build and deployment targets.

Secure Secrets with Secret Manager: Google Secret Manager allows you to store and manage sensitive data, such as API keys, in a secure and centralized location. Integrate Secret Manager with your pipeline to securely access secrets during the build and deployment process.

- name: 'gcr.io/cloud-builders/gcloud'

entrypoint: 'bash'

args: ['-c', 'export API_KEY=$(gcloud secrets versions access latest—secret=api-key)']

●

● **Enable Auditing and Logging**: Enable Cloud Audit Logs to track actions taken within your CI/CD pipeline. Monitoring logs provide a detailed record of who accessed resources, when, and what actions were taken. This information is invaluable for identifying unauthorized access and troubleshooting issues.

6. Optimizing CI/CD Pipelines for Efficiency

OPTIMIZING CI/CD PIPELINES is crucial to minimizing build times, reducing costs, and improving overall efficiency. Here are some strategies to enhance pipeline performance:

Parallelize Tasks: Cloud Build allows you to run tasks in parallel, which can significantly reduce build times. For example, you can run tests, linting, and builds concurrently by specifying multiple steps without dependencies.

steps:

- name: 'gcr.io/cloud-builders/npm'

args: ['test']

- name: 'gcr.io/cloud-builders/npm'

args: ['lint']

- name: 'gcr.io/cloud-builders/npm'

args: ['build']

●

Cache Dependencies: Use caching to avoid reinstalling dependencies on every build. You can cache files like node_modules between builds by using Cloud Build's caching feature, which speeds up subsequent builds and reduces resource consumption.

steps:

- name: 'gcr.io/cloud-builders/npm'

args: ['ci']

cache:

paths: ['node_modules/']

- •

  - **Use Pre-Built Images**: Instead of building Docker images from scratch every time, use pre-built base images or images hosted in Google Container Registry. This approach reduces build time and ensures that your builds start from a known state.

7. Monitoring and Observability in CI/CD Pipelines

MONITORING YOUR CI/CD pipeline helps you understand build performance, detect bottlenecks, and troubleshoot failures. Firebase and GCP offer several tools for monitoring pipeline activities:

  - **Use Cloud Monitoring for Pipeline Metrics**: Cloud Monitoring can track metrics like build duration, success rate, and failure rate. Set up dashboards and alerts to monitor these metrics and respond to any issues that may impact your deployment workflow.

- **Analyze Build Logs with Cloud Logging**: Cloud Logging aggregates logs from all pipeline steps, providing a centralized location to review and analyze build information. Use log-based metrics to identify trends and areas for improvement in your pipeline.

- **Incorporate Performance Monitoring into Deployment**: Use Firebase Performance Monitoring to track app performance after deployment. This helps you detect any issues introduced in the new release, such as increased latency or higher error rates, and quickly rollback changes if necessary.

By implementing these CI/CD practices, you can create efficient, secure, and scalable pipelines for your Firebase and GCP projects. Automating testing and deployment enables you to deliver high-quality applications at a rapid pace, while optimizing pipeline performance ensures that your resources are used effectively. Regular monitoring and security measures protect your infrastructure, allowing you to deploy with confidence and respond quickly to any challenges that arise.

Future Trends in Firebase and GCP Development

AS TECHNOLOGY CONTINUES to evolve, Firebase and Google Cloud Platform (GCP) are positioned at the forefront of innovative cloud solutions. By understanding future trends, developers can better prepare their applications for emerging technologies and evolving user demands. This section explores anticipated developments in Firebase and GCP, covering areas such as artificial intelligence, enhanced automation, edge computing, hybrid cloud solutions, and sustainability practices.

1. Artificial Intelligence and Machine Learning Integration

ARTIFICIAL INTELLIGENCE (AI) and Machine Learning (ML) are increasingly integral to application development, and Firebase and GCP are continually expanding their AI/ML offerings to facilitate smarter applications:

- **Pre-Trained AI Models and AutoML**: GCP offers a suite of pre-trained AI models for tasks like image recognition, text analysis, and language translation. As these models become more sophisticated, developers can expect improved accuracy and expanded capabilities in areas like natural language processing and computer vision. AutoML, which automates model training and optimization, allows developers with limited ML expertise to create custom models that meet specific needs.

- **Firebase ML Kit Enhancements**: Firebase ML Kit provides easy access to on-device ML capabilities, and future enhancements are likely to increase the speed, accuracy, and range of supported use cases. By using Firebase ML Kit, developers can add ML features like barcode scanning, face detection, and text recognition with minimal effort.

- **Real-Time AI with Streaming Analytics**: As real-time AI becomes more prevalent, Firebase and GCP are expected to enhance their support for streaming analytics. Services like Google Cloud Dataflow will likely incorporate more tools for processing data streams in real time, enabling applications to make instant predictions and provide up-to-the-moment insights to users.

2. Increased Automation with No-Code and Low-Code Solutions

NO-CODE AND LOW-CODE development tools are reducing the barriers to creating complex applications, and Firebase and GCP are expanding their offerings in this space:

- **Firebase Extensions for Quick Integration**: Firebase Extensions simplify the integration of common functionalities like payments, authentication, and analytics. As more extensions are developed, developers can expect a growing library of ready-made solutions that streamline application development without extensive coding. Extensions like "Send Email with SendGrid" or "Run Subscription Payments with Stripe" provide plug-and-play modules that are easy to implement.

- **AppSheet and No-Code AI Models**: Google's AppSheet enables users to build apps without any coding experience. Integrated with GCP, AppSheet is expanding to support more complex workflows and ML-driven insights, enabling business users to harness the power of AI directly in their applications. Future developments will likely focus on adding more automation and customization options, making it even easier to create data-driven applications without programming knowledge.

- **Serverless Workflows with Cloud Functions and Eventarc**: Serverless computing is a significant enabler of automation. GCP's Eventarc service facilitates event-driven architectures by enabling developers to route events to Cloud Functions, Cloud Run, or other services. As Eventarc matures, expect better integration with a wider range of event sources, enabling automated workflows across Firebase, GCP, and third-party systems.

3. Edge Computing and the Internet of Things (IoT)

WITH THE RAPID EXPANSION of IoT devices and edge computing, Firebase and GCP are evolving to support applications that require low latency, high availability, and local processing:

- **Firebase for IoT Solutions**: Firebase's real-time capabilities make it well-suited for IoT applications. With expected advancements in Firebase Realtime Database and Firestore, developers can anticipate better support for syncing and managing IoT data in real time. This will allow for faster response times and lower data transfer costs for IoT use cases like smart homes, industrial automation, and connected vehicles.

- **Google Distributed Cloud for Edge Computing**: Google Distributed Cloud offers a managed infrastructure that extends GCP services to edge locations. This enables applications to process data locally, reducing latency and improving performance for geographically distributed users. As edge computing adoption grows, Google Distributed Cloud will likely expand its integration with Firebase, allowing for more sophisticated edge-based solutions that leverage real-time data.

- **Integration with 5G Networks**: The deployment of 5G networks opens up new possibilities for real-time data processing and IoT applications. Firebase and GCP are expected to optimize their services to take advantage of 5G's low latency and high bandwidth, enabling faster and more reliable connectivity for mobile and IoT applications.

4. Hybrid and Multi-Cloud Solutions

THE DEMAND FOR HYBRID and multi-cloud solutions is increasing as organizations seek to avoid vendor lock-in and leverage the unique strengths of different cloud providers. Firebase and GCP are enhancing their support for multi-cloud deployments:

- **Anthos for Cross-Cloud Kubernetes Management**: Google Anthos provides a unified platform for managing Kubernetes clusters across multiple cloud environments. By using Anthos, developers can deploy and manage applications on GCP, on-premises, or on other cloud providers. Future improvements in Anthos are expected to focus on deeper integration with Firebase, making it easier to build hybrid applications that span Firebase and other cloud environments.

- **Data Interoperability with BigQuery Omni**: BigQuery Omni enables multi-cloud analytics by allowing users to query data across AWS and Azure without moving the data. This approach provides a unified view of data stored in multiple cloud environments. Future updates to BigQuery Omni are likely to include enhanced support for real-time data analysis and improved integration with Firebase Analytics.

- **Cross-Cloud Identity Management**: As organizations adopt multi-cloud strategies, managing user identities across different platforms is becoming increasingly complex. GCP's Identity Platform already supports various identity providers, and upcoming enhancements are expected to provide more robust cross-cloud identity management, allowing developers to secure Firebase and GCP applications consistently across different cloud providers.

5. Sustainability and Green Computing

AS THE FOCUS ON SUSTAINABILITY grows, Firebase and GCP are committed to reducing their carbon footprint and providing tools that enable developers to build environmentally-friendly applications:

- **Carbon Footprint Monitoring**: Google Cloud offers tools to monitor the carbon footprint of cloud resources. As these tools become more advanced, developers can expect better insights into the environmental impact of their Firebase and GCP applications. These insights will allow teams to make informed decisions about resource allocation and optimize workloads for energy efficiency.

- **Optimizing Serverless for Sustainability**: Serverless computing inherently promotes efficiency by scaling resources based on demand, which reduces waste and energy consumption. As Firebase and GCP continue to optimize serverless infrastructure, they are likely to introduce more granular controls over scaling and resource utilization, helping developers minimize energy consumption.

● **Promoting Sustainable Application Design**: Firebase and GCP are expected to provide more resources and guidelines for building sustainable applications. This could include best practices for minimizing resource consumption, using renewable-powered data centers, and leveraging Google's carbon-neutral services to build greener applications.

6. Quantum Computing and Its Potential Impact

WHILE STILL IN ITS early stages, quantum computing has the potential to revolutionize many areas of cloud computing. Google is investing heavily in quantum research, and while direct integration with Firebase and GCP may be some years away, it's worth considering how quantum advancements could impact development:

● **Quantum-Enhanced Machine Learning**: Quantum computing could significantly accelerate machine learning tasks, enabling Firebase and GCP to offer more powerful ML capabilities in the future. Quantum-enhanced ML could handle complex data sets and provide insights at speeds that are currently unattainable with classical computing.

● **Advancements in Cryptography**: Quantum computing poses both challenges and opportunities for encryption and data security. Firebase and GCP are likely to stay at the forefront of cryptographic advancements, offering solutions that are resilient to quantum attacks and ensuring the security of cloud-based applications.

● **Google Quantum AI Services**: Google Quantum AI aims to make quantum computing accessible to a broader audience. As quantum computing becomes more mainstream, developers could eventually leverage quantum-powered APIs in Firebase and GCP to solve problems that are currently unsolvable with classical approaches.

By staying informed about these emerging trends, developers can position themselves to take advantage of new technologies and build applications that are scalable, efficient, and ready for the future. Firebase and GCP are continually evolving to address the needs of modern applications, and by leveraging their latest features and tools, developers can create innovative solutions that meet the demands of an ever-changing digital landscape.

Chapter 11: Conclusion and Next Steps

Recap of Key Concepts

AS WE REACH THE CONCLUSION of this book, it is essential to revisit and summarize the core concepts and skills covered throughout the chapters. This will solidify your understanding of Firebase and Google Cloud Platform (GCP) integration, helping you see the big picture and better understand how these tools can be applied to real-world scenarios. This chapter aims to provide a comprehensive overview of what has been covered, reinforce key takeaways, and offer guidance on what to explore next.

Overview of Firebase and GCP Synergy

AT THE BEGINNING OF the book, we explored the synergies between Firebase and Google Cloud Platform (GCP). Firebase serves as a mobile and web application development platform, providing tools and services designed for rapid prototyping and efficient application management. GCP complements Firebase by offering scalable infrastructure and a wide range of additional services, such as BigQuery for analytics, Cloud Pub/Sub for messaging, and AI and machine learning capabilities.

The integration of Firebase with GCP unlocks new possibilities, allowing developers to build applications that are not only highly functional but also scalable and secure. This combination enables rapid development cycles while maintaining the flexibility to leverage GCP's robust cloud services.

Setting Up Firebase and GCP Environments

CREATING AND LINKING Firebase and GCP projects were the first steps toward utilizing their capabilities. This process involved setting up a Firebase project, creating a GCP project, and then linking the two. Managing billing and cloud resources effectively is critical in this setup phase to avoid unexpected costs and ensure that the project remains within budget. Understanding how to navigate both Firebase Console and GCP Console is essential to monitor, manage, and optimize resources effectively.

Authentication and Identity Management

FIREBASE AUTHENTICATION provides developers with various options for user authentication, including email/password, Google sign-in, and other social logins. We explored these options in detail, emphasizing security and user experience. Additionally, we covered advanced authentication techniques, such as using custom tokens and integrating Firebase Authentication with GCP Identity.

User authentication and security are critical components of any application, and Firebase offers tools to implement these seamlessly. However, it's vital to follow best practices, such as using multi-factor authentication (MFA) and regularly auditing authentication settings, to ensure robust security.

Database Solutions: Firestore and Cloud Databases

FIRESTORE IS FIREBASE'S real-time, serverless NoSQL database, known for its scalability and ease of use. Data modeling in Firestore allows developers to structure data in a way that suits their application needs, while optimizing for performance. Integrating Firestore with Google Cloud Datastore opens up additional possibilities, such as exporting data to BigQuery for advanced analytics.

We explored how to optimize Firestore queries to ensure that applications remain performant and cost-effective. Case studies demonstrated how real-time data can be leveraged to create responsive and interactive applications, underscoring Firestore's utility in both small-scale and large-scale applications.

Cloud Functions and Serverless Computing

FIREBASE CLOUD FUNCTIONS enable serverless execution of backend code in response to events from Firebase products or HTTP requests. This serverless approach allows developers to focus on writing code without worrying about server management. GCP Cloud Functions expand this capability by offering more extensive integration options and supporting more complex use cases.

We discussed how to write and deploy functions, trigger them using various Firebase services, and monitor and debug them using Firebase and GCP tools. The ability to create custom server-side logic that can be triggered by events in real-time enhances the functionality of Firebase applications and provides a means for offloading intensive tasks to a serverless environment.

Hosting and Deployment with Firebase and GCP

FIREBASE HOSTING IS designed to serve static files, such as HTML, CSS, and JavaScript, and is optimized for single-page applications. We examined how to deploy web apps to Firebase Hosting, set up custom domains, and secure websites with SSL certificates. Additionally, we explored GCP's App Engine, which offers more flexibility for web app hosting, particularly when applications require dynamic content or more complex server-side processing.

Ensuring that hosted applications are optimized for performance and security is essential. Firebase and GCP provide tools to achieve this, such as enabling HTTP/2, configuring caching strategies, and monitoring application performance.

Storage Solutions: Firebase Storage and Google Cloud Storage

STORAGE IS A CRUCIAL aspect of application development, and Firebase offers Firebase Storage for handling file uploads and downloads. Google Cloud Storage offers more advanced capabilities for managing large datasets and configuring access permissions. Understanding when to use Firebase Storage versus Google Cloud Storage is critical, as each has its strengths and use cases.

For example, Firebase Storage is well-suited for user-generated content in mobile applications, while Google Cloud Storage is ideal for archiving data, storing backups, or handling large media files. By integrating Firebase Storage with Google Cloud Storage, developers can leverage the strengths of both services to create a robust and scalable storage solution.

Analytics, Monitoring, and Performance

FIREBASE ANALYTICS and Performance Monitoring tools provide insights into user behavior and application performance. By leveraging these tools, developers can make data-driven decisions to improve user experience, optimize resource usage, and ensure application reliability. Google Analytics can be integrated with Firebase to gain a deeper understanding of user engagement and to create targeted marketing campaigns.

Additionally, GCP's monitoring tools, such as Stackdriver Monitoring, offer a way to monitor the health of applications and troubleshoot issues before they impact users. These insights are invaluable for maintaining a high-quality user experience and ensuring that applications perform as expected under varying conditions.

Machine Learning with Firebase and GCP

MACHINE LEARNING (ML) capabilities can enhance applications by adding intelligence and automation. Firebase's ML Kit simplifies the integration of ML models into mobile applications, while GCP provides a comprehensive suite of AI and ML services, including AutoML, Vision AI, and Natural Language API. We discussed how to use Firebase ML Kit for common tasks, such as image recognition and text analysis, and how to integrate custom ML models from GCP.

Developers can build intelligent applications that provide personalized and context-aware experiences by combining Firebase and GCP's ML capabilities. A case study on building an AI-driven mobile app demonstrated the potential of integrating these tools to create innovative and user-centric applications.

Best Practices for Firebase and GCP Integration

INTEGRATING FIREBASE and GCP requires attention to resource management, security, and scalability. Following best practices, such as using CI/CD pipelines, managing access permissions, and monitoring costs, ensures that applications remain scalable, secure, and cost-effective. As Firebase and GCP continue to evolve, staying updated with new features and trends is essential for maintaining a competitive edge.

Future Trends and Exploring Advanced Services

THE FINAL SECTION OF this chapter provides guidance on exploring advanced Firebase and GCP services, such as Kubernetes Engine, Cloud Functions for Machine Learning, and BigQuery for large-scale analytics. As cloud technology evolves, Firebase and GCP will likely introduce new tools and features that open up even more possibilities for developers.

Continuing to learn and experiment with Firebase and GCP will help you stay ahead of the curve and build future-proof applications. This book has provided a foundation, but the journey doesn't end here. Firebase and GCP offer a vast ecosystem of services that can transform ideas into reality, enabling you to build powerful, scalable, and intelligent applications.

Exploring Advanced Firebase and GCP Services

AS YOU GROW MORE COMFORTABLE with Firebase and Google Cloud Platform (GCP), you may find yourself looking to deepen your understanding and expand the range of services you use. Firebase and GCP offer a multitude of advanced services that can significantly enhance your application's functionality, scalability, and user experience. In this section, we will explore some of these advanced services and discuss how to leverage them effectively. This includes tools for large-scale analytics, machine learning, infrastructure automation, and much more.

BigQuery for Data Analytics

BIGQUERY IS GCP'S FULLY-managed, serverless data warehouse that allows you to process and analyze large datasets quickly and efficiently. For Firebase developers, BigQuery integration enables you to perform complex queries on your Firebase Analytics data, providing insights beyond what is available through the standard Firebase Analytics dashboard.

To connect Firebase to BigQuery:

1. Go to your Firebase Console, navigate to **Project Settings**, and then **Integrations**.
2. Select **BigQuery** and enable the connection.
3. Choose the Firebase data streams you wish to export to BigQuery.

Once connected, you can run SQL-like queries on your data to analyze user behavior, track long-term trends, or even combine Firebase data with other datasets within BigQuery. For example, to get the top 10 most active users by session count, you can use the following query:

```sql
SELECT user_pseudo_id, COUNT(*) AS session_count

FROM `your_project_id.analytics_events`

WHERE event_name = "session_start"

GROUP BY user_pseudo_id

ORDER BY session_count DESC

LIMIT 10;
```

This query allows you to identify users who are highly engaged with your app, which can inform targeted marketing efforts or product improvements.

Google Kubernetes Engine (GKE) for Containerized Workloads

GOOGLE KUBERNETES ENGINE (GKE) offers a powerful way to manage containerized applications at scale. If your Firebase project grows into a more complex system, you may find it useful to offload certain services to a Kubernetes-managed cluster. GKE automates deployment, scaling, and management of containerized applications.

To deploy an application on GKE:

1. Define your application in a Docker container.
2. Push the container image to Google Container Registry (GCR).
3. Create a Kubernetes deployment and service configuration.

A basic deployment YAML file might look like this:

apiVersion: apps/v1

kind: Deployment

metadata:

name: my-app-deployment

spec:

replicas: 3

selector:

matchLabels:

app: my-app

template:

metadata:

labels:

app: my-app

spec:

containers:

- name: my-app-container

image: gcr.io/your_project_id/my-app-image:latest

ports:

- containerPort: 80

By utilizing GKE, you gain greater control over your application's infrastructure and can achieve a higher level of scalability and resilience.

Cloud Functions for Machine Learning

WHILE FIREBASE CLOUD Functions are excellent for simple server-side logic, GCP Cloud Functions provide broader capabilities for integrating machine learning. For example, you can use Cloud Functions to run predictions with pre-trained models on GCP's AI Platform.

Suppose you have a TensorFlow model for image classification stored in Google Cloud Storage. You can create a Cloud Function that loads the model, processes the input data, and returns predictions. Here is a simplified example of how this might look in Python:

```python
import tensorflow as tf

from google.cloud import storage

from flask import jsonify

def load_model():

storage_client = storage.Client()

bucket = storage_client.bucket("your_bucket_name")

blob = bucket.blob("model/saved_model.pb")

blob.download_to_filename("/tmp/saved_model.pb")

return tf.keras.models.load_model("/tmp/saved_model.pb")

model = load_model()

def classify_image(request):

image_data = request.files['file'].read()

img = tf.image.decode_image(image_data, channels=3)

img = tf.image.resize(img, [224, 224])

img = tf.expand_dims(img, axis=0)

predictions = model.predict(img)

return jsonify({'predictions': predictions.tolist()})
```

This function can be triggered by an HTTP request, making it easy to integrate into your application.

Cloud Pub/Sub for Messaging and Event-Driven Architectures

FOR MORE COMPLEX, EVENT-driven architectures, Google Cloud Pub/Sub is an invaluable tool. It allows you to decouple components of your application, which is especially useful when building systems with multiple services that need to communicate reliably and at scale.

To use Pub/Sub in your Firebase app, you can publish events to a topic whenever a specific action occurs, such as a user sign-up or an in-app purchase. Then, various services can subscribe to this topic and perform actions accordingly. For example, you might publish a message to a topic whenever a user signs up, and then subscribe to that topic with a Cloud Function that sends a welcome email.

Here's a sample Cloud Function in Python to publish a message to a Pub/Sub topic:

```python
from google.cloud import pubsub_v1

def publish_message(request):

publisher = pubsub_v1.PublisherClient()

topic_name = 'projects/your_project_id/topics/your_topic_name'

message = request.get_json().get('message')

future = publisher.publish(topic_name, message.encode('utf-8'))

return f'Message published with ID: {future.result()}'
```

By using Pub/Sub, you can build a system that scales with ease, processing millions of messages per second while ensuring reliable delivery.

Cloud Spanner for Global-Scale Databases

IF YOUR APPLICATION requires a globally-distributed, strongly consistent database, Cloud Spanner may be a suitable solution. Cloud Spanner provides SQL capabilities with horizontal scaling, making it ideal for applications with stringent consistency requirements across multiple regions.

To get started with Cloud Spanner:

1. Create an instance and a database in the GCP Console.
2. Define your schema using SQL statements.
3. Use Cloud Spanner's client libraries to interact with the database.

Here's an example of creating a table in Cloud Spanner using Python:

```python
from google.cloud import spanner

spanner_client = spanner.Client()

instance = spanner_client.instance('your-instance-id')

database = instance.database('your-database-id')

operation = database.update_ddl([
    """

CREATE TABLE Users (

UserId STRING(36) NOT NULL,
```

Username STRING(128),

Email STRING(128)

) PRIMARY KEY (UserId)

"""

])

operation.result()

Cloud Spanner's global consistency and high availability make it a strong choice for applications that require robust and reliable databases across regions.

Stackdriver Monitoring for Proactive Application Management

TO ENSURE THAT YOUR applications remain reliable and performant, Stackdriver Monitoring provides insights into your system's health. You can set up alerts based on custom metrics, create dashboards to monitor application performance, and even automate responses to incidents.

For example, you can create an alert policy to notify you if a particular API has an error rate above a certain threshold. This helps you detect and respond to issues before they impact users. Stackdriver Monitoring integrates seamlessly with GCP and Firebase, allowing you to visualize and manage all your services from a single platform.

Conclusion

THESE ADVANCED FIREBASE and GCP services offer powerful ways to expand the capabilities of your applications.

While the learning curve may be steeper, the potential rewards in terms of performance, scalability, and user experience are significant. As you explore these tools, remember that Firebase and GCP provide extensive documentation and resources to support your journey.

Whether you're processing vast amounts of data with BigQuery, deploying machine learning models with Cloud Functions, or managing containerized workloads with Kubernetes, the key is to continue experimenting and building on what you've learned. By harnessing the full power of Firebase and GCP, you can create innovative and resilient applications that meet the demands of modern users and businesses.

Building for Scalability and Global Reach

IN TODAY'S INTERCONNECTED world, building applications that can handle global traffic is essential. Whether you're developing a mobile app or a complex web application, scalability and global reach are critical for meeting the demands of a growing user base. This section delves into strategies, tools, and best practices for building scalable, globally accessible applications using Firebase and Google Cloud Platform (GCP).

Architecting for Scalability

SCALABILITY IS THE ability of a system to handle increased load by adding resources, such as compute power, storage, or network capacity. Architecting for scalability requires foresight, as well as an understanding of how to optimize resource allocation and handle traffic spikes without impacting performance.

Horizontal vs. Vertical Scaling

- **Vertical Scaling** involves adding more power (CPU, RAM) to an existing server. This approach is limited by the server's maximum capacity and can be costly at scale.

- **Horizontal Scaling** means adding more servers to distribute the load. This approach offers greater flexibility and allows for distributed processing across multiple regions.

FOR GLOBAL REACH, HORIZONTAL scaling is often the preferred option, as it provides better resilience and can distribute load across multiple data centers. Firebase and GCP services like Google Kubernetes Engine (GKE) and Cloud Spanner are designed with horizontal scaling in mind, making it easier to manage growth and ensure availability.

Utilizing Firebase's Global Infrastructure

FIREBASE OFFERS A RANGE of services that automatically scale to meet demand. Firebase Hosting, for example, uses Google's Content Delivery Network (CDN) to distribute content across the globe, ensuring fast load times for users regardless of location.

To enable CDN on Firebase Hosting:

1. Deploy your site using the Firebase CLI.
2. Enable global CDN caching through the Firebase Console under the **Hosting** settings.
3. Configure custom domains if needed, to provide localized experiences.

Firebase Hosting leverages Google's infrastructure, which spans multiple regions and data centers, so you don't have to worry about setting up or managing individual servers.

Google Cloud Load Balancing for Global Traffic Management

GOOGLE CLOUD LOAD BALANCING automatically distributes incoming application traffic across multiple instances, zones, or regions. This ensures high availability and resilience against traffic spikes, even during unexpected surges.

To set up global load balancing in GCP:

1. In the GCP Console, navigate to **Network Services > Load balancing**.
2. Choose **HTTP(S) Load Balancing** and configure a load balancer.
3. Set up backend services and select multiple regions to serve global traffic.
4. Configure a health check to ensure that traffic is only directed to healthy instances.

By using global load balancing, you can route traffic to the nearest available region, reducing latency and improving the user experience for customers around the world.

Multi-Region Database Solutions with Cloud Firestore

FIRESTORE IS A NOSQL database that supports multi-region replication, ensuring data availability even during regional outages. Firestore's multi-region configuration provides automatic data replication, allowing read and write operations to continue seamlessly across multiple locations.

To enable multi-region replication for Firestore:

1. In the Firebase Console, create a new Firestore database.
2. Choose **Multi-region** as the database location setting.
3. Select a region group, such as us-central or europe-west.

Multi-region databases are essential for global applications, as they offer higher availability and resilience. Additionally, Firestore's built-in synchronization ensures that data is consistent across regions, minimizing the risk of data loss or conflicts.

Leveraging Google Cloud CDN for Static and Dynamic Content

GOOGLE CLOUD CDN CACHES content at edge locations worldwide, which reduces latency and improves load times for global users. By caching both static (images, CSS) and dynamic (API responses) content, Cloud CDN can significantly enhance application performance.

To use Cloud CDN with Firebase Hosting:

1. Link your Firebase project with a GCP project.
2. Enable Cloud CDN for Firebase Hosting under **Settings > Integrations** in the Firebase Console.
3. Customize caching rules for specific file types or paths, if needed.

For more advanced caching, such as integrating Cloud CDN with GKE or App Engine, you can configure CDN policies directly in

GCP. By leveraging Cloud CDN, you can deliver content with low latency, regardless of user location.

Implementing Autoscaling with Google Kubernetes Engine (GKE)

GKE PROVIDES AUTOSCALING capabilities that adjust the number of nodes in a cluster based on resource usage. This allows applications to handle varying levels of traffic efficiently without manual intervention.

To configure autoscaling on GKE:

1. Create a GKE cluster and enable autoscaling by setting the minimum and maximum node count.
2. Define autoscaling policies in your deployment configurations.

Here's an example of how to configure autoscaling in a GKE deployment YAML file:

apiVersion: autoscaling/v1

kind: HorizontalPodAutoscaler

metadata:

name: my-app-autoscaler

spec:

scaleTargetRef:

apiVersion: apps/v1

kind: Deployment

name: my-app

minReplicas: 2

maxReplicas: 10

targetCPUUtilizationPercentage: 70

This configuration ensures that as CPU utilization reaches 70%, new pods are added to handle the load. GKE's autoscaling helps maintain application performance during high traffic periods while minimizing costs during low traffic periods.

Using Cloud Pub/Sub for Asynchronous Processing

CLOUD PUB/SUB IS A messaging service that decouples event-producing services from event-processing services. This allows for asynchronous processing, which is crucial for scalability, as it prevents bottlenecks and ensures that different components of an application can scale independently.

To set up Cloud Pub/Sub in your application:

1. Create a topic in the Pub/Sub Console.
2. Publish messages to the topic from one part of your application.
3. Subscribe to the topic from another service, such as a Cloud Function or GKE workload.

Here's a Python example for publishing a message to a Pub/Sub topic:

```python
from google.cloud import pubsub_v1

publisher = pubsub_v1.PublisherClient()
```

```
topic_path = 'projects/your_project_id/topics/your_topic_name'

message = 'Hello, world!'

publisher.publish(topic_path, message.encode('utf-8'))
```

By using Pub/Sub, you can easily scale each part of your application independently, ensuring that messages are processed efficiently without overwhelming any single service.

Global API Management with Apigee

FOR APPLICATIONS THAT expose APIs to external clients, Apigee provides a comprehensive API management platform. Apigee offers features like rate limiting, caching, and analytics, which are essential for managing APIs at scale.

To deploy an API on Apigee:

1. Create an API proxy in the Apigee Console.
2. Configure rate limiting and caching policies.
3. Set up analytics to monitor API usage and performance.

By using Apigee, you can control how clients access your APIs, prevent abuse, and gain insights into usage patterns, which helps in scaling your application effectively.

Monitoring and Logging for Scalable Applications

MONITORING AND LOGGING are critical for maintaining scalable applications. Stackdriver Monitoring and Logging provide real-time insights into your application's performance and health, helping you identify and address issues before they affect users.

To set up Stackdriver Monitoring:

1. Enable Stackdriver in your GCP project.
2. Configure custom metrics and alerts for your application.
3. Set up logging to capture important events and errors.

By monitoring key metrics and setting up alerts, you can proactively manage your application's scalability and ensure that it remains reliable as it grows.

Conclusion

BUILDING APPLICATIONS for scalability and global reach requires careful planning and the right set of tools. Firebase and GCP offer a robust suite of services that simplify this process, from load balancing and multi-region databases to autoscaling and global CDN. By leveraging these tools and following best practices, you can create applications that not only scale effectively but also deliver a seamless experience to users around the world.

As you continue to develop and expand your applications, remember to revisit these concepts and adapt your architecture to meet evolving demands. The journey to building a truly global application is ongoing, but with Firebase and GCP, you have the resources and infrastructure to achieve it.

Staying Updated with Firebase and GCP Developments

IN THE RAPIDLY EVOLVING tech landscape, staying updated with the latest developments is crucial for maintaining a competitive edge. Firebase and Google Cloud Platform (GCP) are constantly evolving, introducing new features, tools, and best practices. This section provides strategies and resources to help you stay informed, explore new functionalities, and effectively integrate updates into your projects.

Leveraging Official Documentation and Release Notes

THE OFFICIAL DOCUMENTATION for Firebase and GCP is the most comprehensive and up-to-date resource available. Both platforms maintain detailed documentation that covers a wide range of topics, from getting started to advanced configurations. Regularly reviewing the documentation will help you understand new features and how they can benefit your applications.

To access the documentation:

- **Firebase**: Visit firebase.google.com/docs.

- **GCP**: Visit cloud.google.com/docs.

In addition to the general documentation, Firebase and GCP also provide **release notes**, which detail recent updates, bug fixes, and new features. Subscribing to release notes for the specific services you use ensures that you stay informed about important changes. You can find Firebase's release notes here and GCP's release notes here.

Engaging with Developer Communities

JOINING DEVELOPER COMMUNITIES can be incredibly beneficial for staying updated and troubleshooting issues. Communities offer a space to discuss updates, share best practices, and gain insights from other developers. Here are some of the most active Firebase and GCP communities:

- **Stack Overflow**: Firebase and GCP both have active tags on Stack Overflow where developers ask questions, share solutions, and discuss new features. Engaging with these communities can provide insights into how others are using the platforms and help you solve common challenges.

- **Reddit**: Subreddits like r/Firebase and r/googlecloud provide a mix of news, discussions, and questions. These forums are helpful for informal discussions and quick updates.

- **GitHub**: Many Firebase and GCP libraries are open source, with their repositories hosted on GitHub. By following these repositories, you can keep track of issues, pull requests, and release updates. The Firebase GitHub repository, for instance, contains a wealth of resources, including sample projects and bug reports.

Attending Webinars, Conferences, and Meetups

GOOGLE FREQUENTLY HOSTS webinars, conferences, and meetups to showcase new developments and provide hands-on training. Attending these events can be a valuable way to learn directly from Google engineers and network with other developers. Some of the notable events include:

- **Google Cloud Next**: An annual conference that highlights new developments in Google Cloud, including Firebase. It features keynotes, hands-on labs, and sessions on various topics, such as security, machine learning, and application development.

- **Firebase Summit**: This event focuses exclusively on Firebase and offers deep dives into new features, case studies, and practical workshops. It's an excellent opportunity to learn about the latest Firebase updates and best practices.

- **Local Meetups**: Platforms like Meetup.com and Eventbrite often list local Firebase and GCP meetups. These events are great for networking, sharing knowledge, and discovering how other developers are using Firebase and GCP in their projects.

Experimenting with Firebase and GCP Beta Programs

FIREBASE AND GCP REGULARLY offer beta programs for new features, which allow developers to test upcoming functionalities before they're widely released. Participating in beta programs can provide early access to new tools and help you prepare for their official launch.

To join beta programs:

- **Firebase**: Visit the Firebase Alpha & Beta Programs page, where you can find a list of ongoing beta programs. Examples include Firebase Performance Monitoring beta features or the latest updates in Firebase Hosting.

- **GCP**: GCP offers Alpha and Beta programs for various services. You can find these in the **GCP Console** under specific services or by signing up through the Google Cloud Console's Alpha and Beta Features.

By experimenting with beta features, you can stay ahead of the curve and gain a deeper understanding of new capabilities before they become mainstream.

Following Firebase and GCP Blogs and Social Media Channels

BOTH FIREBASE AND GCP maintain active blogs and social media channels where they announce new features, share tutorials, and highlight use cases. Subscribing to these channels ensures you receive updates directly from the source.

- **Firebase Blog**: The Firebase Blog covers feature updates, case studies, and tips for getting the most out of Firebase. It's a must-read for Firebase developers who want to stay informed.

- **Google Cloud Blog**: The Google Cloud Blog covers all things related to GCP, including updates, customer stories, and technical deep dives. You can filter posts by topics, such as infrastructure, security, and data analytics.

- **Twitter and LinkedIn**: Follow the official Firebase and GCP Twitter accounts for quick updates, announcements, and links to relevant articles. LinkedIn is also a great platform for longer posts and discussions on new developments.

Implementing Continuous Learning Through Online Courses and Certifications

AS FIREBASE AND GCP evolve, investing time in formal learning can be a powerful way to deepen your expertise. Google offers a range of certifications and courses through **Google Cloud Training** and **Coursera**, which cover both introductory and advanced topics.

Some popular certifications include:

- **Google Associate Cloud Engineer**: This certification provides foundational knowledge of Google Cloud services, including core Firebase and GCP services.

- **Professional Cloud Developer**: Aimed at developers who want to design and build secure, scalable applications on GCP, this certification covers topics like Kubernetes, BigQuery, and Cloud Functions.

- **Firebase Fundamentals on Coursera**: This course provides an in-depth look at Firebase services, covering everything from setup to deployment.

By pursuing certifications, you not only gain in-depth knowledge but also validate your skills, which can be beneficial for career advancement.

Using Experimentation and Prototyping to Explore New Features

EXPLORING NEW FIREBASE and GCP features through prototyping allows you to evaluate their potential impact on your projects. For instance, when a new Firebase Authentication feature is released, you might create a test project to assess how it integrates with your existing system and what benefits it offers.

To streamline experimentation:

1. **Create a test environment**: Set up a sandbox environment in Firebase and GCP specifically for prototyping. This allows you to test new features without affecting your production systems.
2. **Use version control**: Tools like Git can help you manage and track changes as you experiment. This is especially useful when exploring beta features or implementing new configurations.
3. **Monitor performance**: Use Firebase Performance Monitoring and GCP Monitoring to assess the impact of new features on performance and reliability.

Engaging in Open Source Contributions

CONTRIBUTING TO OPEN source projects within the Firebase and GCP ecosystems is a valuable way to deepen your understanding of these platforms. By participating in open source, you can gain firsthand experience with the latest updates and collaborate with other developers.

To start contributing:

- Look for Firebase or GCP libraries on GitHub that match your interests.

- Review issues, especially those labeled as "good first issue," which are typically beginner-friendly.

- Share your improvements and feedback, which not only helps you learn but also benefits the community.

Conclusion

STAYING UPDATED WITH Firebase and GCP developments is an ongoing process that requires a mix of formal learning, community engagement, and hands-on experimentation. By leveraging the resources and strategies outlined in this section, you can stay informed, adapt to changes, and continuously improve your projects.

The world of Firebase and GCP is vast and constantly evolving, offering endless possibilities for innovation and growth. As you continue on your development journey, remember that staying current with new advancements will enable you to build more powerful, efficient, and impactful applications.

Resources for Further Learning

CONTINUING TO EXPAND your knowledge beyond this book is crucial for becoming proficient in Firebase and Google Cloud Platform (GCP). Both platforms are constantly evolving, and staying updated with new resources, tutorials, and best practices will help you make the most of these technologies. This section explores various resources and strategies for deepening your expertise, from official documentation to advanced training and certification programs.

Official Documentation and Tutorials

THE OFFICIAL DOCUMENTATION is the starting point for learning about Firebase and GCP. Both Firebase and GCP provide detailed documentation covering everything from basic concepts to advanced use cases. Regularly consulting these resources will help you stay current with new features and best practices.

• **Firebase Documentation**: firebase.google.com/docs

Firebase's documentation includes guides for setup, product-specific tutorials, and code samples. The documentation is regularly updated and often includes step-by-step examples that can be invaluable for new users.

• **GCP Documentation**: cloud.google.com/docs

GCP's documentation offers extensive resources on cloud services, from Compute Engine to BigQuery. Each service has its own set of guides, tutorials, and reference materials that can be tailored to your project needs.

The **Quickstarts** section within the GCP documentation is particularly helpful for getting a service up and running quickly. It's a great way to familiarize yourself with the basics and start experimenting.

Online Courses and Training Platforms

MANY ONLINE PLATFORMS offer courses on Firebase and GCP, catering to different skill levels. Here are some popular options:

• **Coursera**: Google partners with Coursera to provide a range of courses on Firebase and GCP, from beginner to advanced. Courses like **GCP Fundamentals** and **Firebase for Mobile Development** are designed to help you understand the core concepts and start building projects quickly.

- **Udemy**: Udemy offers a variety of Firebase and GCP courses, often with lifetime access. Courses such as **The Complete Firebase Development Course** and **Google Cloud Certification Training** are popular among learners looking to gain practical skills.

- **Pluralsight**: Pluralsight offers more advanced courses that go deep into topics like Kubernetes, machine learning, and cloud architecture on GCP. It's an excellent resource for developers looking to expand their expertise in specific areas.

- **Google Cloud Training**: Google offers a series of on-demand courses and certifications. This includes the **Google Cloud Platform Fundamentals** course and more advanced training for certifications like **Professional Cloud Architect** and **Associate Cloud Engineer**. These courses are particularly useful for those looking to validate their skills with a certification.

Certifications to Validate Expertise

CERTIFICATIONS PROVIDE an excellent way to demonstrate your proficiency in Firebase and GCP. They are especially valuable if you are looking to advance your career or validate your skills for potential employers. Some of the most recognized GCP certifications include:

- **Associate Cloud Engineer**: This certification is ideal for those starting out in GCP. It covers core services, including Compute Engine, App Engine, and Kubernetes Engine, and is a solid foundation for advanced certifications.

- **Professional Cloud Architect**: This certification is aimed at experienced cloud professionals who want to design, develop, and manage robust cloud solutions. It covers advanced topics like multi-cloud solutions, security, and compliance.

- **Firebase Certification**: While there is no official Firebase certification, completing related courses and achieving GCP certifications will demonstrate your competence in Firebase and GCP. You can also highlight your Firebase experience in your GCP certification projects.

Preparing for certifications often involves hands-on labs, which reinforce learning and allow you to build projects that demonstrate your skills.

Community Forums and Support Channels

ENGAGING WITH THE COMMUNITY can significantly enhance your learning experience. Firebase and GCP have active communities where you can ask questions, share insights, and get help with specific challenges.

- **Stack Overflow**: Stack Overflow has active tags for both Firebase and GCP. It's a valuable resource for troubleshooting issues, as many common problems have already been discussed and resolved by other developers.

- **Google Groups**: Firebase and GCP have several Google Groups that focus on specific services or topics. These groups offer a more focused discussion environment and are a great place to connect with other developers who have similar interests.

- **Reddit**: Subreddits like **r/Firebase** and **r/googlecloud** provide informal discussions and resources. These communities are helpful for staying updated on trends, finding interesting projects, and learning from others' experiences.

- **Firebase Support**: For more direct assistance, Firebase offers a support portal where you can submit tickets and get help from Google engineers. This can be especially useful if you encounter issues that require in-depth technical support.

GitHub Repositories and Open Source Projects

EXPLORING GITHUB REPOSITORIES is a great way to see how others are using Firebase and GCP in real-world projects. You can find open source projects, sample applications, and community-contributed libraries that can help you expand your knowledge.

- **Firebase on GitHub**: TheFirebase GitHub page[3] hosts official libraries and SDKs. It also includes example projects, which are a great way to learn about specific Firebase services.

- **GCP Samples**: Google Cloud's GitHub page includes a wide range ofsample projects[4] that demonstrate how to use various GCP services. These projects can provide inspiration and practical guidance for implementing similar solutions in your own applications.

---

3. https://github.com/firebase

4. https://github.com/GoogleCloudPlatform

Contributing to open source projects is another excellent way to deepen your expertise. By engaging with the community and sharing your own code, you not only learn from others but also help advance the ecosystem.

Firebase and GCP Blogs and Newsletters

SUBSCRIBING TO BLOGS and newsletters can help you stay informed about the latest developments, use cases, and industry trends. Here are some recommended sources:

- **Firebase Blog**: The Firebase Blog covers new releases, updates, and case studies. It's a valuable resource for learning about new features and seeing how other developers are using Firebase.

- **Google Cloud Blog**: The Google Cloud Blog provides updates on GCP services, customer success stories, and technical deep dives. It often includes tutorials and showcases the latest advancements in cloud technology.

- **Firebase and GCP Newsletters**: Subscribing to newsletters from Google or third-party providers can keep you informed about the latest updates and trends. Look for newsletters that focus on cloud development or mobile application development for the most relevant content.

Engaging with Firebase and GCP via Social Media

FOLLOWING FIREBASE and GCP on social media platforms can provide real-time updates and connect you with other developers. Twitter and LinkedIn are particularly useful for staying informed about events, new features, and best practices.

- **Twitter**: Follow @Firebase and @GoogleCloud on Twitter for quick updates, tutorials, and links to relevant blog posts. Many Firebase and GCP engineers are also active on Twitter, where they share insights and answer questions.

- **LinkedIn**: LinkedIn is a good platform for connecting with other professionals in the Firebase and GCP communities. You can follow Google Cloud's official LinkedIn page for announcements and join groups dedicated to cloud computing.

Creating a Personal Learning Pathway

TO MAKE THE MOST OF these resources, it's helpful to create a personal learning pathway tailored to your goals. Here are some steps to consider:

1. **Set Learning Goals**: Define what you want to achieve, whether it's mastering a specific service, earning a certification, or building a portfolio project.
2. **Choose Resources**: Select resources that match your learning style and goals. This might include online courses, official documentation, or community forums.
3. **Create a Schedule**: Allocate time each week for learning and experimenting. Consistency is key to building long-term expertise.
4. **Apply What You Learn**: Build small projects, experiment with new features, and share your knowledge with others. Practical experience is the best way to reinforce your

learning.

5. **Review and Adjust**: Periodically assess your progress and adjust your learning pathway as needed. Stay flexible and adapt to changes in Firebase and GCP offerings.

Conclusion

FIREBASE AND GCP OFFER a wealth of resources for continued learning and professional growth. By leveraging the tools and strategies outlined in this section, you can stay up-to-date, deepen your expertise, and make the most of what these platforms have to offer. As you continue your journey, remember that learning is an ongoing process, and the skills you develop today will prepare you for the challenges of tomorrow.

Chapter 12: Appendices

Glossary of Firebase & GCP Terms

FIREBASE AND GOOGLE Cloud Platform (GCP) offer a range of services and tools for building, managing, and scaling applications. This glossary covers key terms associated with Firebase and GCP to help you better understand the concepts, services, and features discussed throughout this book.

Access Control List (ACL)

An ACL is a list that defines permissions attached to an object in Google Cloud Storage or other services. It specifies which users or groups can access or modify a given resource and what permissions they have, such as read, write, or execute.

App Engine

Google App Engine is a fully managed platform as a service (PaaS) that allows developers to build, deploy, and scale web applications and services. It provides automatic scaling, load balancing, and integration with other Google Cloud services.

Authentication

Authentication is the process of verifying the identity of a user or system. Firebase Authentication provides easy-to-use methods for authenticating users via email/password, social providers like Google or Facebook, and custom authentication mechanisms.

BigQuery

BigQuery is a fully managed, serverless, and highly scalable data warehouse offered by GCP. It is designed to analyze large datasets using SQL-like queries and integrates with Firebase Analytics for advanced data analysis.

Billing Account

A billing account is required to manage costs associated with using Google Cloud services. It allows you to track expenses, set budgets, and receive invoices. You can link multiple Google Cloud projects to a single billing account.

Bucket

In Google Cloud Storage, a bucket is a container for storing objects (files) in the cloud. Each bucket has a unique name and is used to organize data and manage access.

CLOUD FIRESTORE

Cloud Firestore is a NoSQL document database that provides real-time data synchronization and support for offline data access. It is part of Firebase and can be integrated with other Google Cloud services for advanced data handling.

Cloud Functions

Cloud Functions are serverless functions that automatically run in response to events. Firebase offers Cloud Functions for automating tasks like user authentication, database triggers, and more. Google Cloud also provides Cloud Functions for broader use cases.

Cloud Run

Cloud Run is a managed compute platform that lets you run containers directly on Google's infrastructure. It is integrated with Google Cloud services and provides automatic scaling based on request volume.

DATABASE INSTANCE

A database instance is a service for managing a database on GCP. It includes Cloud SQL, Cloud Firestore, and Cloud Spanner. Each instance provides specific features and capabilities, depending on the type of database used.

Deployment

Deployment refers to the process of transferring code from a development environment to a production environment. Firebase Hosting and Google App Engine both offer deployment options for web and mobile applications.

Dynamic Links

Dynamic Links are Firebase-powered URLs that dynamically change their behavior depending on how and where they are opened. They can direct users to specific in-app content, even after installation, and enhance user acquisition and engagement.

ENCRYPTION

Encryption is the process of converting data into a code to prevent unauthorized access. Firebase and GCP provide encryption for data at rest and in transit to ensure data security and privacy.

Event-Driven Programming

Event-driven programming is a paradigm where the flow of the program is determined by events like user actions, sensor outputs, or messages from other programs. Firebase Cloud Functions support event-driven programming for tasks like triggering code upon user login or database updates.

Exponential Backoff

Exponential backoff is a strategy for managing retries of network requests by gradually increasing the delay between attempts. This approach is commonly used in Firebase and Google Cloud services to handle network errors gracefully.

FIREBASE AUTHENTICATION

Firebase Authentication is a service that provides easy-to-use SDKs and backend services for user authentication. It supports multiple authentication methods, including email/password, social providers, and custom authentication.

Firebase Console

The Firebase Console is a web-based interface for managing Firebase projects, services, and settings. It provides access to features like Authentication, Firestore, Cloud Functions, and Analytics.

Firestore Database

Firestore is Firebase's scalable NoSQL database for mobile, web, and server development. It stores data in documents and collections, allowing for flexible data modeling and real-time synchronization.

GOOGLE CLOUD PLATFORM (GCP)

GCP is a suite of cloud computing services offered by Google. It includes a wide range of tools for computing, storage, data analytics, machine learning, and more. Firebase is built on top of GCP, allowing for integration with services like BigQuery, Cloud Functions, and Cloud Storage.

Google Kubernetes Engine (GKE)

GKE is a managed Kubernetes service provided by GCP. It allows developers to deploy, manage, and scale containerized applications using Kubernetes, with full integration into the Google Cloud ecosystem.

Google Tag Manager (GTM)

GTM is a tag management system that allows you to easily add and manage marketing tags, conversion tracking, and analytics code on your website or app. Firebase integrates with GTM for advanced analytics capabilities.

HOSTING

Firebase Hosting is a web hosting service that allows you to deploy and serve web applications, static and dynamic content, and microservices. It provides built-in SSL, custom domain support, and automatic scaling.

IDENTITY AND ACCESS Management (IAM)

IAM is a framework for managing access to Google Cloud resources. It provides tools for defining roles and permissions, enabling fine-grained access control. Firebase integrates with IAM for managing user access to Firebase and GCP resources.

Instance Group

An instance group is a collection of virtual machine (VM) instances managed by Google Compute Engine. It enables scaling and load balancing for applications running on multiple instances.

JSON

JSON (JavaScript Object Notation) is a lightweight data-interchange format that is easy for humans to read and write and easy for machines to parse and generate. Firebase Firestore uses JSON for storing and exchanging data between client and server.

LOAD BALANCING

Load balancing is a method of distributing network or application traffic across multiple servers to ensure availability and reliability. GCP offers load balancing services for managing traffic to applications hosted on Compute Engine, App Engine, and Kubernetes Engine.

Log-based Metrics

Log-based metrics are measurements derived from application or system logs. They provide insights into application performance and are used for monitoring, debugging, and optimizing Firebase and GCP applications.

MACHINE LEARNING (ML)

Machine learning is a field of AI that focuses on developing algorithms that allow computers to learn from data and make predictions or decisions. Firebase ML Kit provides tools for integrating machine learning into mobile apps, while GCP offers a suite of ML services for more complex use cases.

Monitoring

Monitoring is the process of observing system performance and identifying potential issues. Firebase Performance Monitoring and Google Cloud Monitoring both provide tools for tracking metrics, setting alerts, and ensuring application reliability.

NOSQL

NoSQL databases are designed for storing and managing unstructured data. Firestore is a NoSQL database that supports hierarchical data structures, making it suitable for applications that require real-time data syncing and flexible data models.

Notifications

Notifications are messages sent to users to inform them of updates or changes in an application. Firebase Cloud Messaging (FCM) is a cross-platform messaging solution for sending notifications to devices running Android, iOS, and web apps.

PUB/SUB

Google Cloud Pub/Sub is a messaging service that allows applications to communicate asynchronously. It is commonly used for event-driven architectures and can be integrated with Firebase to enable real-time data processing.

Query

A query is a request for data or information from a database. Firestore supports complex querying capabilities, including filtering, sorting, and paginating data, while GCP BigQuery enables SQL-like queries on massive datasets.

Realtime Database

Firebase Realtime Database is a NoSQL cloud database that stores data as JSON and synchronizes data in real-time across all clients. It is designed for low-latency applications where data needs to be updated in real-time.

Roles

Roles in Google Cloud are collections of permissions that define what actions a user can perform. Firebase and GCP use predefined roles to simplify access control management, while custom roles can be created for specific requirements.

SDK (Software Development Kit)

An SDK is a set of tools and libraries provided by Firebase or GCP to enable developers to build applications. Firebase offers SDKs for various platforms, including iOS, Android, and web, to integrate Firebase services into applications easily.

Serverless

Serverless computing allows developers to build and deploy applications without managing servers. Firebase Cloud Functions and GCP Cloud Functions are serverless services that automatically scale based on demand and charge only for the time the code runs.

Storage

Firebase Cloud Storage provides secure file storage with automatic scaling. Google Cloud Storage offers a more extensive range of storage classes and options, ideal for handling large amounts of unstructured data, backups, and archiving.

Token

A token is a piece of data that represents a user's identity or permissions. Firebase Authentication uses tokens to authorize access to Firebase services, while GCP uses tokens for access control and API authentication.

Trigger

A trigger is an event that causes a function to execute. Firebase Cloud Functions can be triggered by events such as changes in Firestore, user authentication, or HTTP requests.

URL (UNIFORM RESOURCE Locator)

A URL is the address used to access resources on the internet. Firebase Hosting allows you to host content accessible via a custom domain or Firebase-provided URL.

User

A user is an individual who interacts with an application. Firebase Authentication manages user accounts and enables authentication through various methods like email, Google, and other social providers.

VIRTUAL MACHINE (VM)

A virtual machine is an emulation of a computer system that provides the functionality of a physical computer. Google Compute Engine allows you to create and manage VMs for various use cases, including web hosting, databases, and machine learning.

Version Control

Version control is a system for tracking changes to code over time. It enables collaboration, rollback to previous versions, and management of code changes. Firebase and GCP support integration with version control systems like Git.

Webhook

A webhook is a method of enabling real-time communication between applications. It allows one application to send data to another application when a specific event occurs, such as a change in a database or a user action.

XML

XML (Extensible Markup Language) is a data format used for exchanging information between systems. While JSON is commonly used in Firebase and GCP, XML may be encountered when integrating with legacy systems.

YAML

YAML (YAML Ain't Markup Language) is a human-readable data format often used for configuration files. GCP services like Google Cloud Build and Kubernetes use YAML for specifying build configurations and container orchestration.

ZONE

A zone is a specific area within a Google Cloud region where resources are deployed. Each zone is independent of others, providing redundancy and availability for resources like virtual machines and databases.

This glossary should provide a helpful reference as you navigate Firebase and Google Cloud Platform services, offering a foundational understanding of the terminology and concepts involved in developing, deploying, and managing applications on these platforms.

Resources for Further Learning

IN THE RAPIDLY EVOLVING fields of Firebase and Google Cloud Platform (GCP), staying updated and continuously learning is essential. This section compiles a list of valuable resources, including official documentation, online courses, tutorials, communities, and more. These resources will help you deepen your understanding of Firebase and GCP, explore advanced topics, and stay current with the latest updates and trends.

1. Official Documentation

Firebase Documentation

FIREBASE PROVIDES COMPREHENSIVE documentation covering its suite of products and services. The documentation includes getting-started guides, API references, and examples for common use cases. Here are some key sections:

- **Firebase Authentication:** Firebase Auth Documentation

- **Firestore Database:** Firestore Documentation

- **Firebase Hosting:** Hosting Documentation

- **Firebase Cloud Functions:** Cloud Functions Documentation

These guides are frequently updated and are the best place to start when looking to understand specific Firebase features.

Google Cloud Platform Documentation

GOOGLE CLOUD ALSO OFFERS detailed documentation for each of its services, with guides for setting up projects, configuring services, and optimizing performance. Some key GCP documentation sections include:

- **Google Cloud IAM:** IAM Documentation

- **Compute Engine:** Compute Engine Documentation

- **BigQuery:** BigQuery Documentation

- **Cloud Storage:** Cloud Storage Documentation

The GCP documentation is invaluable for understanding advanced topics, such as integrating GCP services with Firebase or scaling cloud infrastructure for large applications.

2. Online Courses

ONLINE COURSES CAN provide structured learning paths for mastering Firebase and GCP. Many platforms offer courses taught by experienced professionals, often with hands-on labs and real-world projects.

Google Cloud Training

GOOGLE CLOUD OFFERS a range of training programs and certification tracks, designed to help developers and IT professionals build expertise in cloud technologies. Some popular courses include:

- **Firebase in a Weekend:** A free course on Udacity that introduces Firebase basics and is co-created by Google.

- **Architecting with Google Cloud Platform:** Offered by Coursera, this course covers GCP architecture, networking, and storage.

- **Google Cloud Certification Programs:** Google Cloud offers certifications like Associate Cloud Engineer and Professional Cloud Architect, which can boost your credentials in cloud development and administration.

Udacity

UDACITY'S NANODEGREE programs are project-based, providing practical experience in a structured format. Two recommended courses include:

- **Cloud Developer Nanodegree:** This program covers both Firebase and GCP, with an emphasis on building scalable web applications.

- **Data Engineering Nanodegree:** For those interested in data analytics and big data, this program dives into GCP tools like BigQuery and Cloud Dataflow.

Coursera

COURSERA PARTNERS WITH Google Cloud to offer various courses. Some recommended ones are:

- **Google IT Automation with Python:** Ideal for beginners, this course teaches Python automation on GCP and includes practical projects.

- **Google Cloud Platform Fundamentals: Core Infrastructure:** This course provides an overview of GCP core infrastructure services.

3. Tutorial Websites

Medium

MEDIUM HAS MANY COMMUNITY-contributed articles and tutorials covering Firebase and GCP topics. Search for Firebase or GCP tags, and you will find up-to-date tutorials, project ideas, and case studies. Some well-known publications on Medium include:

- **Firebase Developers:** The official Firebase publication, offering articles from Firebase engineers and community experts.

- **Towards Data Science:** A general data science publication that often features tutorials on GCP's machine learning tools and data analytics.

Dev.to

DEV.TO IS A DEVELOPER community platform where users share technical articles, tutorials, and discussions. It's a great place to find practical, developer-focused content on Firebase and GCP. Popular tags include:

- #Firebase

- #GoogleCloud

- #WebDev

YouTube Channels

YOUTUBE IS AN EXCELLENT resource for video tutorials, walkthroughs, and live coding sessions. Some top channels include:

- **Firebase YouTube Channel:** Official channel for Firebase, featuring tutorials, office hours, and product updates.

- **Google Cloud Platform YouTube Channel:** Google Cloud's official channel provides technical sessions, demos, and recorded webinars.

4. Community Forums

Stack Overflow

STACK OVERFLOW HAS an active community of Firebase and GCP users who ask and answer questions on various topics. You can use tags like **firebase**[5] and **google-cloud-platform**[6] to search for questions and answers specific to these platforms.

Firebase Community on Slack

THE FIREBASE SLACK community is a place to connect with other Firebase developers, share knowledge, and get help with Firebase-related issues. You can join channels focused on specific Firebase services, like Firestore or Cloud Functions.

Google Cloud Community

THE GOOGLE CLOUD COMMUNITY is a forum for GCP users to discuss products, share solutions, and ask questions. You can access it at Google Cloud Community.

5. GitHub Repositories

Firebase Open Source Projects

FIREBASE HAS SEVERAL open-source projects available on GitHub, where you can explore code, contribute, and see how Firebase is being used in various projects. Some key repositories include:

---

5. https://stackoverflow.com/questions/tagged/firebase

6. https://stackoverflow.com/questions/tagged/google-cloud-platform

- **Firebase JS SDK**:firebase/firebase-js-sdk[7]

- **Firebase CLI**:firebase/firebase-tools[8]

- **Firebase iOS SDK**:firebase/firebase-ios-sdk[9]

These repositories are excellent for developers looking to understand Firebase internals or contribute to the ecosystem.

GCP Sample Code

GOOGLE CLOUD'S GITHUB repositories provide sample code for GCP services, covering a range of programming languages and frameworks. Here are some valuable repositories:

- **Google Cloud Platform GitHub Organization**:googleapis[10]

- **GCP Samples Repository**:GoogleCloudPlatform[11]

Exploring these repositories can provide insights into implementing GCP services, following best practices, and building scalable cloud applications.

---

7. https://github.com/firebase/firebase-js-sdk

8. https://github.com/firebase/firebase-tools

9. https://github.com/firebase/firebase-ios-sdk

10. https://github.com/googleapis

11. https://github.com/GoogleCloudPlatform

6. Books and E-Books

Firebase Books

BOOKS ON FIREBASE OFTEN cover topics like authentication, real-time data, and mobile app development. Here are some recommended titles:

- **"The Firebase Workshop"** by Paul Halliday: A beginner-friendly guide that includes projects for building mobile and web apps with Firebase.

- **"Learning Firebase"** by Kato Richardson: Covers Firebase fundamentals and is suitable for those new to mobile backend development.

Google Cloud Platform Books

BOOKS ON GCP OFTEN delve into cloud architecture, data engineering, and machine learning. Here are some recommended titles:

- **"Google Cloud Platform for Architects"** by Vitthal Srinivasan: This book provides a deep dive into GCP services and their use in modern cloud architectures.

- **"Data Science on Google Cloud Platform"** by Valliappa Lakshmanan: A practical guide to building data pipelines and machine learning models on GCP.

7. Blogs and Newsletters

Firebase Blog

THE FIREBASE BLOG OFFERS official updates, product announcements, and tutorials from the Firebase team. It's a must-read for staying up-to-date with new Firebase features and releases. Visit it atfirebase.blog[12].

Google Cloud Blog

THE GOOGLE CLOUD BLOG provides news, case studies, and technical articles on GCP services. It covers a wide range of topics, from AI and machine learning to cloud infrastructure. Check it out at cloud.google.com/blog.

Weekly Firebase Newsletter

THE WEEKLY FIREBASE Newsletter is a community-driven email newsletter that curates the latest Firebase articles, tutorials, and news from around the web. Subscribing to this newsletter can help you stay informed on Firebase trends and updates.

8. Conferences and Events

Google I/O

GOOGLE I/O IS GOOGLE'S annual developer conference, where the company announces new products, features, and updates. Firebase and GCP sessions provide deep dives into

---

12. https://firebase.blog

technical topics and insights from Google engineers. You can attend live or watch recorded sessions on YouTube.

Google Cloud Next

GOOGLE CLOUD NEXT IS an annual conference focused on GCP, offering sessions on cloud architecture, data analytics, machine learning, and more. The event provides a platform for networking, learning, and exploring new GCP offerings.

Firebase Summit

THE FIREBASE SUMMIT is an annual event dedicated to Firebase developers, featuring product announcements, technical sessions, and workshops. Attendees can learn about new Firebase features, hear from the Firebase team, and network with other developers.

By leveraging these resources, you can deepen your understanding of Firebase and Google Cloud Platform, stay current with technological advancements, and build innovative solutions using these powerful platforms.

Sample Projects and Code Snippets

THIS SECTION PROVIDES detailed sample projects and code snippets that demonstrate various use cases for Firebase and Google Cloud Platform (GCP). Each project is designed to showcase specific features of Firebase and GCP, from authentication to real-time data synchronization, cloud functions, and hosting. These projects aim to provide practical examples that you can use as a foundation for building your own applications.

1. Real-Time Chat Application with Firebase Firestore

A REAL-TIME CHAT APPLICATION is a classic project that demonstrates the power of Firebase Firestore's real-time data synchronization capabilities. This project will walk you through setting up Firestore, integrating Firebase Authentication, and using Firestore to manage chat messages in real time.

Project Overview

IN THIS PROJECT, YOU will:

- Set up Firebase Firestore to store chat messages.

- Use Firebase Authentication to allow users to sign in with Google.

- Display real-time chat messages in the app as they are added to Firestore.

- Deploy the application using Firebase Hosting.

Step-by-Step Guide

1. INITIALIZE FIREBASE Project and Set Up Firestore

1. Go to the Firebase Console.
2. Create a new project and enable Firestore.
3. In the Firestore database, create a collection named messages where each document will represent a chat message.

2. Implement Firebase Authentication

Enable Google Sign-In for Firebase Authentication:

1. Navigate to Authentication in the Firebase Console.
2. Go to the Sign-in method tab and enable Google Sign-In.
3. Add your app's OAuth client ID to the project settings.

```javascript
// Firebase initialization

firebase.initializeApp(firebaseConfig);

// Set up Google Authentication

const provider = new firebase.auth.GoogleAuthProvider();

firebase.auth().signInWithPopup(provider).then((result) => {

console.log('User signed in:', result.user.displayName);

});
```

3. Create the Chat Interface and Connect Firestore

Using HTML and JavaScript, create a simple chat interface and use Firestore to store and retrieve messages:

```html
<!—Chat interface—>

<div id="chat-window"></div>

<input type="text" id="message-input" placeholder="Type a message..."/>

<button onclick="sendMessage()">Send</button>

<script>

// Send message to Firestore
```

```javascript
function sendMessage() {

const message = document.getElementById('message-input').value;

firebase.firestore().collection('messages').add({

text: message,

timestamp: firebase.firestore.FieldValue.serverTimestamp()

});

}

// Real-time listener for chat messages

firebase.firestore().collection('messages').orderBy('timestamp').onSnapshot(snapshot
=> {

const chatWindow = document.getElementById('chat-window');

chatWindow.innerHTML = '';

snapshot.forEach((doc) => {

const message = doc.data().text;

chatWindow.innerHTML += `<p>${message}</p>`;

});

});

</script>
```

4. Deploy the App with Firebase Hosting

1. Install the Firebase CLI and initialize Firebase Hosting.

2. Run firebase deploy to deploy your chat application to Firebase Hosting.

2. E-Commerce Platform with Firebase Authentication and Firestore

THIS SAMPLE PROJECT will demonstrate how to build a simple e-commerce platform using Firebase Authentication for user login, Firestore for storing product and order information, and Firebase Cloud Functions for managing complex backend logic.

Project Overview

IN THIS PROJECT, YOU will:

- Set up Firebase Authentication for user sign-up and login.

- Use Firestore to store product details and orders.

- Implement Cloud Functions to process orders and manage inventory.

- Create a front-end interface to display products and handle the checkout process.

Step-by-Step Guide

1. INITIALIZE FIREBASE Project and Set Up Authentication

Set up Firebase Authentication to enable email/password sign-in for users:

```javascript
// Sign up new users

function signUp(email, password) {

firebase.auth().createUserWithEmailAndPassword(email,
password)

.then((userCredential) => {

console.log('User signed up:', userCredential.user.email);

});

}

// Log in users

function logIn(email, password) {

firebase.auth().signInWithEmailAndPassword(email, password)

.then((userCredential) => {

console.log('User logged in:', userCredential.user.email);

});

}
```

2. Define Firestore Structure for Products and Orders

Create two collections in Firestore: products and orders. Store product details such as name, price, and stock in products and store user orders in orders.

3. Implement Cloud Function for Order Processing

Use Firebase Cloud Functions to create an orderProcessing function that decreases the stock of a product when an order is placed.

```
// Cloud Function to handle order processing

exports.orderProcessing = functions.firestore.document('orders/{orderId}')

.onCreate(async (snap, context) => {

const orderData = snap.data();

const productRef = db.collection('products').doc(orderData.productId);

await db.runTransaction(async (transaction) => {

const productDoc = await transaction.get(productRef);

const newStock = productDoc.data().stock - orderData.quantity;

if (newStock >= 0) {

transaction.update(productRef, { stock: newStock });

} else {

throw new Error('Insufficient stock');

}

});

});
```

3. Image Recognition App with Firebase ML Kit and Cloud Storage

THIS SAMPLE PROJECT demonstrates how to use Firebase ML Kit for image recognition, Firebase Cloud Storage for image storage, and Firebase Cloud Functions for server-side image processing.

Project Overview

IN THIS PROJECT, YOU will:

- Use Firebase Cloud Storage to store uploaded images.

- Use Firebase ML Kit to process images and recognize objects within them.

- Display recognized objects in the app interface.

Step-by-Step Guide

1. SET UP CLOUD STORAGE

Create a Firebase Cloud Storage bucket to store user-uploaded images. Ensure you have the proper security rules to allow authenticated users to upload images.

2. Use ML Kit for Object Detection

Initialize ML Kit in your app and process images for object detection:

```
// Initialize ML Kit Object Detector

const objectDetector = new firebase.mlKit.ObjectDetector({
```

```
mode: 'single_image',

classification: true

});

// Function to process image

function detectObjects(imageFile) {

objectDetector.processImage(imageFile).then((result) => {

result.forEach((obj) => {

console.log('Object detected:', obj.class, obj.confidence);

});

});

}
```

3. Deploy Cloud Function for Automatic Image Processing

Deploy a Cloud Function that triggers on image upload to automatically process images with ML Kit.

```
// Cloud Function to process image on upload

exports.processImageOnUpload                                    =
functions.storage.object().onFinalize((object) => {

const filePath = object.name;

const bucket = admin.storage().bucket();

const file = bucket.file(filePath);

return mlKit.objectDetection(file).then((labels) => {
```

```
console.log('Detected objects:', labels);

});

});
```

4. Fitness Tracking App with Firebase Realtime Database

THIS SAMPLE PROJECT will demonstrate how to build a fitness tracking app using Firebase Realtime Database to store workout data, Firebase Authentication for user management, and Firebase Hosting to deploy the web app.

Project Overview

IN THIS PROJECT, YOU will:

- Use Firebase Realtime Database to store and retrieve workout data.

- Implement Firebase Authentication for user sign-up and login.

- Display workout progress in real time on a simple dashboard.

Step-by-Step Guide

1. INITIALIZE FIREBASE Project and Set Up Realtime Database

Set up Firebase Realtime Database to store users' workout sessions and progress:

```
// Write workout data to Realtime Database

function logWorkout(userId, workoutData) {

firebase.database().ref('workouts/' + userId).push(workoutData);

}

// Read workout data from Realtime Database

function getWorkoutData(userId) {

firebase.database().ref('workouts/' + userId).on('value', (snapshot)
=> {

console.log('Workout data:', snapshot.val());

});

}
```

2. Create a Dashboard to Display Workout Progress

Use HTML and JavaScript to create a simple dashboard that updates in real time with data from the Realtime Database.

```html
<div id="workout-dashboard"></div>

<script>

firebase.database().ref('workouts/userId').on('value', (snapshot)
=> {

document.getElementById('workout-dashboard').innerHTML =
JSON.stringify(snapshot.val());

});

</script>
```

3. Deploy the App with Firebase Hosting

Set up Firebase Hosting to deploy your fitness tracking app. Initialize the project using the Firebase CLI and run firebase deploy to make the app available online.

Each of these projects demonstrates a unique aspect of Firebase and GCP, showcasing how these powerful tools can be combined to create scalable, secure, and feature-rich applications. By following these sample projects, you'll gain hands-on experience and a deeper understanding of Firebase and GCP capabilities.

Firebase & GCP API Reference Guide

THIS SECTION PROVIDES an in-depth reference guide for key APIs available in Firebase and Google Cloud Platform (GCP). These APIs are the backbone of the services provided by Firebase and GCP, enabling developers to integrate various functionalities into their applications, such as authentication, database management, cloud storage, and machine learning. This guide aims to give you a comprehensive overview of essential API methods, parameters, and usage examples to help you maximize the potential of Firebase and GCP in your projects.

1. Firebase Authentication API

FIREBASE AUTHENTICATION provides a powerful, easy-to-use API for handling user authentication. It supports various methods, including email/password, social logins, and custom tokens.

Key Methods

CREATEUSERWITHEMAILANDPASSWORD(email, password)

Creates a new user with the specified email and password.

```
firebase.auth().createUserWithEmailAndPassword(email,
password)

.then((userCredential) => {

console.log('User created:', userCredential.user.uid);

})

.catch((error) => {

console.error('Error creating user:', error.message);

});
```

signInWithEmailAndPassword(email, password)

Signs in an existing user with email and password.

```
firebase.auth().signInWithEmailAndPassword(email, password)

.then((userCredential) => {

console.log('User signed in:', userCredential.user.uid);

})

.catch((error) => {

console.error('Error signing in:', error.message);

});
```

signOut()

Signs out the current user.

```javascript
firebase.auth().signOut().then(() => {

console.log('User signed out');

});
```

onAuthStateChanged(callback)

Adds an observer for changes to the user's sign-in state.

```javascript
firebase.auth().onAuthStateChanged((user) => {

if (user) {

console.log('User is signed in:', user.uid);

} else {

console.log('No user is signed in');

}

});
```

2. Firestore Database API

FIRESTORE PROVIDES a flexible, scalable database for real-time data storage. The API supports creating, reading, updating, and deleting documents in collections.

Key Methods

COLLECTION(COLLECTIONPATH).add(data)

Adds a new document with specified data to a collection.

```
firebase.firestore().collection('users').add({

name: 'John Doe',

email: 'john@example.com'

}).then((docRef) => {

console.log('Document written with ID:', docRef.id);

});
```

collection(collectionPath).doc(documentId).set(data)

Sets the data for a specific document, creating it if it does not exist.

```
firebase.firestore().collection('users').doc('user_id_123').set({

age: 30

});
```

collection(collectionPath).doc(documentId).get()

Retrieves the document with the specified ID.

```
firebase.firestore().collection('users').doc('user_id_123').get()

.then((doc) => {

if (doc.exists) {

console.log('Document data:', doc.data());

} else {

console.log('No such document!');
```

```
}

});
```

collection(collectionPath).where(field, operator, value)

Queries a collection based on specified field, operator, and value.

```
firebase.firestore().collection('users').where('age', '>', 25).get()

.then((querySnapshot) => {

querySnapshot.forEach((doc) => {

console.log(doc.id, '=>', doc.data());

});

});
```

3. Firebase Cloud Functions API

FIREBASE CLOUD FUNCTIONS allow you to run server-side code in response to events. Functions are triggered by events such as HTTP requests, Firestore changes, or Firebase Authentication events.

Key Methods

FUNCTIONS.HTTPS.ONREQUEST((req, res))

Creates an HTTP function to handle HTTP requests.

```
const functions = require('firebase-functions');

exports.helloWorld = functions.https.onRequest((req, res) => {

res.send("Hello from Firebase!");
```

```
});
```

functions.firestore.document(path).onCreate((snap, context))

Triggers a function when a document is created in a specified Firestore collection.

```
exports.newUserNotification =
functions.firestore.document('users/{userId}').onCreate((snap,
context) => {

const newUser = snap.data();

console.log('New user signed up:', newUser.name);

});
```

functions.auth.user().onCreate((user))

Triggers a function when a new user account is created.

```
exports.sendWelcomeEmail =
functions.auth.user().onCreate((user) => {

const email = user.email;

// Code to send welcome email

});
```

4. Firebase Cloud Storage API

FIREBASE CLOUD STORAGE provides secure file storage and retrieval. The API allows uploading, downloading, and managing files in a scalable storage solution.

Key Methods

REF(FILEPATH).PUT(FILE, metadata)

Uploads a file to the specified path in Cloud Storage.

```
const storageRef = firebase.storage().ref('images/photo.jpg');

const file = document.getElementById('fileInput').files[0];

storageRef.put(file).then((snapshot) => {

console.log('Uploaded a blob or file!');

});
```

ref(filePath).getDownloadURL()

Retrieves the download URL for a file.

```
storageRef.getDownloadURL().then((url) => {

console.log('File available at:', url);

});
```

ref(filePath).delete()

Deletes a file from the specified path in Cloud Storage.

```
storageRef.delete().then(() => {

console.log('File deleted');

});
```

5. Google Cloud Compute Engine API

GOOGLE CLOUD COMPUTE Engine enables the creation and management of virtual machines on GCP. The Compute Engine API is used for tasks such as starting, stopping, and managing instances.

Key Methods

INSTANCES.INSERT(PROJECT, zone, instance)

Creates a new VM instance in the specified project and zone.

POST   https://compute.googleapis.com/compute/v1/projects/project-id/zones/zone/instances

{

"name": "instance-name",

"machineType": "zones/zone/machineTypes/machine-type",

"networkInterfaces": [{

"network": "global/networks/default"

}]

}

instances.start(project, zone, instanceId)

Starts a stopped VM instance.

POST   https://compute.googleapis.com/compute/v1/projects/project-id/zones/zone/instances/instance-id/start

instances.stop(project, zone, instanceId)

Stops a running VM instance.

POST   https://compute.googleapis.com/compute/v1/projects/
project-id/zones/zone/instances/instance-id/stop

6. Google Cloud Storage API

GOOGLE CLOUD STORAGE provides scalable, secure storage for objects. The API supports uploading, downloading, deleting, and managing permissions for files.

Key Methods

BUCKETS.INSERT(PROJECT, bucketName)

Creates a new bucket in the specified project.

POST   https://storage.googleapis.com/storage/v1/
b?project=project-id

```
{

"name": "bucket-name"

}
```

objects.insert(bucket, object, media)

Uploads an object to the specified bucket.

POST   https://storage.googleapis.com/upload/storage/v1/b/
bucket-name/o?uploadType=media

objects.delete(bucket, objectName)

Deletes an object from a bucket.

DELETE https://storage.googleapis.com/storage/v1/b/ bucket-name/o/object-name

objects.get(bucket, objectName)

Retrieves metadata for an object.

GET https://storage.googleapis.com/storage/v1/b/bucket-name/ o/object-name

7. Google Cloud Pub/Sub API

GOOGLE CLOUD PUB/SUB is a messaging service for building event-driven systems. The Pub/Sub API enables publishing messages to topics and subscribing to receive messages.

Key Methods

PROJECTS.TOPICS.PUBLISH(topic, messages)

Publishes messages to a specified topic.

POST https://pubsub.googleapis.com/v1/projects/project-id/ topics/topic-id:publish

{

"messages": [{

"data": "base64-encoded-message"

}]

}

projects.subscriptions.pull(subscription)

Pulls messages from a specified subscription.

POST   https://pubsub.googleapis.com/v1/projects/project-id/subscriptions/subscription-id:pull

```
{

"maxMessages": 10

}
```

projects.subscriptions.acknowledge(subscription, ackIds)

Acknowledges messages retrieved from a subscription.

POST   https://pubsub.googleapis.com/v1/projects/project-id/subscriptions/subscription-id:acknowledge

```
{

"ackIds": ["ack-id1", "ack-id2"]

}
```

8. Google Cloud BigQuery API

BIGQUERY PROVIDES A fully managed data warehouse that allows you to analyze massive datasets with SQL. The BigQuery API enables you to run queries, manage datasets, and control access to data.

Key Methods

JOBS.INSERT(PROJECTID, configuration)

Creates a new job, which may be a query or a data load.

```
POST     https://bigquery.googleapis.com/bigquery/v2/projects/
project-id/jobs

{

"configuration": {

"query": {

"query": "SELECT * FROM dataset.table"

}

}

}
```

jobs.getQueryResults(jobId)

Retrieves the results of a query job.

```
GET     https://bigquery.googleapis.com/bigquery/v2/projects/
project-id/queries/job-id
```

datasets.insert(projectId, datasetId)

Creates a new dataset in the specified project.

```
POST     https://bigquery.googleapis.com/bigquery/v2/projects/
project-id/datasets

{

"datasetReference": {

"datasetId": "dataset-id"

}
```

}

These APIs provide a foundation for leveraging Firebase and GCP's extensive capabilities, enabling you to build, deploy, and manage scalable applications across various environments. This reference guide should help you understand the essential APIs available and how to use them effectively in your projects.

Frequently Asked Questions

THIS SECTION ADDRESSES some of the most commonly asked questions about Firebase and Google Cloud Platform (GCP). Covering topics ranging from account setup and billing to advanced functionalities like scaling and integrating machine learning, this FAQ aims to provide clear answers to help developers navigate potential challenges and make the most of Firebase and GCP services.

1. Getting Started with Firebase and GCP

Q: HOW DO I SET UP a Firebase project?

To set up a Firebase project, go to the Firebase Console and click on "Add project." Follow the on-screen instructions to create a new project, where you can then enable various Firebase services such as Authentication, Firestore, and Cloud Functions.

Q: Do I need a Google Cloud account to use Firebase?

No, you can use Firebase independently, but linking it to a Google Cloud account unlocks additional features and provides access to GCP's more advanced tools like BigQuery, Compute Engine, and AI/ML services.

Q: What is the difference between Firebase Realtime Database and Firestore?

Both are NoSQL databases, but Firestore is the newer, more scalable option. Firestore offers more flexible data structures, advanced querying capabilities, and automatic scaling for larger applications. The Realtime Database is optimized for real-time data synchronization, especially in mobile applications.

2. Billing and Pricing

Q: HOW DOES FIREBASE pricing work?

Firebase follows a freemium model, with certain services available for free up to a certain usage limit. Beyond that, Firebase offers two pricing plans: the Spark Plan (free tier) and the Blaze Plan (pay-as-you-go). Pricing varies depending on the service, with costs for database storage, authentication, and cloud functions.

Q: Can I use Google Cloud credits with Firebase?

Yes, if your Firebase project is linked to a GCP account, you can use Google Cloud credits towards any Firebase services that are billed through Google Cloud. This includes services like Firestore, Hosting, and Cloud Functions.

Q: How do I set up billing alerts to manage costs?

You can set up billing alerts in the Google Cloud Console by navigating to the "Billing" section, selecting your billing account, and configuring budget alerts. These alerts help you monitor usage and costs, ensuring you stay within budget.

3. Authentication and User Management

Q: WHAT AUTHENTICATION methods does Firebase support?

Firebase Authentication supports various methods, including email/password, phone authentication, and social logins (such as Google, Facebook, and Twitter). It also allows custom authentication for more advanced use cases.

Q: Can I integrate Firebase Authentication with an existing authentication system?

Yes, Firebase Authentication supports custom authentication, allowing you to integrate it with existing user management systems. You can use custom tokens to authenticate users and gain access to Firebase services.

```
// Generate a custom token in your backend

const token = await admin.auth().createCustomToken(uid);
```

Q: How do I ensure secure user authentication?

Firebase Authentication provides built-in security features such as email verification, password strength enforcement, and multi-factor authentication (MFA). Additionally, you can implement security rules in Firestore and Cloud Storage to control access based on user roles and permissions.

4. Data Management and Storage

Q: HOW DO I STRUCTURE data in Firestore for scalability?

For scalable data modeling, follow these best practices:

- Use collections and subcollections to organize data hierarchically.

- Avoid deeply nested data structures, which can impact read performance.

- Use unique document IDs to minimize duplication.

- Leverage Firestore's indexing capabilities to optimize querying.

Q: How can I handle large files in Firebase Storage?

Firebase Storage supports uploading large files through resumable uploads, which allow files to be uploaded in chunks. This approach is robust against network interruptions and improves upload reliability.

```
const uploadTask = storageRef.put(file);

uploadTask.on('state_changed', snapshot => {

console.log('Upload progress:', (snapshot.bytesTransferred / snapshot.totalBytes) * 100);

});
```

Q: Can I back up Firestore data automatically?

Yes, you can set up automated backups for Firestore by scheduling Cloud Functions or using GCP's managed export functionality. Alternatively, you can periodically export data to Google Cloud Storage and automate the process with scripts.

5. Hosting and Deployment

Q: HOW DO I DEPLOY a web app to Firebase Hosting?

First, install the Firebase CLI, initialize your project with firebase init, and select "Hosting." Then, run firebase deploy to deploy your app to Firebase Hosting. You can set up custom domains and manage SSL certificates directly from the Firebase Console.

Q: Can I use Firebase Hosting for dynamic content?

Yes, you can use Firebase Hosting with Firebase Cloud Functions to serve dynamic content. Cloud Functions allow you to run server-side code in response to HTTP requests, enabling dynamic content generation.

```
exports.dynamicContent = functions.https.onRequest((req, res)
=> {

res.send("Hello, dynamic world!");

});
```

Q: Does Firebase Hosting support CDNs?

Firebase Hosting uses Google's global content delivery network (CDN) by default, ensuring fast content delivery worldwide. You don't need to configure anything; the CDN is automatically integrated.

6. Integrating Firebase with Google Cloud

Q: HOW CAN I USE BIGQUERY with Firebase Analytics?

Firebase provides a direct integration with BigQuery. In the Firebase Console, navigate to Project Settings, click on Integrations, and enable BigQuery linking. This allows you to export raw analytics data to BigQuery for advanced querying and analysis.

Q: Can I use Google Cloud Functions instead of Firebase Functions?

Yes, Google Cloud Functions offer additional features and are part of the broader GCP ecosystem. You can use either, depending on your project requirements. Firebase Functions are built on Google Cloud Functions, so transitioning is straightforward if you need the extra capabilities.

Q: What's the advantage of using Google Cloud Run with Firebase?

Google Cloud Run is suitable for deploying containerized applications, offering greater control over runtime environments. It's ideal for complex microservices architectures that might need more than Firebase's serverless functions.

7. Advanced Topics: Machine Learning and AI

Q: HOW CAN I ADD MACHINE learning to my Firebase app?

Firebase ML Kit provides on-device and cloud-based machine learning APIs for image labeling, text recognition, and more. You can also integrate custom TensorFlow Lite models for advanced use cases.

```
const firebaseML = firebase.ml().imageLabeler();

firebaseML.processImage(imageFile).then((labels) => {

labels.forEach(label => {

console.log('Detected:', label.text);

});
```

```
});
```

Q: Is it possible to use Google Cloud AI with Firebase?

Yes, you can integrate GCP's AI services with Firebase to enhance your applications. Google Cloud AI Platform offers tools for training and deploying machine learning models that you can incorporate into your Firebase app using Cloud Functions or API requests.

Q: What are the benefits of using TensorFlow with Firebase?

TensorFlow's machine learning models can be exported to TensorFlow Lite for mobile deployment. Firebase ML Kit allows you to deploy TensorFlow Lite models for on-device inference, providing low-latency and offline capabilities.

8. Security and Compliance

Q: HOW DO I SECURE data in Firestore and Firebase Storage?

Use Firebase Security Rules to define who can access or modify your data. For Firestore, you can set rules based on user authentication status, roles, or document fields. Firebase Storage rules also support access control based on file metadata and user authentication.

```
// Example Firestore Security Rule

service cloud.firestore {

match /databases/{database}/documents {

match /users/{userId} {

allow read, write: if request.auth.uid == userId;
```

```
    }

    }

    }
```

Q: What compliance standards does Firebase support?

Firebase is compliant with various standards, including GDPR, ISO/IEC 27001, and SOC 1, 2, and 3. For HIPAA compliance, you can use Firebase in conjunction with GCP services by signing a Business Associate Agreement (BAA) with Google.

Q: How can I audit Firebase project activity?

You can enable audit logging through Google Cloud Console. This will log project activities and service interactions, providing detailed records of access and modifications for compliance purposes.

9. Scaling and Performance

Q: HOW DO I HANDLE traffic spikes in Firebase?

Firebase's infrastructure is designed to scale automatically to handle traffic spikes. For additional control over scaling, you can configure Firestore's and Realtime Database's concurrency and throttling settings.

Q: Can I use load balancing with Firebase Hosting?

Firebase Hosting automatically provides load balancing through its global CDN. For more complex setups, such as deploying multiple microservices, you may consider using GCP Load Balancer in conjunction with Firebase.

Q: What tools can I use to monitor performance?

Firebase Performance Monitoring provides tools to measure and analyze app performance. You can also integrate Google Cloud Monitoring for more detailed metrics and custom alerts, allowing you to track performance across both Firebase and GCP services.

By addressing these common questions, this FAQ should serve as a helpful resource, guiding you through essential concepts, potential issues, and solutions for optimizing your experience with Firebase and Google Cloud Platform.